THE POLITICAL USES OF HISTORY

THE POLITICAL USES OF HISTORY

A STUDY OF HISTORIANS
IN THE FRENCH RESTORATION

STANLEY MELLON

STANFORD UNIVERSITY PRESS, Stanford, California, 1958

STANFORD UNIVERSITY PRESS
STANFORD, CALIFORNIA

LONDON: OXFORD UNIVERSITY PRESS

LIBRARY OF CONGRESS CATALOG CARD NUMBER: 58-6704

PRINTED IN THE UNITED STATES OF AMERICA

PUBLISHED WITH THE ASSISTANCE OF THE FORD FOUNDATION

TO MY FATHER

Acknowledgment

I wish to express my gratitude to Professor Robert R. Palmer for his aid and encouragement. I also wish to thank the librarians at Princeton University, the University of Michigan, and the Bibliothèque Nationale.

S. M.

Contents

THE POLITICAL USES OF HISTORY

CHAPTER I

Introduction

> History is the muse of our time; we are, I think, the first who have understood the past.
>
> Duchesse de Broglie

This study first seeks to demonstrate that the writing of history in the French Restoration was a function of politics—this might be called the minor thesis. Its major intention is to illuminate the politics of the Restoration by examining the historical writing of the period.

At the very outset of the inquiry, there were several reasons for assuming that history was a natural vantage point from which to study the Restoration. First, there is the suggestive fact that the writing of history began to pick up with the return of the Bourbons, and soon became the most popular form of written communication. Comte Daru, Stendhal's uncle and the author of a history of Venice, estimated that almost forty million pages of history were printed in the year 1825 alone.[1] This is some ten million pages more than the next largest category—belles-lettres—and represented an enormous increase from the three million pages of history published in 1811.

The figures are even more impressive when translated into human terms: Guizot's giant source collections, Thierry's archival labors, Daunou's twenty volumes of lectures, Barante's fifteen volumes on the Dukes of Burgundy, and Montgaillard's nine on the French Revolution.

The enormous productivity of the Restoration has traditionally been explained either as a reaction to the sterility of the Empire (which Renan aptly called an intellectual desert) or as an offshoot of European romanticism, with its exotic interest in the past and its conservative glorification of tradition. This study will offer the explanation that it is not poetry but politics which accounts for the historical-mindedness of the Restoration. History was the most popular subject, attracting the talents of gifted and mediocre alike, because history was the language of politics. Or, as Fiévée put it, "Our century is singular in that it apprehends by memories, as it makes politics with memories."[2]

To whatever area of Restoration life one turns, one will find history at the very center of discussion. In the Chambers, every political issue is given historical dimensions. Questions of foreign policy recall Louis XIV. Indemnifying the émigrés and re-establishing primogeniture compel discussion of the glorious Franks or the intemperate League. The budget for religious affairs is the signal for a debate on the Declaration of 1682 or the Jesuit expulsion of 1764. The student of the Restoration soon learns to take this for granted, but one is occasionally jarred to see a discussion on freedom of the press involving Francis I, or Santo Domingan independence debated in terms of the role of Louis XI. And the politicians of the Restoration do not have to rely on memory. The *Bibliothèque historique* is established, a vast arsenal from which Liberals can draw suitable materials; it has its counterpart in the Conservative *Bibliothèque royaliste,* whose speciality is the French Revolution.

The press of the Restoration is equally revealing. Not only is considerable attention given to the reviewing of historical works, but Thierry has what amounts to a column in the *Censeur européen,* and Trognon contributes a regular series of historical letters to the *Globe.* Indeed only a hyphen separates the journalist and the historian in the Restoration. Every newspaper has its historians: the *Journal des débats* can boast of Guizot and Chateaubriand; Michaud edits the *Quotidienne*; two young historians, Mignet and Thiers, found the *National* in 1830. And in the dramatic months leading up to July, 1830, one finds the press debate dominated by the question: Does 1830 bear more resemblance to the France of 1789 or to the England of 1688?

The university lectures are still another outlet for the spreading of historical ideas. It is in the Restoration that a host of young Liberal professors emerge to confront the Conservative coalition with a Liberal history. Guizot, Trognon, Villemain, and Cousin are the idols of the young generation of students as well as public figures. In fact, there is no better barometer of Restoration politics than the presence or absence in the universities of Liberal professors. The expulsion of Guizot and Cousin in 1822 marked a new phase of Restoration reaction. Their triumphant return in 1828 was the measure of Liberal victory.

Finally, there are the histories themselves. Every effort was made to provide historical works with the largest possible audience. For the Liberals there appeared the *Résumé* series, the *Petite bibliographie,* and the *Bibliothèque du dix-neuvième siècle*; and for the Conservatives, the *Société des bons livres* and the *Bibliothèque catholique.*

Why does the Restoration consider history so necessary, so relevant to politics? Why is so much political energy and talent poured into the writing and propagating of history? A general explanation is possible: some epochs, certain people, have shown a peculiar awareness of their history. But I believe the real answer to the close and continuing relation of history and politics in the French Restoration can best be found in the nature of the Restoration itself.

In 1814, France faced a completely new political experience. Twenty-five years before, the nation had overthrown a thousand-year monarchy, sped through violent and bewildering phases of revolution, and wound up with a military dictatorship. And if that were not enough, there was the Hundred Days. As Bonald writes in 1817: "There was a greater change in the political and moral state of France between the beginning of 1814 and the end of 1815 than there was between 1789 and 1814, and still greater than there was between the reign of Childeric and that of Louis XIV."[3] The acceleration of change was what struck men of this generation.

In the whirl of events, the giant cataclysm of revolution and civil war, it is not surprising that France should have forgotten her past. If the past was confusing, the future was uncertain. France was embarked upon two unprecedented ventures—a restoration and a constitutional monarchy. Even the old fixed classes and groupings could offer little stability. The Restoration acted as a giant prism, deflecting all the forces that entered it—the traditional absolutists emerged as constitutional monarchists, the aristocrats were transformed into royal absolutists, the Liberals of the Revolution became Whigs.

Having faced a rapid succession of Old Regime, Revolution, and Empire, and now saddled with an untried system, the French understandably turned to the more remote past for some precedents to support the future. In addition, it was natural to try to put in order the preceding twenty-five years, to extract out of the whirlwind of the immediate past something that could serve as guide or warning in the Restoration. As Barante observed, in trying to explain this "historical fever": "We had witnessed scenes so great, so diverse, so poignant, we had seen so much history made, that we wished to rediscover in the past something we had seen or experienced."[4]

It seems clear, however, that psychological factors alone cannot account for the torrent of historical writing, or for its largely Liberal bias. The deeper reasons must be sought in the specific nature of the political problems of the Restoration.

The first political task faced by the Liberals—that group which, in speaking for the Revolution, represented everyone from Doctrinaires to the Jacobin Left—was to sell the French Revolution. Their very existence during this period depended upon their ability to justify the Revolution, to acquit it of crimes, to explain away its criminals. There was no better and safer way to do this during the Restoration than to write a history. As Berville, the editor of the *Collection des Mémoires*, noted in defending another historian before a royal court: "An opinion on a historical fact, whatever it be, cannot constitute an offense in the eyes of the law."[5]

The Liberals' second great political task during the Restoration was to split the Conservative coalition of monarchy, aristocracy, and clergy which barred their way. This coalition was the political power of the Restoration, and it was apparent to all Liberals that as long as it remained intact, the Conservative Restoration would linger on.

Formed out of the crucible of the Revolution, united because of their recent common danger, the forces of the coalition had every reason, politically, to remain united. But early in the Restoration, the Liberals discovered that history can be used as a wedge to divide this alliance. It is history that can remind this coalition that it has not always been united, history that can convert old suspicions into present fears, history that can revive dead quarrels and ancient disputations. And this is precisely what the Liberals do. As historians of the aristocracy, they remind the monarchy of the revolutionary character of the French nobility. As students of religious history, they rediscover the Gallican liberties of the seventeenth century and the Jesuit threats of the eighteenth. The effects of these discoveries upon the political coalition will be studied.

A final word of caution. Although, inevitably, some light is thrown on the historiography of the French Restoration, this is primarily a study of politics. I have, in fact, done what I believe the men of the Restoration did: I have turned to history in order to understand politics.

CHAPTER II

The Liberal Version of the French Revolution

> In 1817, preoccupied with a strong desire to contribute to the triumph of constitutional opinions, I began to look into works of history for proofs and arguments which would support my political beliefs.
> Augustin Thierry, *Lettres sur l'histoire de France.*

Napoleon Bonaparte, while carrying the Revolution to Europe, had sought to end it at home, to reconcile the two Frances under the imperial palladium. But with the return of the Bourbons in 1814, all the old questions are reopened. Is France to return to an ante-bellum 1789? What part of the Revolution—if any—can be maintained? To the men who "came back" in 1814, that final wave of émigrés, the answer is clear. The Revolution was a series of crimes, culminating in that most horrendous of crimes, the regicide. Now virtue and justice have returned in the person of the martyred king's brother; the Restoration is to be, in essence and action, a denial of the Revolution. But Restoration France contained two other groups, one uncertain, the other grimly determined to defend the Revolution and its heritage. The first group is the supporters of Royalist France who had slowly dribbled back after Brumaire, the men who had agreed with Napoleon's program of "burying" the Revolution and working for France. The second is the men of the Revolution themselves, the Liberals; from being confused and divided by the Empire's ambiguous attitude toward the Revolution, they emerge in 1814 with the old light of battle in their eyes, determined to renew the struggle, to preserve what they can.[1]

At the outset of the Restoration, the Liberals seem to face a hopeless task. The very word Restoration suggests their difficulty. The brother of the executed Bourbon is on the throne; the men who left France in 1789 have returned in the baggage train of the allied army; Cossacks in the streets of Paris proclaim the triumph of reaction everywhere. The dilemma for the Liberals is, again, how to protect and defend the institutions, interests, and men of the Revolution which were in part preserved by the Empire; how to do this in the face of an avenging aristocracy, a resurgent clergy, a restored monarchy. The control of the Chamber by the Ultras, the launching of a White terror in the South after the Hundred Days—the whole atmosphere of the early Restoration indicates the almost impossible nature of the Liberal task.

A frontal assault is impossible—it is difficult, even treasonable, to proclaim the political principles of the Revolution in an era which owes its very existence to the defeat of those principles. The Liberals must find a way to defend the Revolution, while freeing themselves from the charge of *being* revolutionary.

They discover a method, and that method is history. History would provide an arena in which the Liberals could restage and relive the battles of the Revolution, stating their case while remaining invulnerable under the cloak of an impersonal muse. The men of 1789 had been too busy making and sustaining a revolution to chronicle it. During and immediately after the Revolution, history had become the chief weapon of its Conservative critics.[2] In exile, émigrés like Chateaubriand, Maistre, Barruel, had both the incentive and the time to draw up their indictments. Thus the Conservatives arrive in the Restoration with a formulated historical version of the Revolution, a thorough documentation of its crimes. But in the Restoration, the tables are turned; it is the men of the Revolution, cut off from politics, who turn to history to state their case. "The best way of giving the government your political opinions is to publish a good history of France."[3]

The stakes are high. If the Revolution can be successfully sold to the Restoration, then the very nature of the Restoration is changed, and the gains of '89 can be preserved.

For fifteen years this Liberal version of the French Revolution is to engulf France—histories, biographies, memoirs, polemics and apologetics. To write on the Revolution is the favorite pastime of intellectual France; a list of those who did so reads like an honor roll of nineteenth-century Liberalism. Even collections of sources are ammunition in this campaign: the twenty-four-volume *Choix de rapports, opinions et discours prononcés à la tribune nationale* advertises its purpose as "to offer to our representatives as well as to our young citizens who will one day be called to the tribune, models of enlightened patriotism and clear discussion; to preserve for history precious materials which will forever attest to our achievement and our greatness; . . . to provide a place where the defenders of our liberty, the protectors of liberal institutions, will come to arm themselves with memories, examples, and inspirations."[4]

History is not only the safest terrain upon which to conduct a defense of the Revolution; it is the best possible way to educate the new generation, a generation perhaps blinded by Napoleonic glory and now to be instructed by the Restoration. In 1814 the Revolution is already twenty-five years old; by 1830 a whole generation has emerged without any memory of its actual events. The new generation of the Restoration must be informed of the Revolution, must be taught to regard it as theirs. History, then, serves the primary purpose of keeping the Revolution alive.

In effect, the Revolution is to be taken out of the active realm of politics into the calmer waters of history. Mme de Staël introduces her classic defense of the Revolution by saying, "My ambition shall be to speak of the age in which we have lived as if it were already remote."[5] Twenty-five years have passed since Burke attacked the Revolution for turning its back upon the French past, and Burke's deification of the past can now be turned against the Conservatives—the Revolution is now history, and if you reject it you are rejecting yourselves. In 1817, Benjamin Constant, in the heat of political battle, writes, "It is not necessary to dishonor twenty-seven years of our history,"[6] and Rioust, defending Carnot in the same year, argues that "without doubt he belongs to history."[7]

The Liberals could not be content with converting the Revolution from the realities of politics to the neutrality of history. The Conservatives might willingly concede that the Revolution was in the past, but they would insist that the Revolution was a break with the whole spirit of the French past, a crime against all previous French history. And prior to the Restoration, this version of the Revolution would have been shared by the men of the Revolution themselves. Guizot, lecturing to his students in 1820, was the first to point to the significant change that separates the Liberal first and second generations. He recognizes that in a time of great social crisis and change, "the authority of the past is the obstacle which stands in the way of efforts to create a new society."[8] He admits that the rejection of a nation's history is an inevitable, unfortunate product of revolution, in which the past is always the enemy. However, a view of history hammered out in the heat of a triumphant revolution would not suffice for a restoration. Now the Liberals who had previously "conceded" history to the Conservatives discover—and it is one of their great discoveries of the Restoration—that the Revolution, far from a decisive break with French history, could be seen as merely its latest and most exciting chapter. Instead of glorying in the "newness" of the Revolution, its revulsion from centuries of darkness and tyranny, the Liberals of the Restoration would seize upon the connections with this past; they would counter the Conservative effort to read the Revolution out of French history with a version that would suggest its debt to the past, its continuity.

This effort would involve a second look not only at the Revolution itself but at all of French history—the past would be less black and the Revolution less pure, but the effect would be the same: to bring the Revolution within the pale of French history as the first decisive step in bringing it within the pale of Restoration politics. This determination to relate the Revolution to the French past is a persistent theme of the Liberal historiography in the Restoration, and takes a variety of forms. Mme de Staël, in her bible for Restoration Liberals, the *Considérations* (1817), gives an early example of this effort. Still on the defensive, she admits that the Revolution was an era of great confusion, but:

Men scarcely know any history other than that of their own time, and in reading the rantings of our days we would think that the eight centuries of monarchy which preceded the French Revolution had been peaceful times and that France was then *sur des roses.* We forget the Templars burnt under Philip the Fair; the English victories under the Valois; the Jacqueries; the murder of the Duc d'Orléans and of the Duke of Burgundy; the treacherous cruelties of Louis XI; the French Protestants condemned to ghastly torments under Francis I, at the same time that he was allied to the Protestants of Germany; the horrors of the League and the even greater horror of the massacre of Saint Bartholomew; the conspiracies against Henry IV, and his murder, that frightful work of the League; the scaffolds raised arbitrarily by Richelieu; the dragonnades; the revocation of the Edict of Nantes; the explusion of the Protestants, and the war of the Cevennes under Louis XIV; and, finally, the milder but nonetheless important struggles of the parlements under Louis XV.[9]

When seen in this special light, the French Revolution emerges not as the decisive introduction of the principle of change in French society, but as one battle in a history studded with conflict. In reply to the Conservative myth of French history—fourteen centuries of unbroken order—Mme de Staël offers a living past, with all the turbulence, error, and crime her generation had been led to associate exclusively with the Revolution. Further, these centuries of conflict have a definite pattern, an unconscious unity:

In France endless strife has been caused by the efforts to achieve liberty, whether that liberty was conceived of as feudal, religious, or representative; . . . we shall not find, in the space of eight centuries, an interval of twenty-five years without a conflict of nobles against the sovereign, of peasants against nobles, of Protestants against Catholics, or, finally, of parlements against the court—all struggles to escape from arbitrary power, the heaviest burden a people has to bear.[10]

This is Mme de Staël's great contribution to the Liberal arsenal—"liberty is ancient"—and this is to become the battle standard of the Liberal historiography. For if liberty is ancient, the French Revolution is no isolated outbreak without roots in French history, but rather the latest effort in a thousand-year struggle for liberty. Thus the Liberal of the Restoration not only discovers that the past can be used as a weapon generally, but uncovers a specific past, a Liberal past, which can sustain him. No longer need he commence French history with the Revolution; rather history can be given a fresh reading, and a new Liberal revision emerges.[11] Mme de Staël's dictum gave Liberals the impetus to go back to the French past—even to the blackest eras of feudal domination—and find their ancestors. But the immediate purpose for this new direction in historical thinking was clear: by finding such a tradition, a Liberal filiation, the Revolution could be brought into history—as French as the Fronde. Rather than something aberrant, foreign, and antinational, it is seen as the culmination of a persistent tradition.[12]

In 1819, Carrion-Nisas, an ex-Napoleonic officer, vigorously seconds the proposition that liberty is ancient. He chides writers of the past for ignoring this tradition, through either ignorance or perfidy.[13] "We have seen the spirit of liberty presiding over the primitive institutions of Gauls and Franks, enchained by feudal despotism, almost freed by and finally succumbing to royal despotism, gradually freeing itself from these new bonds, to the profit of the renaissance of letters and commerce."[14]

Carrion-Nisas admits the erratic course of this liberty, that victories were squandered and advantages lost, but the important fact is that it did exist. He lashes out at those who think that French history begins with the anarchy of feudalism or the despotism of Richelieu.

It is despotism which is of recent date in France, and one can say as much for all nations, and since the enemies of liberty force us to do so, it is necessary to repeat to them ceaselessly this obvious truth: that liberty is the natural state of man and has thus watched over the cradle of all peoples.[15]

This is the philosophical counterpart to Mme de Staël's historical formulation, but Carrion-Nisas goes to history to reinforce his case. His first chapter documents the basic freedom of the Gauls, even under Frankish domination. Charlemagne is presented as "this monarch, this friend of liberty who was so much ahead of his time and who has been so often and so gauchely compared to Napoleon."[16] Next comes feudalism, which is treated as a nightmare in the best Enlightenment tradition, but with a peculiarly Restoration note: "The spirit of liberty was never entirely destroyed; it lived, it matured, it fretted in the heart of this chaos[17] . . . and seized all occasions to burst forth."[18] When Carrion-Nisas comes to consider the Constituent Assembly, he is able to classify it as the beginning of the fourth epoch in the history of French freedom, closely resembling the "primitive times of liberty."[19]

Between 1817 and 1827, Augustin Thierry, perhaps the greatest French historian of the Restoration, published a series of letters in the *Censeur européen* and the *Courrier français.* These articles, which achieved the stature of classics during the Restoration, were collected and printed in 1827 and 1828.

In a well-known passage Thierry has described how a reading of Chateaubriand excited his historical imagination. Less celebrated are the passages in which he indicates that it was the deplorable state of historical writing in France as much as Romantic prose that spurred him into history.

To these prejudices, born of a lack of solid and conscientious study, I oppose the original documents of the past as well as that experience of political life which is among the privileges we enjoy in our own eventful era. No man of sense need accept the empty monarchic or republican abstractions offered by the writers of the old regime when all he has to do is call upon his own recollections and use them as a check on what he has read or heard about events long past: before long he will sense something alive stirring in the dust of vanished times. For there is not one among us children of the nineteenth century who does not know more on the score of rebellions and conquests, of the dismemberment of empires, of the fall and restoration of monarchies, of popular revolutions and the consequent reactions, than did Velly or Mably, or even Voltaire himself.[20]

As early as 1817, Thierry writes in the Liberal *Censeur européen*: "We are always told to imitate our forefathers. Why don't we follow this advice? Our ancestors were the artisans who founded the communes which invented modern liberty."[21] Again, in the following year, he recalls those who preserved the arts and customs of civilization during the feudal darkness:

These saviors of our arts were our ancestors; we are the sons of those serfs, those tributaries, those citizens whom conquerors pillaged at pleasure; we owe them all that we are. Virtue and glory are associated with their names; and yet these memories glitter but little, for history, which should have transmitted them, was hostage to the enemies of our fathers.[22]

Note the dedication to finding a history deliberately ignored by monarchist historians:

Here is the legacy of our national honor; here is what our children should read. . . . But slaves only lately freed, we have long had our memories filled only with the families and actions of our masters. It was only thirty years ago that we were advised that our ancestors were the nation. We have admired all, learned all, except what they were and did. We are patriots, but we leave in oblivion those who for fourteen centuries tilled the soil of our country, a country so often laid waste by other hands. The Gauls existed before France.[23]

Thierry blames the Revolution itself for this shameful neglect; the conquered Gauls deserve to be remembered as the first Frenchmen who fought in defense of liberty.[24]

The theme of Thierry's enterprise, indeed the motto of the Liberal history, is clearly stated in his first letter to the *Courrier français* in 1820:

The history of France as it has been written by modern writers is not the true history of the country, the national, the popular history; this history is still buried in the dust of contemporary chronicles. . . . The best part of our annals, the most serious, the most instructive, remains to be written; we lack a history of citizens, a history of subjects, a history of the people.

But it is no mere scholarly lacuna that concerns Thierry:

This history would present us, at the same time, with examples of conduct and that feeling of sympathy which we vainly seek in the adventures of the small number of privileged persons who alone occupy the historical scene. Our minds would be occupied far better with the destinies of the masses of men who have lived and felt like us than with the fortunes of the great. . . . The progress of the popular masses toward liberty and well-being would appear to us more imposing than the march of conquerors, and their misfortunes more touching than those of deposed kings.[25]

Calling for a "historiography of French liberty," Thierry attacks both the older historians and the modern revolutionaries, as much for ignoring this tradition as for propagating the myth that the Revolution was something new under the French sun. "And yet they are the same men. Just as we can trace ourselves back to them by name and descent, so we could trace to them our ideas, hopes, and desires, if their thoughts and actions were faithfully bequeathed to us."[26]

The one large task of the Liberal historians is to document Mme de Staël's dictum that liberty, no matter how obscured by circumstances and deliberate neglect, is ancient. For ten years, Thierry pours forth a steady stream of articles, letters, notes—all designed to recall the glorious past. He pays tribute to municipal liberties, freedom of the communes, and the irrepressible Jacques Bonhomme.[27] Thierry selects as his special subject the conquered races, first establishing their original freedom and then dwelling sympathetically upon their defeat and loss of liberty. This interest in conquered races culminates in his master work (1826) on the Norman conquest of England, in which he identifies himself with the defeated Saxons.

Thierry's attentions to these conquered peoples have given him the reputation of a racial historian, but he is equally concerned with discovering the tradition of resistance to despotism. The rise of the Estates is a lifelong interest.* He writes: "I wished to emphasize the democratic character of the process that led to the establishment of the communes. . . . A naïve account of the insurrection of Laon and the civil disturbances will teach us more than a learned theory on the origin of the Third Estate, which many people think suddenly sprang up from the earth in 1789."[28] The eighteenth-century Liberal gloried in an Estate produced by revolutionary demand, but the young Liberal Thierry senses the excitement and importance of giving this struggle the dimension of history. It was not until 1840 that Thierry submitted his full glorification of the Third Estate, but earlier in the Restoration he realized the value of resurrecting it.

It is true that this Third Estate, preferring peace to all other goods, feigned sleep during two centuries and thus caused itself to be forgotten: but its first appear-

* This question is treated gingerly by the Liberal historians, since, throughout the Restoration, some Conservative historians attempt to capitalize on this tradition. The Liberal must be careful, in praising the Estates, not to agree with their ancient principles of organization, in order to avoid attacking the changes made in 1789.

ance on the stage of political events foreshadowed those displays of energy, patriotism, and violence by which it was to distinguish itself in our times. Perhaps history has no place in the struggles and clashes of the ideas of our days—but since it is persistently drawn into these debates, *as happens every day*, an important lesson may be drawn from it: that no one in France is anyone's freedman; that none of our rights is of recent origin; and that the present generation owes all its liberties to the courage of the generations that preceded it.[29]

Another element in the French past to be resurrected is the middle class:

Our distant predecessors in our quest for political freedom were the medieval townsmen (*bourgeois*) who six hundred years ago restored the walls and the civilization of the ancient municipalities. Let there be no mistake: these were worthy men, and the most numerous and most forgotten class of our nation deserves a new life in our history. . . . Where did the aid come from which chased the English and raised the throne of Charles VII . . . ?

Not only is the Liberal tradition to be resurrected; the middle class, the Third Estate, is to be equated with the national interest. These forgotten members of the lower orders fought for France as did their descendants in the Revolution. Thierry cites the *Chronique de Saint-Denys* on the role of the *roturiers* in defending France. "The nobility, the royalty, in spite of the place of honor they occupy in our annals, did not contribute more than the Third Estate."

Thierry's motive for this opening of the past is always present:

Our sense of security, our confidence in the future, would be strengthened if we all realized that even in the most difficult times this country never lacked champions of justice and liberty. The spirit of independence is as firmly stamped on our history as on that of any other nation, ancient or modern. Our forefathers understood the meaning of liberty, they desired it as strongly as we do, and if they have failed to hand it down to us in its fullness and entirety, the fault was not theirs but that of human imperfection, for they overcame more obstacles than we shall ever encounter.[30]

In 1820, François Guizot, whose career in the Restoration is the most striking example of the enmeshing of politics and history, produced a defense of the Revolution as French and nothing but French. In a political broadside called *Du Gouvernement de la France depuis la Restauration et du ministère actuel* (which ran to five editions within the year and brought forth innumerable replies), Guizot made explicit the connection between past and present.[31] Borrowing heavily from the political-historical controversy of the eighteenth century (Montesquieu, Boulainvilliers, Dubos), Guizot takes as his starting point the traditional question—the rival races in French history. Abbé Sieyès had taught him that the Third Estate could be identified with the defeated Gauls, and Guizot takes the final step: the French Revolution is nothing less than the latest skirmish in an age-old campaign. "For more than thirteen centuries France has contained two peoples, conquerors and conquered. For more than thirteen centuries the conquered people battled to throw off the yoke of the conquerors. Our history is the history of this struggle. In our time, a decisive battle has been waged. It is called the Revolution."[32]

This struggle had taken many different forms, but from the vantage point of the Revolution it was now possible to see that it had been one struggle. "The battle continued in every age, under every form, with all weapons; and when in 1789 the deputies of all France were united in a single assembly, the two peoples hastened to reopen their old quarrel."[33] Guizot's brilliant synthesis enabled him to subsume the struggle of Frank *vs.* Gaul, seigneurs *vs.* peasants, nobles *vs.* middle class, under a single heading. Two decades before Marx, Guizot has the concept of a class struggle clearly in hand. With Carrion-Nisas and Thierry, he provides the men of '89 with a full and active past; from that point on, the Revolution is not alone. The struggles of the Gauls, peasants, States-General, and middle class are all honorable preludes to 1789. The Revolution discovered that history could be on its side. And this is the lesson that Guizot sought to drive home to Restoration France, including his students at the Collège de France. When he mounted the rostrum on December 7, 1820, to launch his famous series of lectures, he proudly claimed the past as the possession of Liberal France.

It is not true that injustices and abuses cannot find shelter except under the authority of antiquity. . . . Truth, justice, and rectitude are also graced by venerable titles, and at no period has man allowed them to be proscribed. Taken in succession, all the moral deeds, all the legitimate interests, of our society exist throughout the history of our country—you will find them constantly asserted and defended—all epochs will afford you innumerable proofs of struggles endured, of victories won, of concessions obtained in this holy cause . . . There is not a truth or a right which cannot call forth, from any period of history, monuments to consecrate it and facts to vindicate it.[34]

Not only is the past the faithful mirror of the struggles of the present, but there is a real historical connection between them. "There is no age that has not had its part in the grand struggle between good and evil, truth and error, liberty and oppression. And not only did each age carry on this laborious struggle on its own account, but whatever advantage it managed to maintain, it transmitted to its successors."[35]

Guizot selects as theme for the course the eight-hundred-year struggle for representative institutions. In fifty lectures, he manages to get through the fourteenth century, clearly establishing that the struggle is an ancient one. For Guizot, representative institutions are the significant fact of European history, and their continued presence is no accident. "They have existed in European society as the basis of all its deepest wants and most enduring tendencies."[36]

Guizot never completes his course; in 1822 he is ousted from the university. In virtual political exile, he turns to history and these are his productive years; he edits the thirty-one-volume *Collection des mémoires relatifs à l'histoire de France,* and writes the history of England. With the Martignac ministry, he returns to the university in triumph, his great theme in hand—the struggle of the European middle class from the time of the eleventh-century communes.[37] Guizot held his chair to the very eve of the Revolution of 1830, when he presented the French middle classes with the historical rationalization for this victory.

When deposed in 1822, Guizot was succeeded at the Collège de France by another young, brilliant, and Liberal professor—Auguste Trognon. In his opening discourse, he echoes the determination of the Liberal historian to have ancient France yield up her true secret, her hidden past. "It is time, gentlemen, that ancient France be avenged for the reproach of having left only sterile memories to the succeeding centuries."[38] Attacking any simple reading of the past as orderly progression, he sees it as marching from revolution to revolution.

Trognon proceeds with a bitter attack upon the romanticizing of French medieval history, singling out as culprits Sir Walter Scott and the Romantic poets. This is necessary, for these romancers are the impediments that must be cleared away if the genuine past of conflict and Liberal opposition is to be discovered. "Gentlemen, history is not poetry. The latter embellishes all that it touches; it loves to place, in the mists of ancient times, those brilliant phantoms of virtue and happiness . . . History is something else; it is designed to bear true witness of the past; that is what it owes to the future. Our ancestors have rarely been happy."*

Trognon devotes his energies to uncovering this seamy, though exciting, side of the French past. Of particular interest are two letters he publishes in the *Globe* on the communes of Vézelay and Laon. He quotes at length the story of a twelfth-century struggle of the people and the Comte de Nevers

* Auguste Trognon, *Etudes sur l'histoire de France* (1836), p. 401. This is a persistent theme of the Liberal discovery of the Middle Ages. And it is consistently confused by students of historiography, who have taken the tributes paid to Scott by historians like Thierry and Barante at their face value. What they admired in Scott was his sense of life, his ability to portray vividly, not his politics. They were vigorous in denouncing any attempt to "romanticize" the Middle Ages. See Guizot's criticism of Scott's view of the medieval burgher in *History of Civilization,* I, 140. See also Barante's Preface to *Histoire des Ducs de Bourgogne,* 4th ed. (1826), I, 43: "One remains convinced that even in this barbarous time when force reigned . . . the thoughts and views of the people were already exercising an immense power." Both Barante and Thierry were impressed by Scott's handling of the struggle between rival races. (See Thierry's article IX in *Dix ans,* pp. 392–97.) The Liberal "Romantic" historians of the Restoration did not admire Scott for the same reasons that the ante-bellum American South did. Closer to the true Scott of the novels *Ivanhoe* and *The Heart of Midlothian,* they decisively rejected the golden age of medieval history propagated by Conservative historians like Chateaubriand.

against the abbé of Vézelay. The Church was victorious, and the twelfth-century chronicler concludes his pious account with, "Thus were re-established the liberties of the monastery by the arms of the very excellent Abbé Pons." Trognon adds his comment: "I, who am of the nineteenth century, I mourn; thus were destroyed the liberties of the commune of Vézelay."[39] This is the Restoration historian feeling his way back into French history, finding his lineage. The Liberal historian can extract the liberal tradition, even out of a hostile chronicle.

In a second letter on the commune of Laon, Trognon traces still another manifestation of this twelfth-century resistance to oppression. Here is chronicled a struggle between bourgeoisie and nobility, in which the people buy the neutrality of the bishop. The bishop reneges on his bargain; the people revolt, torture and kill the bishop. "Such were the people in all times, in the days of innocence, in our golden age of monarchy . . . same needs, same passions, same fury. Every time they were made too miserable they revolted; every time they revolted it was bloody. It is silly to speak of things so well known today. Why is it that there are still so many who do not understand them?"

Trognon concludes, summing up his intention in both letters as, "I have sought to establish the two ways, unique in our history . . . in which the communes of France were founded. The historiographers of the court have been accustomed to regard them as beneficent emanations of royal power."[40] What emerges clearly from Trognon's work is the relevance of the past to the present, the destruction of the myth of a golden age, the ever-present revolutionary tradition. This is what a Liberal examination of the French past can offer to the French Revolution.

The clearly propagandistic intent of these Liberal historians should not blind us to their real achievement. In their forays into the past, Guizot and Thierry ransack the archives; it would be no exaggeration to say that these politically inspired historians laid the groundwork for a serious consideration of the French past.* Nor should we forget the state of history that confronted these Liberals of the Restoration. The Liberals of the eighteenth century (when not worshiping classical Greece or Rome) had rejected the past, abandoning French history to the Conservatives. The Conservatives were content to blindly extol the past, to glorify traditional monarchy or aristocracy. Thus, what faced the Liberal historian of the Restoration—what he inevitably reacted against—was a tradition of official monarchist history and aristocratic apologia. Though not yet in the tradition of scien-

* In the period of the July Monarchy the Liberal historians fulfill their Restoration mission. Guizot, as Minister of the Interior, sets in motion a vast program centering around the Comité de Travaux Historique et Scientifique. Among the historians who serve are Mignet and Michelet. Thierry is given charge of his own project, the publishing of the *Monuments inedits de l'histoire du Tiers État.*

tific history, Liberals like Guizot, Thierry, and Trognon see themselves as redressing the balance. In discovering the Liberal French past, long ignored by the eighteenth-century *philosophe* and the traditional monarchist, the Liberal historian performed a necessary shift of emphasis and, incidentally, came a good deal closer to the scientific truth.*

This idea of giving the French Revolution roots was not limited to French history. In their eagerness to make the Revolution respectable, the Liberals embraced all history. The Revolution was not only a logical development of the French past, but also the culmination of a general European revolution, the end product of three centuries of European history. It was as if the Revolution could be made more acceptable by widening its ancestry, by placing it in a context broader than French history, by giving it a European dimension and a world-wide significance.

The Liberals have no difficulty in selecting their pedigree. The French Revolution is the climax of the great European revolution for liberty: religious in the sixteenth century, constitutional in the seventeenth, and philosophic in the eighteenth. In an age of reviving Catholicism (Maistre, Bonald, Lamennais), it would seem unwise to stress the relationship between the Protestant Reformation and the French Revolution. Indeed, Lamennais offered this connection as grim evidence that the Revolution was a war against God.[41] But Protestants like Guizot and Mme de Staël were obdurate: "Far from concealing the fact that liberty of conscience is closely linked to political liberty, the Protestants ought, in my opinion, to make a boast of the alliance."[42] Speaking of the sixteenth-century religious wars, Trognon asks, "Is it an illusion of our liberal spirit of modern times to see engaged among these religious quarrels, the imperishable cause of liberty?"[43] Thiessé, in his popular résumé of the French Revolution, locates the decisive change in the sixteenth century, when "the human spirit received a vast thrust. . . . From then on the human spirit was on the march; it continues to march."[44]

Liberty is Protestant in the sixteenth century and English in the seventeenth. In 1824, when Guizot turned from a consideration of France to a history of England, he did so to demonstrate what every Restoration Liberal was prepared to believe on faith—that the eighteenth-century French

* The position of the eighteenth century on history is a matter presently undergoing revision. The Enlightenment which produced a Gibbon and a Voltaire cannot easily be dismissed as unhistorical. See N. Shargo, *History in the Encyclopedia*, and Eberhard Weiss, *Geschichtsschreibung und Staatsauffassung in der französischen Enzyklopädie.* One must also consider the great debate of the eighteenth century on the rival races in French history; see Jacques Barzun, *The French Race.* Yet it is still a question of emphasis; placed alongside of the nineteenth century, the Enlightenment still appears fundamentally antihistorical. History, for the *philosophe,* is still largely the dark ages, the Gothic past, an accumulation of errors and misery. As Arthur Wilson says in his review of Weiss's book, "It is still true to say that the Encyclopedists had little faith in history. It was a case of history without Historismus." A.H.R., July 1957.

Revolution was only the latter-day version of the seventeenth-century English Revolution. "Passionately preoccupied with the political future of my country, I wished to know precisely through what truths and what errors, by what persevering efforts and by what prudent transactions, a great people had succeeded in conquering and in preserving a free government."[45] Says Carrion-Nisas: "Read about the English Revolution and you will find that this revolution was the prophecy which ours fulfilled."[46] Mignet begins his history of the Revolution with a statement of the parallel; Bodin and Carrel echo it. By 1826 it is a cliché of the Liberal history; by 1830 the ominous parallel of the "two restorations" is a stand-by of Liberal politics.

Montgaillard, another political holdover from the Empire, concludes his nine-volume defense of the Revolution by affirming "a propagation of ideas, an association of theories across the centuries," and he sees the Revolution as communicable, moving from Puritan England to the New World and then to France.[47] Generally, the Liberal historian was committed to defending the eighteenth century as the necessary last link in the great chain of European revolution, but he was careful to deny that it *alone* was responsible for 1789.[48] It was rather the Conservatives who tended to hold the eighteenth century "responsible" for the Revolution; once they had assigned it a single specific cause, they had merely to "treat" that cause and prevent further revolution.*

The problem of how to defend the eighteenth-century ancestors of Restoration Liberalism, without admitting the Conservative charge that a band of conspirators was directly responsible for subverting French society, was a ticklish one. Perhaps it was best solved by Victor Cousin, for whom the eighteenth century, far from being the conscious perpetrator of the Revolution, is simply the helpless summation of the preceding centuries[49]—a product, like the sixteenth and seventeenth centuries, of the undermining of the Middle Ages. This undermining, according to Cousin, is the great theme of European history; the Revolution is its climax. "Heir to the centuries that preceded it, the eighteenth century accomplished its work. The sixteenth and seventeenth centuries had mined and shaken the Middle Ages; the mission of the eighteenth was to overthrow them." "The French Revolution finished the work of the preceding revolutions and carried on its flanks the accumulated storms of two centuries." Indeed, Cousin argues that the end result of the Revolution—the spirit of political liberty—was present in one form or another in all these earlier movements, the Revolution was merely the last act in the drama.[50]

This attempt to "lose" the Revolution in history, to give it respectability by emphasizing its antecedents, had an additional advantage. It reinforced

* Barante on Charles X: "For forty years he was convinced that the Revolution would have been easily avoidable except for the weakness of his brother Louis XVI." A. G. P. de Barante, *Souvenirs* (1890–95), III, 487.

one of the most persistent and important of the themes of the Liberal historiography of the Restoration—the inevitability of the Revolution.* Early in the Restoration, the Liberals realized that one of the best ways to absolve the Revolution from any guilt was to insist that it *had to be,* that it had been a long time in the making, that it represented an accumulation of history, and therefore that to deny it was to deny time itself.

Mme de Staël, recognizing the Conservative tactic of assigning the cause of the Revolution to some specific catastrophe, denies that French participation in the American Revolution was *the* cause; rather, "The Revolution must be attributed to everything, and to nothing: every year of the century led toward it by every path."[51] For the *Archives,* Guizot's magazine, it was "social necessities which led to the Revolution." For Le Sur: "In 1789, we had arrived at the epoch when it was necessary to enact into laws the changes that had occurred in customs."[52] Thiessé, characteristically more radical, and writing in 1826, gives the notion of inevitability a new twist: the eighteenth-century Enlightenment was the inevitable response to centuries of abuse, "only a consequence of the principle that the action is equal to the reaction."[53] Montgaillard goes even further: the Revolution itself was the "forced consequence, the political corollary, of the *ancien régime.*"[54]

Tocqueville, writing after a generation of Liberal historians, noted this emphasis upon inevitability as a tendency of all democratic historians.

> According to them, each nation is indissolubly bound by its position, its origin, its antecedents, and its character to a certain lot that no efforts can ever change. They involve generation in generation, and thus, going back from age to age, and from necessity to necessity, up to the origin of the world, they forge a close and enormous chain which girds and binds the human race. . . . They take a nation arrived at a certain stage of its history and affirm that it could not but follow the track that brought it thither.[55]

In 1820, Dupin, defending the Abbé de Pradt from charges of having attacked the king, shouts to the court, "The Revolution of 1789 was not made in a day; it was propelled by the weight, the irresistible weight, of preceding centuries."[56]

The Restoration Liberal sees the inevitable process as continuing. For Rémusat, the party opposed to the Revolution is "condemned to inevitable extinction; it cannot retard for a moment the march of society."[57] Guizot, in 1821, warns that "The social movement has not stopped; its direction has not changed; the classes which join its ranks continue to rise; those which refuse to take part in it live increasingly in its backwash."[58] And Montgaillard in 1825 adds, "You cannot stop the movement of the earth."[59]

Closely allied to this thesis of inevitability is the insistence upon the popularity of the Revolution—the totality of the demand for change. In-

* This notion is a constant one in the historiography of the Revolution, receiving modern formulation as the "thèse de circonstances" by Augustin Cochin.

deed, popularity may be regarded as a kind of proof of inevitability. Mme de Staël again lays down the line that the Liberal historians are to follow, arguing that the eighteenth century was of one mind.

The Empress Catherine fawned over Voltaire; Frederick the Great was almost his rival in literature; Joseph II was the most determined *philosophe* in his realm; the King of France had twice, in America and Holland, taken the part of the subjects against their prince; . . . M. Necker was then perfectly right when he said . . . that the voice of Europe invited the King to consent to the wishes of the nation.[60]

Mme de Staël is at pains to describe the atmosphere of the eighteenth century as conducive to change, to insist that there was a kind of *Zeitgeist* for change to which the Revolution was the welcome response. She notes that the delegates would not kneel to the King in '89 because "the public at large, not excepting the proudest aristocrats, would have termed the action ridiculous, that is, wholly inconsistent with the opinions of the age."[61] Le Sur notes that even the Catholic Church was affected by the Enlightenment, and Richard states flatly, "The Revolution was the work of the immense majority of Frenchmen. They who accuse it, then, of all the things which accompanied it, accuse the nation whose doing it is."[62] If the Revolution was wanted, if it sprang from some universal demand, if those who later fought it were among those who brought it into being, there could no longer be any question of guilt—everyone was guilty. Listen to Thiessé:*

The Monarch seated on the throne desired a change in the lot of the people and looked for every means to accomplish it; the nobility, still bruised from the blows of Louis XI, of Richelieu, of Louis XIV, called for liberty at least for the aristocracy; the magistracy, armed with its remonstrances, . . . not only wanted a revolution, but gave the signal for it, assigned it its character, fixed its principles.[63]

Here we have another plank in the platform of the Liberal historians—the shift or the sharing of blame. Long before Tocqueville, this first generation of Liberal historians presents a fully developed statement of the aristocratic revolution.

A transitional figure between the Revolution and the Restoration, Jacques Antoine Dulaure, links the efforts of two generations in his attempt to familiarize Restoration France with the aristocratic revolution. Author of a history of Paris and a history of phallic cults, Dulaure began his career in 1790, at the age of 25, writing an *Histoire critique de la noblesse, depuis le commencement de la monarchie, jusqu'à nos jours; où l'on*

* Thiessé, born in 1793, had the typical diversified career of the Liberal journalist-historian of the period. He was a dramatist, a poet, a translator of Byron. He contributed to the Liberal house organs, the *Constitutionnel* and the *Revue encyclopédique*. His own publication, Les Lettres normandes, was banned. For the *Résumé* series, he also published an *Histoire romaine* and an *Histoire de Pologne*.

expose ses préjugés, ses brigandages, ses crimes, où l'on prouve qu'elle a été le fléau de la liberté, de la raison, des connoissances humaines, et constamment l'ennemi du peuple et des rois. In 1815 he returned to his theme. This time he sets about explaining the *Causes secrètes des excès de la Révolution,* in which he reveals his purpose: "If I prove . . . that the leaders of the French émigrés are the principal authors of all the excesses that the Revolution is reproached for . . . I will have absolved the principles of the Revolution from the crimes imputed to them."[64] Thus he presents us with the minor theme of the Liberal version of the aristocratic revolution—the nobility is responsible not only for the Revolution, but for the unfortunate course it took. In 1823, Dulaure introduces his five-volume study of the Revolution with a detailed analysis of the activities of the parlements, concluding,

that the resistance of the royal will, these civil dissensions, these bloody revolts, indeed these preliminaries of the Revolution, were the work of the ministers, of the parlements, and of the nobility of some of the provinces; and that the men of the Third Estate were strangers to this and played only a secondary role. Soon they will be seen imitating the example of the upper classes.[65]

In his *Mémoire au roi* (1814), Lazare Carnot seeks to shift the burden of guilt onto the aristocracy; they are the true regicides,

you who by the perfidy of your counsels drew him into a labyrinth from which he could not be extricated. Why did you refuse him the *dons gratuits* that he asked for? Why did you refuse to grant him the increase in taxation which your depredations made necessary? . . . What did the notables do for him? The clergy? The nobility? Who incited the States-General? Who placed all France in a state of revolution? . . . Louis XVI, you say, was the best of kings, the father of his subjects. Well, what did you do to save this father, this best of kings? Didn't you abandon him in the most cowardly manner when you saw him caught in that very danger you had led him into? Wasn't it your duty to form a rampart around him with your bodies?[66]

Here, in 1814, are the two basic accusations: an aristocrat-inspired revolution, plus the charge—echoed throughout the Restoration—desertion of the king. Carnot is emphatic: "You draw a frightful picture of the Revolution, and the more frightful it is, the more criminal you are, for it is your work—you are the authors of all the calamities that have resulted from it."[67]

In 1816, Chateaubriand's famous pamphlet *De la Monarchie selon la charte* had drawn the distinction between the men and moral interests of the Revolution. In a reply, Jubé de la Perrelle picked up the phrase "men of the Revolution" and gave it a Liberal definition, arguing that we are all men of the Revolution, all products of 1789: "Since the king forgets and wishes that we forget, let us not reproach the nobility, or the clergy, or the parlements, or the financial situation, or the people."[68] In short, the Liberals do not intend to allow the nobility to sponsor a revolution and then, with a restoration, allow this same nobility to point the finger of guilt at them.

Mme de Staël was equally firm in assigning aristocratic responsibility, but with her usual intelligence she saw the Liberal dilemma—could one attack the aristocracy for helping hatch a revolution that the Liberals were busy trying to prove was inevitable and desirable? Her resolution of this difficulty—consistent with her historical admiration for the nobility—is to praise the aristocracy for participating in the Revolution, but criticize it for doing an about-face. She charges the aristocracy with desertion, not of Louis XVI, but of the Revolution:

These men forget that they themselves, with courage and reason, launched the first attack against the royal power, and what little resistance they encountered because the nation was with them. Have they any right to complain that, after having proved too strong for the crown, they should have proved too weak for the people?[69]

Her version of the aristocratic revolution is that the nobility failed to follow through. Scorning the example of the English aristocracy, they did not place themselves at the head of the Revolution. They preferred to quit their country in a mass, and "allied themselves with foreigners."[70]

Guizot, less sympathetic to the historic role of the aristocracy, sees the Revolution as primarily the work of his beloved middle class, and offers still another version of this aristocratic revolution. It *did* take place, but its motive must be distinguished from that of the real Revolution. For Guizot, the historian, this was no struggle for liberties, but merely the traditional selfish struggle of the aristocracy against the throne, a struggle which happened to coincide, in 1789, with the demands of the French people. Thus the aristocrats bear the onus of revolt against the king, while the ignoble nature of their motives absolves them from any credit—a perfect Liberal compromise. "In 1789 as today, and today as in 1789, they have not been the Royalist party but the Aristocratic party, battling for their personal interests."[71]

Once again it is Thiessé who best sums up the Restoration Liberal attitude: The aristocracy unleashed a revolution which it then proceeded to fight; it is guilty on both counts.

The first blows were raised against the monarchy by the very castes most interested in its survival, so general was their impatience for revolution. But after having aroused all the passions, after having unleashed the torrent of democracy, these castes retreated before their own work. Capable of finishing the Revolution by the same means with which they had begun it, they preferred to betray it and to fight it; they raised Europe against it. Reduced, then, to the necessity of saving itself . . . the Revolution descended to the lowest classes and took on the character and tastes of the multitude.[72]

Thiessé's account is close to Mme de Staël's reading, but it goes one step further. By relinquishing control of the Revolution they had begun, the aristocrats were responsible for its falling into the hands of the mob.

This conception of an aristocratic revolution is not without contradictions. The Liberals are, after all, committed to defending the Revolution; in shifting the blame, they risk admitting that the Revolution is blamable. Nevertheless, the practical advantages of labeling the aristocracy a revolutionary party are enormous. First, by widening the category of the guilty to include the aristocracy, the Liberals confuse the whole question of guilt, making it meaningful only in theological terms. Second, by labeling the aristocrats as revolutionary in the 1780's, they cast doubt on the purity of their intentions during the Restoration. Finally, this line of attack is consistent with the basic Liberal strategy of the Restoration—to drive a wedge between monarchy and aristocracy by recalling to both their historic conflicts. Ultimately, it was this same concept, carefully nurtured, that enabled the men of 1830 to charge the Ultras with trying to overthrow the Restoration.

As we have seen, the Liberal historians of the Restoration countered the Conservative attempt to dispose of the Revolution as accidental with the thesis of inevitability, and met the Conservative indictment of conspiracy by (1) asserting the Revolution's general popularity, and (2) giving due "credit" to the aristocratic revolution. However, these are essentially defenses of the origins of the Revolution; granted its inevitability, its popularity, even its aristocratic phase, the Revolution did succeed, did rule, the aristocrats ultimately did emigrate. The Revolution had to confront its own record. Were its crimes also "inevitable"—as the Conservatives would have it? The Restoration Conservative did not forget and was determined not to let France forget.

This was a difficult problem for the Liberals; they were being called upon to defend what seemed, in the Restoration, indefensible. Here again, their historians found the solution. For the Conservatives had gone too far in their rejection of the Revolution. They had attacked the whole revolutionary experience, regarding it as one deadly drama, commencing with the *philosophes* and culminating with Bonaparte. But a glance at the Revolution shows that it was more complicated than that; it had its phases, its internecine struggles, its own dialectic. The Liberals could take advantage of its very nature, could cut it up into clearly defined pieces, identifying one as the true Revolution and everything else as a falling-away, a betrayal. This became the basic Liberal stratagem in the Restoration. They met the Conservative attack with "That isn't what we meant at all."

In 1797, under the relative calm of the Directory, Benjamin Constant anticipated this theme: "Let us separate then, in the history of the revolutionary period, that which is part of the government, those measures which they had the right to take, from those crimes which they committed and which they did not have the right to commit."[73] The key concept is government, as opposed to the Terror; the key word is "separate." In the

1829 edition of this work, Constant, with the battles of the Restoration behind him, points up the relevance of this conception for the Restoration:

I would not have recalled any memories of the Terror, but I thought it important for the future of France that she not confuse what is worthy of admiration and what is worthy of horror. To justify the reign of '93, to picture its crimes and frenzies as a necessity that weighs inevitably upon peoples when they seek freedom, is to harm a sacred cause, to do it more damage than its most avowed enemies.[74]

This is the reasoning of the Restoration Liberals on the crimes and excesses of the Revolution. Not only can we dissociate ourselves, it is our *duty* to do so, for in defending the Terror we weaken our whole case. We must defend only what is morally defensible.[75]

Another voice from the past is brought to the aid of the Liberal effort at dissociation in 1817, when the *Archives* reprints Mounier's 1801 reply to Abbé Barruel's classic attack on the Revolution. The Liberal finds Mounier an ideal source, a Liberal who broke with the Revolution because of its excesses. Summing up the contents, the magazine transmits Mounier's message to the Restoration.

Mounier is trying to distinguish those doctrines which contributed to the first *élan* of the Revolution from those which owed their force and their influence to the Revolution itself. He carefully separates what preceded 1789 from what followed it, this separation being more important than is thought by those who devote themselves to confusing everything in order to decry it.[76]

In his pamphlet of 1816, *Du Gouvernement représentatif*, Guizot admits that the Revolution went astray: liberty and justice were its clearly proposed ends, but "ambitions supplanted opinions, realities regained the upper hand," and the Revolution degenerated into class warfare, "a war not for liberty, but for power."[77] Here is the explicit Liberal theme—the Revolution is a good thing gone wrong. In 1820 Guizot specifically attacked the Conservatives for their insistence upon seeing the Revolution *en bloc:* "Do you realize that it is most dangerous to curse the Revolution in its entirety, and not to allow one to discriminate between good and evil, between sound principles and errors, between excellent results and deplorable straddling?"[78]

In 1821, Guizot complains that the government "exploits the fear that the Revolution still inspires," that it can do this because men still habitually "take the past *en bloc.*"[79] This is wrong; there was not one revolution, there were two; you must not confuse the two, you must distinguish between them. This is the Liberals' plea, the argument that will give them a lifeline in the Restoration. It gives them also their Revolution, a revolution without a blemish, achieved by the simple expedient of reading out of it all that is disfiguring.

For Carrion-Nisas, it is the peculiar advantage of the Restoration Liberal that *he* can adopt this happy procedure, that he can be a connoisseur of the Revolution, slicing it up and selecting the desirable portions for defense.

The new generation, which grows and advances with the new institutions, owes to its age the precious advantage of having inherited the Revolution without having directed it, of having taken no part in its political excesses and for that reason having the right to blame everyone; it eagerly welcomes all the good that the Revolution has done during the thirty years which have passed, and it freely repudiates the evil; it blesses the great results of '89, but it wants no more of the bloody aftermath; it will uphold the principles and not the pernicious consequences deduced from the principles by base or perverse minds.[80]

This is the version the Liberals are trying to sell to the Restoration—a revolution purely conceived, but unfortunately corrupted. Carrion-Nisas takes to task the Conservative effort to enmesh Revolutionary Jacobins and Restoration Liberals in one net. Are those men to be called Jacobins who "experienced the disasters of our long Revolution without departing for a single instant from the route mapped out by their patriotism and their love of the public good?"[81]

This process of drawing the line is actively pursued by the Liberal historians. For Félix Bodin, editor of the popular Liberal *Résumé* series, the Jacobins are "that illegal and violent power which raised itself to the level of the national representation in order to oppress it one day."[82] Before beginning to treat the Convention in his own *Résumé de l'histoire de France*, Bodin takes the Liberal pledge, "I embrace none of the parties which existed then and which seem so far from our present ideas"[83]—suggesting the distance between this untouchable part of the Revolution and the Restoration. Marat is "horrible"; Hébert, "frightful"; Robespierre, "a man whose calm façade of patriotism and moderation masked a cold and vicious soul, a man whose cruelty could only be explained by envy."[84]

So deeply embedded is this notion of dissociation that, even in the heat of debate, General Foy (an intrepid defender of the Revolution in the Restoration Assembly) does not let down his guard. The Conservatives, raising the specter of '93, press the Liberals to accept the whole Revolution, but Foy has the answer: "They also speak to us of '93; to us, three quarters of whom were victims of the regime of '93. It is not us, it is not any of us, who made '93."[85]

The pattern of the Liberal attitude emerges: by identifying themselves with a part of the Revolution, the Liberals can deny any historical responsibility for or any personal sympathy with the Terror, the Noyade, and so on. Thus, the Liberals' defense of the Revolution clusters about the Constituent Assembly; 1789–91 was *their* revolution. Glorification of the Constituent Assembly becomes part of the Liberal catechism. Mme de Staël feels it necessary, "before entering on the distressing events which disfigured the French Revolution," to "examine the principles proclaimed by the Constituent Assembly. . . . It is perhaps the only one in France that fully represented the national wish."[86] Norvins bemoans the fact that so little is known about it; and Carrion-Nisas feels that the French preserve for it a "mémoire du cœur."[87] In the ostensibly neutral *Collection des Mémoires*, the Constituent Assembly is treated as the golden age of the Revolution. Berville, one of the editors, finds in the Ferrières memoirs "a picture of the most important epoch of our history."[88] For Montgaillard, the Assembly is where representative government was born, and he attacks Burke for having "painted it in the most odious colors."[89] For Bodin, it was nothing less than "the most glorious assemblage of virtue, talent, and light that has ever been offered any civilized people."[90] For Thiessé, August 10 is the turning point, after which "violence and crime dishonored the popular victory."[91]

Splitting up the Revolution into acceptable and reprehensible phases was a neat trick, but it left one major question unanswered: How did it happen that the acceptable constitutional revolution had given way to the reprehensible Terror? Burke had prophetically argued in 1790 that at the end of every vista is a gallows, and the Restoration reactionary held that the connection between revolutionary ideals and revolutionary realities was one of cause and effect. That there was a revolutionary rhythm, that change would lead to violence, was an article of Conservative faith, and to discourage Liberal reform in the Restoration one had only to point to the results of the great reform started in 1789. The problem, then, for the Liberal historian, after dissociating himself from the crimes, is how to account for them, since the Conservatives would not allow them to be forgotten. The Liberals, seldom at a loss for fresh ways to defend their revolution, come up with three methods of handling the delicate question.

First, they can adopt the attitude of the defense attorney who holds "society" responsible for the acts of the accused. As counsel for the defendant, historians of the Revolution argue that it was the *ancien régime* that was responsible. It was the persistence of the Old Regime in the Revolution that produced the unfortunate excesses. The original resistance, the emigration, foreign intervention—all the revolutionary crimes can be seen as responses to some provocation. Two striking examples of this approach can be found in Mignet and Laroche. Mignet, whose account was unusually restrained, saw that

> the Revolution had obstacles to overcome. . . . The privileged sought to prevent it, Europe to subject it; and thus forced into a struggle, it could not set bounds to its efforts, or moderate its victory. Resistance from within brought about the sovereignty of the multitude, and aggression from without, military domination.[92]

For Laroche, whose edition of the letters of Abbé Grégoire forced him to flee to England, it was the emigration and the foreign intervention that transformed a family quarrel into a national war. The guilty are those who "caused a humane and generous nation to settle matters by the sword. . . . They alone must bear the responsibility for all the bloodshed that stirred up the people and directed their weapons against their fatherland."[93]

This line of defense—guilty with an explanation—is an obvious one; indeed it had been employed in the very heart of the Revolution. Here, perhaps, is its weakness—the very crimes now universally decried were committed in the name of provocations. Far more original and even bolder is the attempt to mitigate the Revolution by a comparative approach. Here the historian is in his element; he cannot excuse the crimes, but he certainly can place them in a context of fourteen centuries of crime. Moreover, he can deny the Conservative claim that the Revolution was an especially loathsome and unnatural event, outside of humanity and history. All of French history lay open, and the Liberals attack it with relish: "Yes, we were bad," is their refrain, "but you—you're worse!"

In Richard's *Aperçu de la Révolution* (1820), we find one of the earliest examples of this approach. After trying to pin the blame for the horrors of the Revolution on a single faction, he switches ground and in a footnote, without comment, lists the horrors of French history, as if to say "Even if there were horrors, they are not new to French history."[94]

In 1823, the editors of the *Collection des memoirs*, stung by criticism that theirs is a Liberal source collection designed to whitewash the Revolution, devote a series of four volumes to the September Days. Actually this is perfectly consistent with the Liberal version; September 1792 is the great dividing line of the Revolution, the frontier of respectability. Here as elsewhere the editors reveal their Liberal bias in a long paragraph on the relativity of crime:

It is a sad thing for a nation to find in its annals . . . the spectacle of the same passions aroused for different reasons. This sad and painful recital involuntarily recalls the massacre of the Protestants, prepared with such artifice and executed with such cruelty by the Leaguers, and, in even more distant times, the execution of the Armagnacs, sacrificed to the vengeance of the Burgundian party. The quarrels of the aristocracy, religious fanaticism, and the horrible excesses of popular rage have too often produced scenes of carnage.[95]

Note the "reluctance" with which the editors turn to an examination of the French past. History speaks and offers this terrible equation: crime is a constant factor of the French past.

Whether these similar projects were conceived in the palace of the Dukes of Burgundy, in the middle of the court where the Medici reigned, or in the heart of the commune of Paris, . . . the outrage done to justice, the outrage done to men and to God, remains the same: always the bloodshed, always the outcries against the executioners. France will forever number among its days of mourning, history will brand with its judgment, the massacres of the Armagnacs, the night of Saint Bartholomew, and the detestable September Days.[96]

No attempt is made to deny the horrors of the Revolution. It is simply pointed out that the Revolution's victims (monarchy, aristocracy, clergy) have, if one goes back far enough, as black a record as the Revolution itself. Once again history is with the Liberals: its dark side can be used to mitigate the indefensible part of the revolutionary record.

Montgaillard, having chronicled the story of the Revolution—good and bad—feels compelled in his conclusion to compare the Revolution with the record of the French monarchy. In a roll call reminiscent of the eighteenth century's total rejection of the French past, he singles out distinguishing crimes of France's rulers: Philip the Fair persecuted Templars and Jews; Charles IX was soaked in Protestant blood; Henry III was tyrannical and debauched (Louis XV, just debauched); Richelieu and Louis XIV violated all the sacred treaties. How pale September 1792 seems, says Montgaillard, alongside Saint Bartholomew's Day, 1572: "One cannot recall too vividly to the memory of the French the crimes of ultramontanist fanaticism." As for the National Convention, "It is certainly more excusable than the despot Louis XIV for violations comparable to his."[97]

There is a touch of the ludicrous about this newest of the Liberal sciences, comparative criminology, with its effort to palliate the crimes of one generation with a recital of the misdeeds of an older one. But historians like Montgaillard and Thiessé are not content with merely reminding France of her wicked past; they go further and suggest a connection. Just as the Liberal historians had shown the roots of the French Revolution to be deeply embedded in French history, they now discover that the errors of the Revolution can be rooted in the errors of the past. "Francis I, Henry II, Charles IX, Henry III, Richelieu, Louis XIV, even the effeminate Louis XV, had tortured consciences, imposed dogmas, determined rules for religion, required oaths, profanations of the sacraments, *billets de confession*, etc., and the revolutionaries of '91, '92, '93, and '94 copied these hideous examples."[98]

This is the charge, that the Revolution at its worst was only imitating the French past; for every crime there was a grim precedent. Thus, after listing a choice selection of crimes, persecutions, massacres, Montgaillard says, "The Jacobins of 1793 only copied the Acts of Proscription exercised under the Valois and Bourbon princes. . . . This spirit of almost servile imitation in crime is seen in so many details that it seems the revolutionaries of 1792, '93, and '94 can only be charged with resurrecting the crimes of our history."[99]

Thiessé brings this charge right down to the Revolution itself. "These tendencies were inspired by the upper classes; the spirit of sedition descended from above."[100]

The attempt to excuse the crimes of the Revolution, however morally detestable they may have been, as politically necessary, is an early defense set up by Restoration Liberalism. The shift to comparative criminology is a sign of growing truculence. The crimes are still crimes, though they seem less shocking with all French history as a backdrop. There remains one further development, certain proof that, in the closing days of the Restoration, the Liberals are winning their battle to enshrine the Revolution. It is the ultimate sophistication: the crimes of the Revolution are to be judged by the results that were achieved, the forces that had to be overcome; you cannot have a great revolution without some excess. You cannot make an omelet without breaking some eggs.

As early as 1818, Rémusat, a young Doctrinaire writer, had wondered about the "mistakes" of the Revolution. "Among the faults which were committed, some were inevitable. The National Assembly has been reproached for having committed too many: could it have been otherwise? One cannot remove a stone of the edifice without upsetting it entirely."[101] This is a remark made by a man of the new generation (he was born in 1797), a man who has not experienced the Revolution directly. Rémusat's remarks are not published—1818 is too early—but by 1829, Victor Cousin, speaking to the new generation at the Faculté des Lettres, can trumpet Rémusat's observation into a full-blown defense of the Revolutionary era.

Cousin starts with the premise that the French Revolution was the last of the great European revolutions for liberty. In 1829 he can truly observe that it has been general and it has been successful. But, he asks, "Did it escape the law of all great upheavals? Did it regenerate the world without violence? Was it violent without being extravagant, was it extravagant without being criminal?"[102]

Having suggested by his question the improbability of any such revolution's proceeding peaceably, Cousin answers, "No, gentlemen, no revolution has been able to escape this sad cortege. Clearly these details are far from attractive. You know the horrible excesses, the still unforgettable outrages, which bloodied and soiled the English Revolution."[103]

Here Cousin suggests that the crimes of the Revolution must be weighed against the tremendous achievements of the Revolution. These crimes are unfortunate, but somehow necessary, given the magnitude of the results. The French Revolution, according to Cousin, was indeed deserving of more forgiveness for its crimes, because the changes it wrought were even more fundamental than those wrought by earlier revolutions: "The French Revolution must surpass preceding revolutions in violence as it surpassed them in greatness."[104]

We have seen thus far that the task of the Liberal historian was to rescue the Revolution from the stigma it would naturally bear in a restoration. Whatever the tactics employed, whatever the defense adopted—be it providing the Revolution with respectable antecedents, stressing its inevitable and popular character, dissociating it from its crimes, or explaining and excusing those crimes—the Liberal was proceeding on one central assumption: that the Revolution was right. The Liberals dissociated all the more to insist upon the purity of the original Revolution; they could extenuate crime only because they were convinced that the Revolution was, in essence, just.

And occasionally, in the midst of all their apologies and explanations, this essential faith and belief in the Revolution steps out from behind the façade and we catch a glimpse of it. The Revolution was "right," and the corollary was that the Old Regime was in some way "wrong."[105] One could hold with Mme de Staël that Old France was despotic, or with Carrion-Nisas that it was feudal, or with Rémusat that it was simply corrupt—whatever abuse one chooses to single out, the Revolution was desirable. And in 1820, as if tired of the defensive attitude, endless apologies, and rationalizations that are the Liberal historians' lot in the Restoration, Guizot captured the real basis for the Liberal's belief in the Revolution: that, taken all in all, crimes included, the Revolution was worth having.

Illuminate all its errors, establish all its faults, seek out and assemble all its crimes, then what have you proved? . . . I am more generous than you, I do not wish to disown anything of the revolution, I do not claim to discharge it of anything. I seize it as a whole, its truths and its errors, its virtues and its excesses, its triumphs and its reverses. . . . You will tell me that it violated justice, oppressed liberty. I will agree with you, I will even join you in examining the causes of these lamentable digressions. I will go further: I will grant you that the germ of these crimes was present in the very cradle of the Revolution.[106]

Having made these concessions, Guizot makes the leap, gives us the heart of the Liberal matter:

I will still say that the Revolution, brought on by the necessary development of a society in progress, founded on moral principles, undertaken with the design of the general good, was the *terrible* but *legitimate* battle of right against privilege, of legal liberty against despotism, and that to the Revolution alone belongs the task of regulating itself, of purging itself, of founding the constitutional monarchy to consummate the good that it has begun and to repair the evil it has done.[107]

The use of the word "legitimate" is deliberately ironic. The European Restoration, the Holy Alliance, had claimed legitimacy as its justification, but the effort of the Liberal historians of the Restoration can be seen as an attempt to steal the word, to legitimatize the Revolution. Guizot, in 1821, holds that the Conservatives have no right to monopolize the word.[108]

In 1817 Camille Jordan boldly proclaimed the Liberal position in an address to his constituents: "We do not hesitate to proclaim that the wishes and the hopes of the French nation in 1789 were legitimate. . . . If these hopes were cruelly deceived, much of the blame must be placed upon the corruption bred in the past, on the violent opposition that liberty encountered both inside and outside of France."[109]

Thiessé, at the outset of his history, offers us still another insight into the assumptions of Restoration Liberalism: "We would ask if all was so well under the *ancien régime.* Were there not innumerable abuses? Had the thirteen centuries of French monarchy given fifty years of peace to the people? It would be difficult to deny that immensity of evil which, after having weakened the French nation under a thousand successive forms, had become by the end of the last century more intolerable than ever."[110]

At the conclusion of his work, after establishing the fundamental proposition that France was in need of a change and showing how the Revolution answered this need, Thiessé draws up a balance sheet. Like Guizot, he is willing to concede much, and like Guizot's, his fundamental faith is unimpaired.

> The Revolution was filled with sublime acts and enormous crimes. . . . Everything was confused and confounded in this frightful and ever-changing drama, and yet the Revolution, surviving so many days of woe, so many crimes and disasters, attained its end. Out of chaos came light. France changed its face; Europe was first conquered, then regenerated; human reason took a great stride forward.[111]

The Liberal catechism on the Revolution is now complete. It could read as follows: The Revolution had roots in France and Europe; it was inevitable and popular, even partly aristocratic. There were crimes, but we did not commit them; besides, there were provocations. Worse crimes were committed in the past, and the crimes of the Revolution were justified by its achievements.

This formula for the defense of the Revolution is a milestone in the development of European Liberalism. Looking back to the eighteenth century, we can see the distance traveled. The Liberal historians of the Restoration succeed in freeing Liberalism from the traditional charge of being antihistorical; they bring the *philosophe* up to date, converting him into a kind of Whig historian. Looking ahead into the future, their achievement is equally impressive: they establish the broad lines of that defense of the Revolution which is to serve Liberals throughout the nineteenth and twentieth centuries.* Like most men caught in a historical situation, of course, these historians looked neither backward nor forward; they could scarcely take the time to congratulate themselves on their improvements of the Enlightenment or to speculate on their legacy to the future. They lived in the urgent present and they looked to the immediate problem: to perfect their version of the French Revolution and present it to a Restoration France that was sitting in judgment.

* As an example of the political uses of this Liberal history at a later period in French history, see Paul Farmer, *France Reviews Its Revolutionary Origins* (New York 1944). Farmer chiefly concerns himself with the political-historical debates of the Third Republic. The work of this later generation of historians is impressive, though one cannot escape the conclusion that nothing very new has been added.

CHAPTER III

The Revolution in the Restoration

> . . . to support in its honor, in its moral dignity, as well as in its material needs, the France that the Revolution made, and whose children we are—such, sir, is what I conceive to be my mission as deputy.
>
> From a letter addressed by candidate Guizot to the electorate.

> Dialogue historique entre un Royaliste et un Libéral (1830):
>
> ROYALIST: They hide their ambitions under the mask of popularity, but the unhappy days of the Revolution taught us by what epithet we must henceforth characterize them. Robespierre also called himself *philanthrope*, friend of the people, protector of humanity, and each day he executed thirty or forty people. Can you deny these bloody memories?
>
> LIBERAL: You confuse Liberals and Revolutionaries.
>
> Ollé de Mantet

The defense of the Revolution on historical grounds is, for the Liberals, the most convenient way of waging the basic political campaign of the Restoration: to compel the Restoration to accept as much of the Revolution as possible. The first Liberal historians of the Revolution write in the tradition of party literature: they are not content to simply set the record straight; their purpose is to protect and preserve the Revolution in a hostile Restoration. And the Revolution is in need of protection, for the Restoration threatens its interests, assaults its principles, and, above all, endangers its men.

The need to defend the men of the Revolution is obvious: From the Second Restoration till the dissolving of the Chamber in 1816, the Conservatives sought to rule with men who were free of any Revolutonary association. During the following fifteen years they sought to use involvement in the Revolution as a yardstick for denying participation in political life. For the Liberals, there is no more pressing task than to persuade the men of the Restoration to accept the men of the Revolution; failing this, they forfeit any chance for political power.

The first candidates for this political salvaging operation are the men whose role in the Revolution closely resembled the political position of the Liberals in the Restoration. These political ancestors of the Restoration Liberal are the Revolutionary Moderates, the men of 1789, the men who opposed the regicide, resisted the Terror, and were frequently victims of the revolution they had made. The defense of these men is linked with the general strategy of dissociation—they are innocent representatives of an innocent era.

Here the fifty-six-volume *Collection des mémoires* is an arsenal of Liberal propaganda, a source book in which the Moderates and Constitutionals of the Revolution have their day. The selection of Bailly's memoirs as Volumes VIII, IX, and X in the series is typical. Bailly is ideal: he resigns as mayor of Paris in 1791 and is executed under the Terror. The memoirs cover the first five months of 1789, the idyllic, defensible phase of the Revolution. To the editors, Berville and Barrière, Bailly "will always be numbered among the most courageous and respectable victims of our civil troubles."[1]

One characteristic of the series is that it seeks constantly to classify as Moderates men who would normally be regarded as extremists, to take members of the National Convention and distinguish them from the real criminals. Thus, Louvet de Couvray, we are reminded in an introduction, denounced Robespierre and Marat.[2] Apologizing to their readers for the necessity of including some violent remarks in the text, the editors note that, "accused by the Jacobins of Moderatism, but detesting their excesses, Louvet de Couvray exaggerated . . . his hatred for royalty, in order to escape their reproaches."[3]

In a Notice on Durand de Maillane's *Histoire de la Convention nationale*, he is pictured as another reluctant member of the revolutionary government. Though he was sent out on a mission, the editors insist that he was "never a passionate Republican. He wished sincerely and firmly, in 1789, for the reform of abuses." The distinction between the reformer and the revolutionary is a useful one for the Liberals—these men were reformers, and Lally-Tollendal's tragedy *Strafford* is quoted approvingly: "to reform a state is not to overthrow it."[4]

In the same volume is a fragment by the Comte de Lanjuinais, the man who best serves as a link between Revolutionary Moderate and Restoration Liberal. As the central surviving figure of these Moderates (Lafayette was too closely identified with the extremists during the Restoration; he had participated in the plot of 1821), Lanjuinais is a living example that the Revolution was not a unit, that it contained a party of sanity as well as a party of terror.[5]

Attacked by Saint-Aignan for comparing a proposed law unfavorably with a similar law of the Revolution, Lanjuinais replies in a *Mémoire justificatif*: "I have spoken, I have written, for justice and for a moderated liberty, for the oppressed of each epoch, against the errors and crimes of all parties which have reigned in France." Then, defending his own revolutionary record: "I was always opposed to confiscations and proscription lists; I worked energetically and successfully so that families might keep either their entire fortunes or at least the debris of their inheritance; in the legislature I denounced, in vain, the laws on subversives."[6]

This is a typical Restoration case: A Liberal, being accused of compromising relations with the Revolution, cites his record to show that he opposed all that was wrong in the Revolution.[7] In answer to this defense, another pamphlet accuses Lanjuinais of being one of the "seditious *philosophes*" who did not oppose the proscription laws of 1793.[8] Lanjuinais shows the first charge to be based upon a case of mistaken identity—another Lanjuinais! As for not opposing the laws of the Convention, he laconically notes, "I was not there; I was in hiding."[9]

Defending the conduct of the Moderates in the Revolution is a method of preserving the Liberals' political existence in the Restoration. In addition, it is part of the general fabric of defense of the Revolution. These Moderates, however, are still controversial figures; more important, by defending the Revolution in their person the Liberals were faced with the same difficulties as when they tried to defend the Constitutional phase of the Revolution—the Moderates *were* defeated, leadership *did* go to Robespierre and Napoleon and not to Lanjuinais and Lafayette; the Moderates could not prevent the regicide or Brumaire. There is, however, a group of men which seems to offer the strongest possible ground on which to defend the Revolution. These are the military, the men who had been successful, had defended France, and had carried the flag to the four corners of the Continent. Therefore, the Liberal Restoration puts its best foot forward when it unleashes a flood of military histories, vindicating memoirs, and glorifying biographies of Revolutionary generals. The motive is apparent: the glories of the military record, the individual feats of the soldiers, the patriotism of the army, are that part of the revolutionary performance most likely to be outside of controversy, to be a source of pride to the French nation. The military memoir serves the dual purpose, a personal *mea culpa* as well as a reminder to France of her decade of military triumph and revolutionary fame. Tissot, in his *Précis ou histoire abrégé des guerres de la Révolution Française*, describes the intention of his volume as recalling "to our old warriors the exploits in which they have taken part. The present generation will find there great and noble memories, and future generations will find in this recital of our wars examples of the most sublime devotion. The campaigns of the Republic will indicate what efforts and prodigies a generous nation is capable of, when it is influenced by the love of liberty and independence."[10]

Further, the military achievement of the Revolution offers the clearest link with the French past, reinforcing that general Liberal conception of the Revolution as continuous with French history. As with the defense of the Moderates, the *Collection des mémoires* is an important source in which the military exploits of the Revolution are kept alive in the most favorable light. Between the years 1821 and 1825 there appear in this series alone the memoirs of Doppet, Turreau, and Dumouriez, as well as a volume on the wars in the Vendée and against the Chouans.[11] Doppet is a revolutionary general with service in Spain; Turreau has been accused of atrocities in his campaign against the Royalists and this series presents his side of the story. Savary, the "historian" of the Vendée and the Chouans, claims that he will be the first to use all the documents, including those of the Convention. Dumouriez's memoirs are introduced as containing "so many memories dear to the national pride."[12]

It is General Foy who takes upon himself to do for his military colleagues in the Chamber what Lanjuinais has done for his fellow Moderates in the House of Peers. With Sebastiani and Lafayette, Foy becomes part of a triumvirate of Revolutionary generals who protect the warriors of the Revolution from the attacks of the Restoration. Foy's particular forte is to stress the military tradition of France, linking the Revolution's military success with the ancient triumphs of French arms. Challenged on the floor of the Chamber for having referred to the tricolor, the flag of the Revolution, he refuses to backtrack, arguing that if the King ever wishes to reestablish this flag, "the ghosts of Philip Augustus and of Henry IV would not be indignant in their tombs to see the fleur-de-lis of Bouvines and of Ivry on the flag of Austerlitz."[13]

The activity of General Foy in the Chamber is echoed by the activities of Dupin Aîné in the courts of the Restoration. Dupin, as he tells us proudly, made a career by defending the interests of the soldiers of the Revolution and Empire. This provides him with a bewildering variety of activity. The Restoration is launched with the execution of Marshal Ney, and so is Dupin's career. Marshal Moncey is deprived of his duties for refusing to sit on the board that tried Ney; Dupin publishes a memoir on the subject, insisting that the title of Marshal is not revocable. In 1815, he offers help to Carnot, and defends General Travot, who was sentenced to death for atrocities committed during the Revolution. In the same year, he represents General Poret de Morvan, being determined (as with Travot) to have the amnesty of 1816 enforced. In 1818, he defends the veteran Cantillon from the charge of attempting to assassinate Wellington. The following year, at the request of the widow, Dupin pursues the killer of Marshal Brune, despite the fact that the Marshal had been declared a suicide by a packed court.[14]

Dupin busied himself with still another type, the military exile; he took on the affair of General Allix in 1818, and the return of the Duc de Rovigo in 1819, who hoped for a better verdict than the one that had condemned Ney. In 1820, he finds himself involved with the aftermath of the Duc d'Enghien case, representing Generals Caulaincourt and Hulin.[15]

Dupin never forgot this battle, typical of the early Restoration, that earned him the title "avocat des Maréchaux."[16] In 1827, on a point of protocol—Marshals were announced at an official reception without their titles—he publishes "Les Maréchaux de France, défense de leurs titres" in the *Constitutionnel.* The Marshals themselves address a letter to Charles X, holding that "titles won by our armies and awarded by victory, noble attributes of a glory acquired by France and adopted by the Bourbons themselves, were recently contested in the very heart of the capital."[17] Here is the revolutionary case in a nutshell: the military and its triumphs are indisputably French; acceptance of the military side of the Revolution is an opening wedge for the acceptance of the entire Revolution.

Perhaps the most striking example of what was at stake in this defense of the military tradition can be seen in the 1818 debate on the Recruitment Law. Briefly, this is a proposal, strongly supported by the Liberals, which would (1) establish a system of conscription, (2) set up a system of liberal promotion, and (3) integrate the veterans of the Revolution into a national army of the Restoration. The men of the Right see it correctly as an effort to have the Restoration covertly accept the Revolution by adopting its military system—conscription—and its military personnel. They attack the notion of conscription as being unconstitutional, but their basic fear is the proposed formation of "légionnaires vétérans" which seemed to Salaberry, spokesman for the Right, as a "decisive concession . . . to all those internal enemies who have never stopped hoping and plotting since the Restoration." He harks back to a promise made in 1815, that public employment will be "confined to those men of proven integrity, enlightenment, and especially devotion to King and country,"[18] revealing the fear of Conservative France, that this army bill represented the opening salvo in the campaign to let the Revolution "in." For Labourdonnaye, the training of forty thousand new men each year establishes "a principle destructive to the Charter and a germ of revolution."[19] Marcellus plays upon Conservative fears, advising the Chamber to "think of the terrible Revolution that devoured France, the misfortunes of your country, the tears you shed."[20] Corbière states it as a simple proposition: conscription is the invention of the Revolution. Conscription, Bonaparte, and the Revolution fell together—"The legitimate government is obliged by its very nature to depart from the path of the Revolution; never have we had to remember this in a more important deliberation."[21]

Baron Bignon, aide-de-camp to Napoleon and later to be his first great biographer, answers for the Liberals. The question for him is simply one of the glory of the army. He attacks the fears and phantoms of the opposition, recognizing the conservative effort to keep the Revolution as something distinct and outside of the Restoration. There is only one remedy for the crisis France has come out of—forgetfulness: "Error has been in all camps, it has been inside the walls and outside the walls, it has marched under all banners. . . . All of us have made more or less serious mistakes; over whom would the King reign, if he did not know how to pardon?"[22] Here is the Liberal tactic of divided guilt and responsibility in the service of the revolutionary veteran.

The high point of the debate was the defense of the legislation by Gouvion-Saint-Cyr, Minister of War. Written by Guizot, and delivered by a Royalist Marshal of France, it is an amazing confrontation of the question of the Revolution in the Restoration, and a landmark of Liberal success.[23] He notes that fear has motivated the debate, not fear of the veterans as an institution, but "fear of the *men* who will be called first to take their places there." Then, with the absolute attention of the Chamber, he comes to grips with the question:

It is necessary to know if there exist among us two armies, two nations, one of which will be struck with anathema and regarded as incapable of serving the King and France. . . . It is necessary to know if we will still call to the defense of the country the soldiers who have given it glory, or if we will declare them dangerous to her safety. The latter course would be harsh and unjust because these soldiers were admirable in combat, they were inspired by a superb spirit, they were sustained by heroic patience; never did they stop believing that they were sacrificing their lives and honor for France, and when they abandoned their colors they still had immense reservoirs of strength and bravery to offer. Must France renounce calling upon them? Must France, in her adversity, cease to take pride in these men whom all Europe has never ceased admiring? [Tumultuous reception.] No, gentlemen, I do not believe it. Our safety does not lie in forgetting so many services, in rejecting so much courage, in abandoning so sure a road. Gentlemen, empires are not founded on mistrust; the King knows this, the King does not want a single national force which does not belong to him, a single generous sentiment he has not earned. Our soldiers have atoned for much because they have suffered much. Who will insist upon still rejecting them?[24]

Contemporaries vie in describing the riotous reception when Gouvion-Saint-Cyr stepped down.[25] Behind the protective screen of France's military heroes, the Liberals were advancing toward their objective, which was what the Conservatives feared most: to thrust the French Revolution into the Restoration, by asking—demanding—forgiveness, reconciliation, and recognition. As Charles Pouthas has put it, with this speech "for the first time in the Restoration, and in a magnificent flight, the Royalist government adopted the heroes of the revolutionary and imperial epochs, and asserted their glory."[26]

The Liberals, then, find military heroes and political moderates a strategic way of staking a claim for the Revolution in the Restoration. But, just as Liberal historians cannot finally ignore the crimes of the Revolution, Liberal politicians cannot evade the necessity of dealing with the criminals. Here the Conservatives force the issue. From the very beginning of the Restoration there is a ready-made scapegoat through which the entire Revolution can be assailed. This is the regicide, and it was a powerful weapon in the hands of the Conservatives, a weapon which they never relinquished. Statues to the martyred King, observances of January 21, national expiations—again and again they singled out the central crime in a decade of crime![27] The Conservatives want their countrymen to equate the Revolution with regicide, to see in this crime the last work, the ultimate revelation, the unanswerable argument.

In the first years of the Restoration, the subject of the regicide is treated as taboo by the Liberals. By 1818, as part of the general Liberal resurgence under the Decazes regime, there are stirrings; the *Bibliothèque historique* is fined and censured for pleading clemency for regicides.[28] Later in that year, an opportunity for the Liberals is presented when Abbé Grégoire, a venerable figure from the revolutionary past, is elected to the Chamber from the Isère. On December 2, 1819, his name is read off on the list of delegates to be seated, but cries of "point de régicide" interrupt the reading.[29] A short, violent debate follows. Swirling around this figure from the past, the New France fights to defend its right to exist, to be represented; if the Liberals can get Grégoire accepted, bring a regicide within Restoration grace, the Revolution has succeeded. For the Conservatives, the issue is even more crucial: here the Revolution is challenging the Restoration on grounds of its own choosing. The seating of this regicide is a fundamental attack upon the very nature of the Restoration. Lainé leads off for the Conservatives: "The presence in this assembly of a man whose name is associated with such frightful notoriety is incompatible with liberty, with royal legitimacy."

The Liberals reply with their heaviest artillery, Benjamin Constant. First, says Constant, there is article XI of the Charter, which specifically bars any penalties for past votes and opinions; then, switching adroitly, he reminds his audience that there was Fouché, another regicide, whom Louis XVIII did not scruple to use in the hectic first days of the return of the Bourbons.[30] Labourdonnaye, the impassioned conscience of the Ultras, takes the floor. He begins by blaming the government for the events which have led to Grégoire's appearance before the Chamber. Earlier in the year, the Comte de Serre, under attack from the extreme Right, had let slip words of praise for the Convention.[31] It was this praise that "gave the Revolution the insolence to raise its bloody and hideous head in order to brave the majesty of the throne." For Labourdonnaye, the crime is so terrible that when a nation does finally recover its liberty, its first duty, on penalty of being declared an accomplice, of sharing the shame, is to reject completely the actual authors of the crime, to separate their cause from its own, at the same time holding them up to public contempt and branding them with the seal of infamy. . . . If not, by admitting them into its body, the nation would adopt the guilty, it would affirm its own guilt, it would justify their crime.[32]

In reply, Manuel returns to article XI of the Charter: "What you propose today is nothing more than to prosecute someone who once held an opinion that you regard as a crime." He is interrupted: "The crime is evident." It is interesting to note the shift in the Liberals' emphasis: when defending the military they encourage an examination of the past; they want the military reputation of the Revolution to survive. But in defending the regicide, the Liberals (consistent with the Charter) call for a wiping out of the past. Here the tables are turned: the Conservative wants the past to be remembered; the Liberal wants memory to be memory of the Charter. But Manuel goes further; he brings the arguments of the Liberal history to the defense of Grégoire: "After thirty years of revolution, who has not taken some part in the disorders we have experienced? Who has not been, in his turn, agent or victim? Who has not frequently changed his role?"

In this effort to divide responsibility, to share the guilt, the regicide is dealt with as merely a more extreme form of involvement in the Revolution. Manuel argues that responsibility was so diffused in the days of the Convention as to make individual guilt meaningless. He deals at length with the difficulties of any such mass condemnation: "Consider what a lot of misery and trouble you will cause. Each, individually, will have to be examined." He is interrupted by Castelbajac: "There are not so many regicides in France."

Corbière sees the question as: Does the "regicide have the right to appear in our midst, trailing in his wake the entire revolution"? If Grégoire *is* the Revolution, then the Chamber is voting on the Restoration *vs.* the Revolution. The Liberals desperately try to shift the debate to the constitutional question—the right of the Chamber to deny Grégoire his seat—and to the larger question, the attitude of the Restoration toward men of the Revolution. But the Conservatives steer clear of any constitutional tangle—it is for them purely a matter of principle. As Marcellus put it:

I ask that an election which threatens throne and altar be declared null and void, and for the single reason that the fourth deputy from the Isère, as a member of the Convention, gave his support to the judgment and condemnation of Louis XVI. I protest any other alleged motive for his exclusion.

The debate, then, resolves itself into which issue is to be voted on: seating Grégoire or validating the election. The Right insist it is a question of seating Grégoire, and the Chairman decides in their favor. To cries of "Vive le Roi," the delegates begin to rise, the Right first, then the Center, finally the Left. Then the Conservatives demand that the Liberals stand and be counted on this question, but this is precisely the ground they do not want to be caught on—disrespect for the monarchy—and only one member votes for Grégoire.

The attempt to seat Grégoire at the end of 1819 marks the high-water mark of Liberal influence (until the Martignac administration of 1828); a few months later, the Duc de Berry is assassinated and reaction takes over, not to yield the reins until the fall of the Villèle regime in 1827. From 1816 to 1819 France was undergoing a Liberal restoration: the Revolution was being sold successfully. But the attempt to seat Grégoire was going too far—France in 1819 was still too close to the memory of '93.

The Grégoire affair was just one incident among many; other figures offered equally good battlegrounds for the struggle. Among them was Lazare Carnot. As both a great military leader and a regicide, Carnot embodied the best and worst arguments for the Revolution. His career in the Restoration is only a dim afterglow of his revolutionary reputation, but the controversies over the effect of the survival of this reputation offer an insight into the Liberal campaign *for* the Revolution.

Shortly after the return of the Bourbons, Carnot addressed a memoir to the King, seeking to defend his past conduct. In reply to the basic charge of regicide, he turns on his accusers:

> The regicides are the people who took up arms against their native country—you yourselves. The others have voted as judges appointed by the country as a whole; they are not obliged to account for their judgment to anyone. If they fell into error, they are in the same circumstances as any other judges who have erred. They have erred together with the entire nation which provoked that judgment, urged, as it were, by thousands of appeals sent in from the departments. . . . They have erred in common with all the nations in Europe who dealt with them.[33]

Thus, Carnot pitches his defense on the lines that the Restoration historian is to adopt—the totality of the Revolution and the consequent impossibility of judgment. Again: "The French Revolution was a combination of heroism and cruelty. But all families which remained in France were obliged to take a more or less active part in that revolution. . . . All have made sacrifices. . . ."[34]

Carnot never allows us to forget his strongest claim to forgiveness—his military service. He charges that "Glorious events are forgotten or disfigured; an affected contempt is turned toward acts of devotedness," whereas, in fact: "The military veterans of the Revolution were the instruments by which our nation's glory was preserved . . . an inconvenient glory, which certain men now seem inclined to tarnish. . . . Be it known to those brave men that that glory today is more than just their reward, that it is the safeguard of whatever liberty remains to us."[35]

As for the men who seek to deny this glory:

Do they think they can take us back to those days of 1789, as if reason itself could turn back? Do they hope to make us confess aloud that the entire Revolution was but a heap of crimes, when it really represented no other crimes than those of which they themselves were the first cause? It is the defenders of the soil who form the indestructible body of the nation, . . . of this nation, powerful and victorious for so many years! We will not let our laurels be touched. We will share them in a fraternal manner with those who are worthy of them, but certainly not with those who dishonor them.[36]

The charge again anticipates a favorite charge of the Liberal historians: the Conservatives seek to deny history, to impugn the military glories of the past. Carnot opposes the Conservative equation, revolution equals crime, with his own formula: revolution equals military glory. He continues with a general defense of the Revolution:

This Revolution which appears so terrible when viewed at a short distance: How will it rank in the annals of the world? What are these events we have just witnessed alongside of the barbarian invasions of the Roman Empire? What are they compared to the massacres which followed the discovery of the New World, or those wars of extermination which have so often depopulated Asia?[37]

This attempt to place the Revolution in perspective and to measure it against the atrocities of world history is a striking anticipation of the comparative criminology of the Liberal historian.

The following year (1815), Carnot produced a supplement to this memoir, bringing his apology up to date, accounting for his conduct during the Hundred Days, and offering a fresh appraisal of his revolutionary career.[38] He insists that he was never a blind worshiper of the Emperor; that he always believed in constitutional government; that he was the mortal enemy of Robespierre; that he was an army man, pure and simple, and besides, was too busy to make out proscriptions. Admirers of "the great Carnot" might find this summation of his revolutionary leadership somewhat disconcerting, but we must remember Carnot's position in the first year of the Restoration. In defending himself, he comes up with the defense which the Liberal Restoration is to adopt as official. Beneath the absurdity of Carnot's explanations can be discerned the triparite Liberal apology for the Revolution and its sons: dissociation from its crimes and "criminals," emphasis upon moderate constitutionalism, reliance upon the army and its achievements.

There is a great deal at stake in Carnot's effort to rehabilitate himself; far more than Grégoire, Carnot is a great revolutionary. If he can be defended, the Revolution that fathered him has taken a giant step toward its vindication. The challenge is recognized; Carnot's two works drew an avalanche of replies, including Chateaubriand's famous *Réflexions politiques* of December 1814.[39]

The next engagement in the Restoration battle over Carnot occurred in

1817, when Rioust published his laudatory biography. Immediately, 605 copies of the work were seized, and Rioust was hauled before a royal court, charged with a long list of offenses, chiefly with having insulted the King.[40] The subsequent trial and verdict provide an excellent illustration of the Restoration's concern with the figures of the Revolution.

Vatimesnil, the public prosecutor, charges that Rioust's work "presents the most seditious characters, proclaims dangerous opinions, and indicates culpable intentions. The author lavishes the most exaggerated eulogies upon Carnot. The work includes passages intended to justify the Revolution and the most criminal outrages to which it has given rise."[41] Vatimesnil accuses Rioust of having written a biography of Carnot in order to justify the Revolution; the intention of the work is the crucial question. Rioust somehow must defend his biography, yet deny its transparent motive. His general defense and his answers to particular charges afford a fascinating example of the tortuous difficulties of being a spokesman for a revolution during a restoration.

First, Rioust denies he is a friend of the Revolution; indeed, in the preface of the biography he takes pains to clarify his position: "I suffered from the revolutionary excesses."[42] Having dissociated himself, he is free to answer the charges one by one. He is accused of applying the phrase "idolâtre de sa patrie" to Carnot. He defends his choice of words thus: "If I had known of a Frenchman with a life more patriotic than Carnot's, I would have written of him."[43] He is prepared to defend his choice of subject in the very way that Carnot defended himself—by presenting Carnot as the patriot, the revolutionary defender of France. Again Rioust strikes the note closest to the Liberal line, denying he has insulted the king: "I attacked neither directly nor indirectly *the person of the King and his authority*; when speaking of Carnot, I praised the prodigious success of the French armies, of which the King was surely not unaware, since he was always King of the French."[44] The Liberal finds the army the most satisfying part of the Revolution, since its triumphs were plainly in the name of all France.

The prosecution has reproached Rioust for the use of the phrase "accablante pour des cœurs française," referring to Carnot's message after Waterloo. "To this reproach, a word. Who perished at Waterloo? Were they Frenchmen or savages?"[45]

Rioust is further charged with having "advocated philosophy, attacked religion, and praised the Revolution and its disasters."[46] After a formal denial of the first two charges, he proceeds to the serious part of the accusation. He admits that he has praised the Revolution: "The Revolution! . . . yes, if . . . one gives this name to useful changes in political situations; to the principles lately developed in the Preamble to the Charter, . . . in which His Majesty prohibited the prosecution of citizens for their opinions and votes."[47]

The charge forces Rioust into the open. Driven back upon his deepest beliefs, he proclaims his liberal faith in the Revolution, which he quickly justifies by the two favorite "proofs" of the Restoration Liberal—the Charter has accepted the Revolution, and article XI makes it nobody's business anyway. He also performs the Liberal ritual of separation: "The Revolution, yes"; the crimes, no. The crimes shock him.

Nonetheless, he advances all the usual mitigating circumstances. The National Convention committed crimes, "but are we forgetting the almost supernatural efforts with which she tore French territory from the hands of the foreigner?" He does not defend the Terror, but the worst of the lot *were* from the upper classes; there were misfortunes, but they were caused by the "encroachments of the nobility on the rights of the people."

Rioust's self-defense can be read as a compendium of Liberal devotion to the Revolution. The necessity of defending himself and justifying the Revolution does not cause him to lose sight of his hero; before the royal court he reiterates his faith in Carnot, and this leads him to espouse everything from the sovereignty of the people to Carnot's use of the pike. To the basic charge that Carnot is a regicide, Rioust's reply is a model of Liberal restraint, calling for nothing less than a suspension of judgment on the grounds "that . . . this disastrous event is still too close to us to be judged sanely, that it is in the realm of passions too recently and too deeply aroused, that we must leave to the future the men and events of this period of our history."

He asks the Restoration to leave the regicide to history, "to the scrutinizing eye of the impartial Clio," with the hopeful thought that "the ages to come will recognize the true authors of this political calamity." In the meanwhile, he emphasizes that Louis XVI himself had pardoned France, and that Louis XVIII has "placed under the protection of the Charter . . . all those whose names are associated with this dread memory," seeking to extend the conception of amnesty to the regicide. Vatimesnil's final summation notes that Rioust has neither denied the charge nor shown any regrets, and the official *Moniteur* echoes this astonishment: "He has not sought to excuse himself; on the contrary, he is concerned with justifying the principles that he has been reproached for having included in his brochure."[48]

Rioust's bold stand is rejected; he is sentenced to two years in prison and fined two thousand francs. He is held "to have weakened, by calumnies and insults, respect for the person and authority of the King. . . . He has professed . . . principles which he qualifies as liberal and which are only seditious."[49]

Though Rioust is found guilty, and Carnot dies in exile in 1823, the Liberals seek to have the final word. In the year following Carnot's death, a volume, *Mémoires historiques et militaires sur Carnot*, appears in the *Col-*

lection des mémoires series, designed to show "our respect for the public and for the memory of a great man."[50] In the Introduction, Carnot is treated by Tissot as a simple man, a *politique* in a great French tradition: "Suddenly the conspiracy of Europe forced the Convention to form, in its bosom, a government commensurate with the force and magnitude of the perils of France, and the same genius which created Jourdans, Hoches, Pichegrus, Moreaus, in the lowest ranks of the army chose Carnot to lead these emulators of our greatest leaders."[51]

Moderates, regicides, soldiers—the Liberals embraced their cause in the first years of the Restoration in the persons of Lanjuinais, Grégoire, Carnot. Each man represented a special group in the Restoration which was seeking recognition: the Moderates were the political equivalent of the Liberals in the Revolution; the regicides stood for all those who were compromised by their revolutionary conduct; the military represented a strong and persistent national, patriotic tradition. Each category presented a special problem, each required a different line of defense; the Moderates were to be clearly separated from the criminals, the criminals were to be forgiven or forgotten in the interest of Restoration harmony, and the military were to be remembered for their sacrifices.

Although the Liberals' identification with controversial revolutionary figures was in part emotional, they advanced the most practical kinds of arguments to make these men acceptable to the Restoration. Chief among these was the simple proposition that it was impossible to punish the men of the Revolution because the Revolution *was* France. Benjamin Constant, in 1817, summed up this argument: "One should not pronounce political excommunication against all those who served either Bonaparte or the Republic, declare them born enemies of our present institutions, or find in these institutions all that is antipathetic to them, without reflecting that these men are France itself."[52]

The *Archives* offers an even more practical piece of advice: one should not punish the men of the Revolution because times have changed, because the Revolution is perfectly willing to serve the Restoration. In 1821, Guizot echoes this reasoning: "How contemptible to scrutinize the most obscure events, to form categories, to classify men by their past, as if these men had chosen their circumstances."[53]

In defending the men of the Revolution, the Liberals were preserving the link between the revolutionary past and the Liberal present. However, in so doing, they were exposing themselves to the most damning of the Conservative indictments. The Conservative attack during the Restoration always featured the charge that the Liberals were revolutionary, by pedigree and by intention. They never lost the opportunity to label the Liberals as a fundamentally subversive party, plotting to overthrow the Restoration as the

Liberals of '89 had overthrown the *ancien régime*. Thus, the Liberals' program of defending and identifying themselves with the Revolution seemed to justify the worst fears of the Conservatives.

The Liberals' problem was a real one: how to exonerate and defend the French Revolution and yet deny any revolutionary intention of their own. One general answer to this problem was the Charter, but there was a more specific line of defense available, an opportunity to defend *the* Revolution without advocating a continuing revolution in France. This opportunity was present thanks to the political climate of the European Restoration; one could identify with and support any revolution that was taking place outside of France—in Haiti, Greece, Italy, Spain.

In 1823, the government of Louis XVIII, seeing an opportunity to reestablish French power while still remaining faithful to the Holy Alliance, indicated its willingness to intervene in behalf of the Spanish Restoration, to restore the Bourbon Ferdinand deposed by a Spanish Liberal Revolution. The French Restoration is now nine years old, and the two sides look on at a disturbing drama—a revolution, a Bourbon losing his throne. The plot and characters are the same, only the time and place have changed. In restoring the Spanish throne, in defeating the Spanish Revolution, the French Right are presented with a golden opportunity to redress history; by acting with resolution, they can symbolically "kill" their own revolution, atone for past weakness and error. Further, they have the opportunity to succeed where Napoleon failed—victory in Spain, a double vengeance on Revolution and Empire—and thus appropriate some of the military prestige that is one secret of the Revolution's popularity. Billecocq, in a work significantly entitled *De l'Influence de la guerre d'Espagne sur l'affermissement de la dynastie légitime et de la Monarchie Constitutionnelle en France*, is convinced that "the result of this struggle against the spirit of evil in Spain will be to consummate for France the work of the restoration of 1814, to affirm the throne of the Bourbons and, with it, our new institutions."[54]

The men of the Revolution are equally quick to see the implications of the Spanish adventure. The French Liberals, their revolution safely history, have been at work hammering out a version of this controversial past that will be acceptable to the Restoration. Now a revolution emerges, wearing Spanish dress, but recognizable nonetheless: it is 1789 south of the Pyrenees. The issue is even more sharply drawn for the Liberals because France is acting on the instigation of that same Holy Alliance which fought the Revolution. France is being forced to play the role of killing her own child—the Spanish counterpart of her great revolution. The Liberal has been conducting his defense on historical grounds, but in Spain history seems to be repeating itself, and defending the Spanish Revolution in 1823 is the most direct way of defending the principles and interests of the French Revolution. The Chamber of Deputies gives us the best vantage point from which to observe the way in which the Two Frances identify themselves with the two Spains.

Louis XVIII proclaimed France's readiness to march on January 28, 1823. President Ravez on February 8 read the report of the commission studying the advisability of such action. The report is clear. Spain is undergoing revolution; France has shown how revolutions are to be solved; why doesn't Spain learn from her example? The Restoration is presented as the great lesson to all revolutions, and France, thanks to her special experience, is seen as "destined by Providence to close the abyss of revolutions."[55]

Taking up the question of Spain, Royer-Collard, in one of his great defenses of the Revolution, defines the Liberal position.[56] Opposing the granting of credits, he first argues for peace. It is one of the ironies of this debate that the Revolution, so long identified with anarchic violence or military triumph, emerges as the pacifist party. Royer-Collard finds in the proposed intervention, "in this profound assault on the laws of nations, a no less profound assault on our principles of government and the generous spirit of our Restoration." For the Liberals as well as the Conservatives, the Spanish Restoration reopens the grand debate of the French Restoration. ("In pronouncing this word restoration, . . . I deliberately raise in your minds a flock of memories.") For Royer-Collard in 1823, the Restoration monarchy is the old monarchy, but it is also fundamentally different in character from its ancestors; it is "a new monarchy, separated from the old by events which are like centuries." By pointing out that France herself has accepted the Revolution, he seeks to undercut the Royalist argument that Restoration France must resist revolution wherever it appears: "See the Charter, the expression of the King's will. Of the entire Revolution, the King repudiates only the errors and the crimes."

The lines are drawn. The Liberals' effort to plant the Revolution in the Restoration will be repudiated if France can intervene in the Revolution in Spain. If the Royalists carry the day, the Revolution will still be equated with crime. The King, Royer-Collard continues, needs no Spanish enterprise to establish his glory, because the glory acquired by the revolutionary armies is also his. "The King adopts it; even more, he makes it the ornament of his throne." This inevitable comparison between the revolutionary army and the army now poised on the frontier of Spain leads Royer-Collard into a general defense of the role of the revolutionary army which, for the Liberals, is always a prelude to a defense of the cause for which that army fought: "Was it for the Committee of Public Safety or for the Directory that we conquered at Fleurus, at Zurich, and on so many battlefields? . . . No, France did not defend wicked or contemptible governments; she defended her independence; she fought the Prussians, the Russians, the Austrians; she would do it again today."

This is to remind France of her old enemies, whose bidding she is doing today. The greatness of the French army—and its peculiar relevance for the Restoration Liberals—is that it has always represented France. This was the secret of her success: "The glory is pure because the cause is just. The memories of this great war will never be effaced among us because it struck home to every family; there is no family which did not give its blood."

The revolutionary army could achieve glory because its cause was just, but now, with the positions reversed and France the invader, no glory is possible. The King cannot contemplate such a war, Royer-Collard insists; the true culprit is that party "which has understood the Restoration simply as a punishment." He correctly analyzes the heart of the Conservative interest: "Today it attacks the independence of Spain because the cause of independence was for a long time ours; it undertakes this aggression in the cause of absolute power because absolute power is dear to it, and is necessary to accomplish its designs."

The following day, Bignon makes the same point succinctly—there are two sides to this debate: the productive, useful people (the Revolution), and that handful of courtiers "and passionate gentlemen who believe that they will find in Madrid the privileges that France deprived them of in 1789."[57]

The remarkable thing about the debate is that the Conservatives accept the Liberal analysis of what they are doing; they see Spain as nothing less than the battleground of the European revolution. "It is at Madrid that the fate of revolutions will be decided."[58] Labourdonnaye identifies the party of "peace" as "radicals and carbonari." To him the compelling reason for intervention is that there is revolution in Spain and "revolutions never forgive."

It remains for Chateaubriand, architect of the Spanish policy, to render the classic defense of that policy and the most candid statement on what is actually involved. He begins by accepting the parallel urged throughout the debate by the Liberals: France is doing here in 1823 what England tried to do in 1793. However, he definitely rejects the Napoleonic parallel:

> Permit me to address myself to the comparison which has been made between the invasion of Bonaparte and what France is considering today, between a Bourbon who marches to deliver a Bourbon, and the usurper who has just seized the throne of a Bourbon . . . between a conqueror who proceeds by breaking altars, killing monks, deporting priests, overthrowing the institutions of a country, and a descendant of Saint Louis who comes in order to protect what is sacred among men. . . . The arms turned against Napoleon will fight for us.[59]

Chateaubriand has seen that, cutting across national lines, a new ideological division has formed; the Spanish peasants who fought Napoleon will welcome a royalist army. And the ideological interest that dominates, the question that divides all Europe, is the Revolution. This is the most compelling reason for intervention, the fact that the Spaniards are reenacting the French Revolution. "Ferdinand is still only a prisoner in his palace, as Louis XVI was in his before going to the Temple and from there to the scaffold. I do not wish to vilify the Spaniards, but I do not wish to honor them more than I do my compatriots. Revolutionary France gave birth to a Convention; why would not revolutionary Spain produce hers?"

Apparently, for the Conservatives, all revolutions are equal; the pattern of the French Revolution must reappear in the Spanish. Chateaubriand is led to this rigorous conclusion by the realities of the political situation: "Hasn't the Spanish revolution taken ours for a model, has it not copied ours slavishly, hasn't it proclaimed the same principles, hasn't it already despoiled altars, assassinated priests in the prisons, set up the instruments of torture, decreed confiscations and exiles?"

The problem for the Liberals now was to find a way in which their own revolution, newly conceived and freshly resurrected by the Liberal historians, could be allowed to exist in the Restoration. What evidence could the Liberals find that could enable them to demonstrate that, far from rejected, the French Revolution had been recognized by the Restoration?

The Liberals find what they are looking for—the link between Revolution and Restoration, proof of the continuity—in the Charter of 1814. This Charter, a highly ambiguous document, was the product of compromise between the demands of the Ultra-Royalists and the interests of the New France. It became for the Liberals of the Restoration an untouchable shrine, the proof and guarantee of their rights, the symbol that preserved in practice their men, principles, and interests. The story of how the Liberals "claim" the Charter—fight off all rival claimants, place it upon a pedestal (even above the king), wage political warfare under its banner, and finally make a revolution in its name—is the story of the Restoration.

According to the Liberal historians, the Revolution was a good thing gone wrong. Now, with the Charter, it became possible to complete the catechism—the Revolution is over and has triumphed. By proving that the Revolution is over, the Liberals can claim that they are no longer revolutionary, that they can be as royalist, as loyal to the Restoration, as any émigré. By guaranteeing the triumph of the Revolution, the Restoration becomes the extension of the Revolution rather than its rejection; the Liberals become the true royalists, the Ultras the true revolutionaries. This political turnabout actually occurs in 1830 when, thanks to their reading of the Charter, the Liberals claim that they are the true Conservatives, conserving the Charter itself, the conserver of the Revolution. Thus, the Charter becomes the last link in the chain forged by the Liberal historian: it is the climax of the story.

In the first years of the Restoration, the Liberals tend to regard the Charter as a mediator between the Two Frances, a truce between the Revolution and the counterrevolution. For Guizot, in 1816, it is king and Charter that will heal the wounds.[60] Later, a more positive view of the Charter begins to emerge. Consistent with the Liberals' determination to separate themselves from the crimes of the Revolution, the Charter is seen in the *Archives* (1817) as miraculously preserving the best part of the Revolution: "It is neither to the crimes nor to the misfortunes of the Revolution that we owe the Charter; it is solely to those legitimate and healthy principles of the Revolution, to whatever was noble and generous in it."[61] Thus it is the Charter that is the wedge by which the Liberals slip into the Restoration free of the incubus of revolutionary guilt, the Charter that is the realization of that "healthy" revolution with which the Liberals have sought to be identified.

The article stresses the theme of the transaction, a compromise which "recognized in the present state of France the principles and interests of conquerors and conquered; it placed the monarchy on the site of victory." The Liberals have just succeeded in passing the Electoral Law of 1817, and the article sees this action as the consummation of the contract. It urges the voters to make the law work by "electing as deputies men interested in upholding the compromise, and not men interested in renewing the battle; for the former, the Revolution is over; for the latter, it must begin again."[62] Two important features of the Liberal argument emerge in this article: (1) The Charter is a transaction between the Two Frances which terminates the Revolution, while preserving its best elements, and (2) since it is a settlement of the Revolution, there can be no question of a revolutionary party in the Restoration—those who accept the Charter accept its terms. Indeed, those who do not, the Ultras, are the revolutionaries, in revolt against the solemn compact that unites Restoration France.

In the following year (1818), this idea is ready for extension, and once again it is Guizot, the spokesman of the Doctrinaires (the ideological wing of the Liberals), who presents the challenge in the *Archives*. Reprinted in the *Moniteur*, his statement produces an explosion. Guizot proclaims the Charter, not merely as a compromise between the Two Frances, but as proof that the Revolution has been accepted. Speaking for the Ultras, Chateaubriand had insisted that France must choose between being royalist or revolutionary, but for Guizot this is a false dichotomy. The Revolution is composed of men, principles, and interests; an examination of the Charter can lead to but one conclusion: "We are, by the very fact of the constitutional monarchy, on the terrain of the Revolution. It is this terrain which produced the Charter; it is in the Charter that the Throne is established; there is in the Charter one single fact stated and consummated, and that fact is the Revolution."[63]

If the Charter is the Revolution, as Guizot would have it, then Chateaubriand's distinction between revolutionaries and royalists is meaningless, and the whole basis of Conservative action in the Restoration is undermined. Guizot's contribution is to insist that there is no contradiction between Liberal and Royalist, nothing incompatible between Revolution and Restoration. This is a fact of Restoration political life, a fact which had become increasingly clear since the dissolution of the *Chambre Introuvable* in 1816. Although the Liberals had become good Royalists, it remained for Guizot to rationalize this change into a political philosophy.

Turning back to the revolutionary past, Guizot professes to find nothing surprising in the Liberals' allegiance to the royal Restoration, for the *Revolution was never opposed to royalty.* Here is the dynamite in his article, the suggestion that opens up bewildering possibilities: If the Revolution was not aimed against royalty, there is no reason why the Liberals cannot be Royalists in the Restoration. But the real brilliance of this thesis lies in its corollary: If royalty was not the object of the revolutionary attempt, who was? The aristocracy, of course; the aristocrats were the counterrevolutionaries in 1789, as they are the counterrevolutionaries today. Today, however, thanks to the Charter, the Revolution is accepted; therefore, in being counterrevolutionary the aristocrats are being anti-Royalist, and they are thus the real revolutionaries of the Restoration.[64]

This dramatic effort to rearrange the political patterns of the Restoration is the practical counterpart to the historians' effort at persuasion. In a single maneuver, the Revolution—thanks to the Charter—becomes the legitimate parent of the Restoration. Guizot supports his view with a historical analysis which can be summarized briefly: The Revolution was directed not against the king but against "the interior constitution of society";[65] the enemy was the aristocracy, and victory was victory over the aristocracy; royalty's mistake was to have forgotten that the aristocracy was a faction "from which royalty had suffered a great deal and for a long time," and to have allied with it briefly. Now, as Guizot sees it, the aristocracy is seeking to reverse that choice and, by so doing, threatening the very security of the throne, which rests upon the Charter and upon acceptance of the Revolution. The aristocracy is compelled to do this because "the throne is overturned for them, reestablished without them, no longer dependent upon them."

The key element of this analysis of the Charter as a revolutionary document—the element that gives it political bite and relevance—is the argument that it is the aristocrats, then and now, who are the real revolutionaries (revolution now being defined as violation of the Charter), in revolt against King and Charter.[66] This Liberal line—you, not we, are the revolutionaries—is one of the astonishing phenomena of the Restoration, astonishing in its persistence and in its ultimate success.

This particular line is most clearly associated with the Doctrinaires, who, once again, provide the most effective arguments for the Liberals. For

Guizot, it is the aristocrats, left out of the compromise between Revolution and royalty, who have "revolutionary needs."[67] At one stroke, the Liberals are absolved from the stigma of the Revolution and the burden is shifted to the aristocrats. Rémusat, another Doctrinaire, insists that the Liberals are not revolutionaries, objects to the very use of the word Restoration; and Royer-Collard, the Doctrinaire in the Chamber, echoes Rémusat: the Liberals are "innocent of revolution."[68]

In a word, the Charter, thus conceived as the acceptance of the Revolution, allows the Liberals—trailing their Revolution with them—to be legitimate in the Restoration. The importance of this conception can hardly be exaggerated. The Charter proclaimed by an exiled Bourbon is a weapon in the hands of its creators; as such, it is first looked upon with great suspicion by the Liberals. But, step by step, the Doctrinaires succeed in converting it into a truce, a contract, finally a victory for the Revolution. Once this is done, the Charter becomes the banner around which all the great battles of the Restoration are waged.

In 1820, Guizot gives the most extreme statement of this Liberal adoption of the Charter, calling the document nothing less than the triumph of the Revolution, the unconditional surrender of one part of France to another. In a battle that has been waged throughout French history, the Charter represents not only a decisive victory, but a reversal of previous losses.

> The outcome of the Revolution was never in doubt. The people formerly conquered had become conquerors. In their turn they conquered France. By 1814 they controlled it beyond dispute. The Charter recognized their possession, proclaimed this fact to be law, and provided representative government as its guarantee. . . . By this one act alone, the king became the leader of these new conquerors. He placed himself in their ranks, at their head; he pledged to defend, with them and for them, the gains of the Revolution. . . . The Charter spelled out this agreement explicitly because the war was clearly ready to break out anew.[69]

Here in a single passage, Guizot offers a Restoration political program consistent with a larger vision of French history. The Revolution is the triumph of a faction in French history. This conquering faction would not, could not, give up its victory in 1814, and indeed, did not. According to this version of the granting of the Charter (and this was one of the hotly debated issues of the Restoration), it was not the King magnanimously holding out the hand of friendship to a defeated Revolution, but the King accepting the Revolution and placing himself at its head, doing, in fact, what the Liberal historians had argued Louis XVI should have done in the first days of the Revolution. It is no wonder that Guizot's work stirred up a Restoration furor; if he was correct, the King had accepted the Revolution, the Revolution was a natural ally of the King, and those who opposed the Revolution were also opposed to the King. A major virtue of Guizot's argument is that it is an accurate picture of the politics of the Liberal Restoration, where an Ultra wing frequently found itself fighting a political coalition of Liberals and Royalists.[70]

Guizot's ideas on the fundamental relation of the Restoration to the Revolution are sharpened by political defeat in 1821; with reactionaries in the saddle, the Liberals' version of the Revolution seems far from reality. He concedes that those who have interpreted the Charter as a rejection of the Revolution have temporarily won; he devotes himself to attacking the assumptions of this counterrevolution. He finds that the chief justification for the counterrevolution is its conception of the Revolution as something dangerous, ungovernable, anarchic. He grants that the true principles of the Revolution—the sovereignty of the people, attack upon privilege, government as a servant of the people—were at one time revolutionary and are now susceptible of abuse. But he demonstrates that these were revolutionary as objectives, not as essences; that now, having been achieved, these principles have lost their revolutionary impact.[71] Because the Revolution has won, its supporters are no longer revolutionary; they have, in fact, become the new conservative force, even the new aristocracy.

In effect, Guizot presents Restoration France with a newly conceived Liberal party, descended from the Revolution but transformed by its victory into a conservative interest: "Today all is changed. . . . Interests formerly aggressive and out to conquer are now on the defensive, because their rights have been recognized, not only in fact, but in law. The Charter, which found them strong, recognized them as legitimate."

Guizot sees that the mistake of the Liberals in 1821 was to have lost the leadership of France to a defeated party, a party defeated by history. The Restoration has misunderstood itself, has mistaken its friends for its enemies. He characterizes this party as "weak because they have been vanquished . . . illegitimate because they are outside of the Charter; . . . revolution is a necessity for them."

Here are Guizot's three basic charges: the Ultras are a defeated party in history; they are illegitimate; and they are truly revolutionary. To this party, exposed as historically corrupt, dangerous, but now impotent, Guizot contrasts the party of the future—the party born of the Revolution. Unlike the Ultras, this party has everything that is necessary to construct a stable society. Though "perhaps difficult to lead in the beginning, [its members] have this immense advantage: since the future belongs to them, it is in their interest to settle down and regulate themselves as they move forward."

As for the Conservative course being followed in 1821, it rests upon two miscalculations: first, the Ultras' illusion that the Restoration has been successful "in its assault on the France which made the Revolution and exacted the Charter" (the aristocracy has revealed "a degree of ignorance that I am scarcely able to conceive"); second, their refusal to recognize the emergence of the middle class. According to Guizot, the only road open to Restoration France is to deal with this middle class.

In his work of 1821, Carrion-Nisas, concerned like Guizot with proving the "triumph" of the Revolution in a period of reaction, takes a different tack. The proof he offers is an actual listing of the principles and institutions of the Revolution that have survived in the Restoration: the uniformity of laws and administration, equality of taxation, progress in the physical sciences, the breaking up of large estates, the extinction of prejudices against industrial enterprises, and so on.[72]

For the full statement of this Charter worship, however, we turn once again to that touchstone of Liberal sentiment, Cousin's lectures of 1829:

> The Charter carried a peremptory judgment on the eighteenth century. . . . It condemned what was condemnable, legitimized what was legitimate. Every charter, every constitution, is only a historical résumé, a recognition of the essential elements of an epoch. . . . The Charter vindicated the principles and impressive results of the French Revolution and of the eighteenth century, . . . and in vindicating them, it vindicated the two centuries which preceded and prepared them. The revolution of the sixteenth century is recognized and extended in the Charter by the article which consecrates the freedom of religion; the political revolution of the seventeenth century is equally recognized by the introduction of the Chambers into the government of the King, and the participation of the people in the affairs of the country. . . . Thus the Charter itself adopted the religious and political reforms of the sixteenth and seventeenth centuries, and the great Revolution of the eighteenth. The final result of the progressive conquests of humanity, the Charter represents and protects them all.[73]

Here is a charter that connects perfectly with the propositions of Liberal history. The Charter is the culmination, not merely of the French Revolution, but of that great Liberal European revolution, preserving the best that has been wrung not only from the French past but from all history.

Emerging out of this construction of the Charter as the embodiment of the Revolution is a set of Liberal axioms under which the Liberal campaign of 1830 is to be conducted. The Liberal "reading" of the Charter construes it as proving that the Revolution is concluded, that it has won; that the Restoration descends from it logically as well as chronologically; and that those who oppose this guarantee of the Revolution are the true revolutionaries.

If we turn to the two significant areas of political controversy in 1830—the press and the Chamber—we will be able to register the impact of these notions, to observe how the establishment of the Charter as the legitimate triumph of the Revolution becomes the justification for the July Revolution, enabling the Liberals to overthrow the Bourbons in the name of law and order.

This Liberal capture of the Charter does not go uncontested in the Restoration. From its proclamation in 1814 to the closing days of July, 1830, the Conservatives fight a desperate losing action, disputing the Liberal version. They argue that the Charter is theirs, that it was *proclaimed* by the King after the defeat of the Revolution, that it decisively rejects the preceding twenty-five years.[74]

The question of the nature of the Charter is fundamental; it is taken up by the *National* in 1830; two weeks after its founding. "The Charter was not proclaimed, it was exacted; it is not the gift of royalty, it is the prize of the Revolution; it is not the result of any anterior rights, it is itself the foundation of all rights. No powers that it establishes can be touched without destroying it, . . . without beginning again the battle in which the public power perishes, but the nation remains."[75]

Two days later, this view is defended in the form of a series of questions and answers:

> In 1789, did Royalty grant a Charter? No.
> When did it grant one? In 1814.
> What happened between 1789 and 1814? A Revolution.
> What did this Revolution seek? A Charter.[76]

It is, then, literally true that the Charter is the prize of the Revolution, its granting seen in retrospect as fulfilling the true purpose of the Revolution; thus, the Charter is held to be the justification of the reasonable intentions of the Revolution.

Turning, a few days later, to the group which persists in misinterpreting the Charter, the *National* accuses "the party which, in less than fifteen years, has forgotten the origins of the Charter, has forgotten those origins with reason. In making the Charter flow from the royal prerogative and not the royal prerogative from the Charter, one knows what its desires are. It conspires against representative government."[77]

Here the immediate political importance of the historical debate over the granting of the Charter is revealed. If the Charter was merely granted, it can be revoked; if the Charter takes its authority from its royal origins, it is vulnerable to that same authority. If, however, the Charter was wrung from the monarch and if his throne rests upon an agreement, then sovereignty resides in the Charter and the agreement is decisive.

On January 29, 1830, the *National* boldly deals with the question that troubles all France. The Conservatives have discerned a pattern in events, have charged the Liberals with being precisely what they were in 1789, a revolutionary party. By this means they seek to justify the measures of the Polignac regime and urge it to still more extreme action in order to head off the threatened revolution. The *National* calls its article "1789 and 1830."

> Does 1830 resemble 1789? Are some of us knaves and many others dupes marching toward a new revolution, the former knowing it, the others ignorant of it? From 1789 are we going to pass to 1792 and 1793? . . . In 1789 all that was obtainable had not yet been obtained . . . [whereas today] instead of a unique,

humiliating, absurd situation, society finds itself perfectly constituted and, in order to prosper, needs only to be left to itself. . . . All those who say that we want a revolution, or that without wanting one we are preparing for one, lie equally. People do not revolt twice in forty years; this never has happened; it is especially unlikely when, in the interval, they have exhausted themselves by wars of unheard-of duration and violence. The passions let loose in 1789 are not possible today.[78]

The Revolution of '89 is used here to prove the good intentions of the Liberals of 1830; then there was cause, today there is not. This echoes an argument used by Carrion-Nisas nine years before: the prosperity of France is proof that its middle class is no longer revolutionary. And the Liberal Martignac regime of 1828–29 has matched the economic advance of the Liberals with political concessions. Therefore, in 1830 the Liberals do find themselves in the position of a group which has, in a sense, won. But this is precisely why a real revolutionary situation exists. The Polignac regime, installed on August 8, 1829, is beginning to threaten the gains already achieved by the Liberals, just as in 1788 the aristocracy threatened the improved position of the peasants.

Having insisted that there is no actual revolutionary threat, the *National* comes to the crux of the Restoration dilemma: the Liberals have won, but their victory is threatened by those now in control, who are "worrying a nation that has acquired a great deal and wants to preserve it, by opposing its . . . opinions, by seeking to impose their religious and political ideas upon it." By examining the actual state of France in 1830, the *National* thus comes to the same conclusion laboriously hammered out for a decade by Liberal strategists: that the revolutionary impulse is no longer to be found in the classes that had supported the Revolution of '89.

Yet there is an explosive situation in 1830. Who is responsible for it? The *National* replies: "These sentiments are found not in the lower classes but in the upper. It is they who have more foresight, who are more susceptible to anxiety and alarm; it is they who control the government. . . . It is not the spirit of sedition which is formidable, then; it is rather this conviction that things cannot progress, circulated among those very classes which are charged with making them progress."

The paradox of the situation is that the Conservatives are shouting "Revolution!" and girding themselves for the thrust when, in fact, it is these very efforts to "cut off" the Revolution which are making the middle class restive. "It is absurd, senseless, to arm oneself, to draw one's sword, believing that one is going to be assailed by a people broken loose, when on the contrary, what is needed is to reassure them, to win over a people who are falling away." It is significant to note that six months before the July Revolution, the Liberal press is insisting that the threat of a revolution is fantastic, something cooked up by the Conservative press.

The *Journal des débats* is equally decisive in rejecting the Conservative parallel, ridiculing those who insult the elected Chamber by recalling the atrocities of '92 and '93 and by invoking the specter of the Convention. "Never again will those dreadful days and those terrible nightmares afflict France. Let us deplore the memories of August Tenth and January Twenty-first. Let us profit from those memories, but let us feel no resentment."[79]

Note how carefully the *Journal des débats* picks its path through the Revolution—the two dates mentioned were dreadful, but they bear no relation to the present demands of the Liberals, and it is mischievous of the Conservatives to pretend that they do. As history, they deserve to be remembered; as politics, they must be forgotten. The Liberals insist that, as the party of the Charter, they are the party of the present; and that the Conservatives, who are trying to reverse the present, are the party of the past. Thus, oddly enough, in the year 1830, the Liberals who have "adopted" history as their own special weapon in the struggle to secure the Revolution, now turn around and accuse the Conservatives of being too consciously historical, of reading 1789 into 1830. The *Journal des débats* complains: "Liberty appears to them only under the bloody colors of the Revolution. Freedom of religion reminds them of the cult of the Goddess of Reason and the Theophilanthropists; the left side is the Mountain, the center left is the Gironde. . . . Each step the New Order takes they believe to be a fall into the abyss of revolution."[80]

For the Liberals these parallels are odious and invalid, for being no longer a revolutionary interest, they have ceased to identify themselves with their ancestors of '89. Nevertheless they must refute this argument because, in 1830, it is the very basis of the Polignac regime.

> This ministry has recalled many tragic memories, has resurrected strange-sounding words which France believed had been abolished from her political language. In order to keep itself in office it must din terrible threats daily into the King's ears, . . . as if one could frighten a Bourbon who wants and has sworn to uphold the Charter. This is how this strange ministry, doomed from the moment of its birth, still hopes to survive . . . constantly holding up to the gaze of France and its King the scaffold of Charles I and of Louis XVI.[81]

In essence, the Liberal case in 1830 charges that the Conservatives are raising the false alarm of revolution though *they* are the real revolutionaries. Support for this view came from an unexpected quarter; the arch-Royalist Cottu, an active publicist throughout the Restoration, produced a pamphlet in 1830 which called upon Charles X to stop shilly-shallying with the Revolution, to eliminate the Liberals by changing the basis of representation, by abandoning the Charter, and by establishing a kind of dictatorship.[82] Cottu's proposals were the desperate suggestions of a Royalist badgered too long by the opposition's successes in the Restoration. But for the Liberal press, he was a godsend, proof that the real demand for change in French society emanated from the Right. The *Globe* notes triumphantly: "It is not the people that he calls to insurrection, it is royalty."[83]

Here, in embryo, is the justification for July—royalty's mutiny against the Charter, the breaking of the sacred contract. The *Globe* reminds its readers that the Charter is a transaction between those who believe that sovereignty resides in the king and those who believe that it is to be found in the people. "Between the two opinions, the Charter is a compromise; withdraw it and the battle begins again. . . . After forty years of trouble, France is finally peaceful and happy. A treaty of alliance has been signed between those forces which had for so long contended for victory."[84] This is the Charter as seen in 1830, a sacred peace treaty whose violation means war—not revolution, but justifiable war.

To turn from the Liberal press to the Liberal bloc in the Chamber is only to shift one's vantage point; the propositions are the same. Perhaps the most striking summary of the revolutionary commitment, as it prepared itself for the struggles to come, was the statement of Agier on March 15, 1830.[85] In it are caught up the themes so patiently developed in fifteen years of historical analysis and political debate.

First, he denies any revolutionary intent: "Who in France desires a revolution unless it is those who need catastrophe in order to be someone? A great many possess, a great many wish to acquire by legitimate means; and for owning as for acquiring, for industry as for property, order and calm are necessary."

Second, the Revolution of 1789 was a response to European history: It "had taken its source, its beginnings, in the remotest events and ages."

Third, the Revolution has been accepted: It "is for the Restoration a *fait accompli* and can be nothing else." To reopen it would lead to disaster. "It is an abyss closed by our institutions."

Fourth, as for the parallel between 1789 and 1830:

> It is only complete ignorance, or a sign of bad faith, that enables one to compare the present period to that of 1789, because everything that was demanded then, we now have. Through crimes and great deeds, through blood and glory, through anarchy and despotism, France has found a haven. She wants to remain there, and threatens with all her indignation those who wish to hurl her back to the midst of storms.

Fifth, the Liberals are the true conservatives:

> In 1789 the spirit of innovation produced turbulence; in 1830 the spirit of conservation produces moderation; and the spirit of conservation cannot separate the Charter from the princes who granted it. Who then is the party of the Revolution? Who then makes the revolution? . . . Those who wish to destroy our parliamentary regime at the risk of seeing the monarchy itself led to the precipice created by their violence.

Sixth, the Charter which recognizes the Revolution as the basis for the Restoration is an irrevocable contract:

> He [Louis XVIII] is free to give France the form of government he wishes, but enlightened by experience and misfortune—knowing very well that if monarchies can be established by force of arms, restorations are ordinarily founded only by compromises and are only consolidated by good faith—he proclaims a Charter to his people and the people accept it with enthusiasm and gratitude; from that point on, the contract is made. . . . Has there ever been a contract in the world more reciprocal, more solemn, more binding?

Thus, in the very twilight of the Restoration, we see emerging a Liberal rationale that will ensure its triumph. The Liberals have worked out a complete defense of the Revolution of 1789 in the Restoration. They insist that 1830 is not 1789, that in fact the roles of the two parties are now reversed: the men who are standing by Polignac and Charles X are the real revolutionary interests. As descendants of the Revolution of '89, the Liberals of the Restoration have maneuvered themselves into the position of Conservative protectors of a Restoration "contract." The Charter is theirs, the government is theirs, the Restoration is theirs.

The Charter is the synthesis that has enabled the Liberals to see themselves in the glorious tradition of '89—revolutionaries by descent, yet Conservatives in the present. Historically revolutionary, politically conservative, these are the men of 1830 and that is the character of the July Monarchy they are to create. And the historians of the Restoration have played a part in the creation of this new character; they have provided France with a view of history that allows Liberals to make a Conservative revolution in 1830 in the name of the Liberal Revolution of 1789. By making the Revolution history, they have nurtured it in the early days of the Restoration, keeping it from the Conservatives' assault. By making it French history, they have given it national roots and respectability; by making it a response to all history, they have extended its claim to greatness. By conceiving of it as inevitable, they have taken it out of the category of crime. By reminding France of the variety of its origins and the popularity of its results, they laid a foundation for its consideration in the Restoration. By dissociating the Revolution from its crimes, they undercut the Conservative effort to conduct the Restoration in the spirit of an inquisition, while still preserving the Liberal right to defend the criminals. Above all, by justifying the Revolution, they allow its men, principles, and interests to survive in the Restoration. Finally, by interpreting the Charter as the prize and not the penalty of the French Revolution, they gave the men of 1830 a justification for their version of revolution.

CHAPTER IV

The Conservative Reply

> When I have seen the same errors repeated for thirty-two years, restored in reputation, propagating themselves in Europe with more ease and even more deplorable success than in 1789, menacing us with their terrible and shameful return, I believe myself to be acting like a good Frenchman in writing the history of the Constituent Assembly.
>
> Charles Lacretelle, *Histoire de l'Assemblée Constituante* (1821)

One major way of attacking the Liberal Revolution of the eighteenth century was to charge it with being committed to abstractions—such as the rights of Man—which were unrelated to experience, to theories whose practical consequences were disastrous. Burke was the first to oppose the abstractions of philosophy with the experiences of history. Central to his indictment was the charge that the French Revolution was an assault upon French history, an insurrection against the past. To the Conservative, Burke's analysis seemed confirmed; the revolutionaries seemed determined to extinguish the monarchy, impoverish the aristocracy, and enslave the clergy. They were unconcerned with the charge of being antihistorical; indeed, they seemed bent on severing all connections with French tradition: costume and forms of address were altered, the map was redrawn, the calendar revised, and Notre Dame converted into a Temple of Reason. The men of the Revolution were willing to see themselves as a party of the present and future, abandoning the past to those who had made such a mess of it.

But in the Restoration, the Liberal descendants of the Revolution—themselves now in the position of a defeated party of the past—cannot afford to "concede" history to the Conservatives. Instead, the Liberals of the Restoration—1789 now safely history—abandon philosophy for history, finding that a precise examination of the Revolution itself is the best means of defending it. The Liberals' discovery of history and their successful exploitation of it during the Restoration have been traced in the preceding chapters. To the Conservative, accustomed to thinking of history as his exclusive preserve, a comfortable abstraction, a convenient generality to fling at the Revolution, this Liberal assimilation of history is a shock. He finds himself compelled to enter the arena, to fight to establish his version of history.

And with what weapons? He can no longer confidently wield "history" against the Revolution; nor can he merely resurrect the original Conservative attack upon the Revolution. The Liberal history of the Restoration had raised fresh questions, had adopted new lines of defense, which rendered the émigré attack on the Revolution obsolete and unsuitable. One has only to consult Joseph de Maistre's classic of 1796, *Considérations sur la France,* to see its inadequacy for the Restoration. Maistre, refusing to assign particular guilt, takes for his theme the total guilt of the French nation.[1] This illustrates the gulf that separates the exiled émigré from the one who returns triumphant. By insisting that everyone was guilty, Maistre sought in 1796 to remind his fellow émigrés that they had much to atone for. It may be valuable to remind a defeated party in exile of its past errors, but this is highly irrelevant to a restoration, which is predicated upon the return of the innocent and the punishment of the guilty. Maistre speaks of the Revolution as a blessing in disguise for the French clergy: "the crimes of the tyrants of France became the instruments of Providence."[2] Here again the hope for purification through ordeal is a private message addressed to fellow sufferers. It may be useful to tell an exiled clergy that it was growing soft and corrupt—but again, once it has returned, it is its innocent martyrdom which must be stressed.*

Maistre's conception of the Revolution as a just punishment for an age of Liberalism led him to accept the Revolution as inevitable—a notion popularized by the Liberal historians of the Restoration: "The French Revolution leads men more than men lead it. . . . Those who established the Republic did so without wishing to and without knowing what they were doing; they were conducted by events; an earlier attempt would not have succeeded." Thus Maistre in 1796 specifically rejects the notion of the French Revolution as conspiracy which is a key to Conservative thought and practice in the Restoration. Further, Maistre comes suspiciously close to arguing that the Revolution was necessary and desirable when he says, "never has the Divinity shown itself more clearly in a human event. If it employs the basest means, that is because it punishes in order to regenerate." Finally, that "it is impossible to have a great revolution without producing

* Note that the argument of the Revolution as the salvation of the clergy becomes, in the Restoration, the Liberal Gallican line, to be found in such writers as Abbé de Pradt and Abbé Grégoire.

some misfortunes" is a shrewd and generous observation for a Royalist in 1796, but one which the Conservatives in 1814 cannot afford.[3] Exile may give the critic of the Revolution a certain detachment—even a certain freedom and frankness—which are political liabilities in a Restoration.[4] The Restoration Conservative has learned the need for closing ranks—enough of self-criticism and speculation, the enemy is at hand.*

These first attacks, contemporary with the Revolution, are never entirely abandoned in the Restoration; but the Conservatives soon recognize that, thanks to the Liberal historians, the battleground has shifted considerably. As early as 1818, the Liberal line has solidified sufficiently for Chateaubriand to summarize it accurately while dismissing it sarcastically:

On all sides we hear repeated in a subtle jargon that it is good to have done what was done, to have taken what was taken; that if the nobility had their throats cut, if the priests were denounced and the landowners robbed, this was patently their own fault; that these nobles were tyrants, these priests fanatics, these landowners aristocrats; that it was they who, by their resistance, killed Louis XVI; that the throne perished only by accident, and that if the monarchy was destroyed, it was for its own good; that nothing is as good as the Revolution; that there was a natural alliance between this Revolution and legitimate royalty.[5]

Riambourg sees his *Les Principes de la Révolution française* being written in an atmosphere of "eulogies delivered to this Revolution which caused such great evils."[6]

In a preface to his précis of the French Revolution, Achille de Jouffroy wonders if 1820 is not too early to write the history of the Revolution.[7] He feels that the Restoration has settled nothing, has simply left the basically antagonistic forces in French life drawn up against each other: "the veterans of the revolt and the disabled loyalists; the authors of the proscriptions and their victims; the bloody organizers of the circuses of the sovereign people and the sons of martyrs." The Empire has silenced this great debate, but, as Jouffroy wisely observes, the return of the Bourbons has been as much a restoration for the men of the Revolution as for the Royalists. Surveying the Liberals' activity, he laments that "once again they want to lead us to the same abysses where their companions are swallowed up helter-skelter with their victims; . . . they seek to arouse all the old passions. . . . In such circumstances . . . one would not dare describe the events of the past accurately." This seems to be a good reason for *not* writing a history of the Revolution—it would simply stir things up. And

* Maistre's work of 1796 (*Considérations*) is reprinted three times in the Restoration: once at the outset in 1814, once in 1820, and again in 1829. It is given surprisingly little attention considering its popularity throughout the rest of the nineteenth century (nineteen printings in all, fourteen between 1843 and 1868), and compared to the popularity of Maistre's other works in the Restoration (i.e., *Les Soirées de Saint-Pétersbourg*). As has been pointed out, the explanation of this relative neglect after 1814 is that many of its ideas dovetail with Liberal history.

yet, the new generation must be reminded of past errors "at this time, with Spain about to repeat our fateful experiences." Jouffroy's work is a warning to those "born since the epoch of our troubles," those who remember only the military triumphs of the Revolution.[8]

In 1824 Madrolle bitterly remarks that, despite the age of the Revolution and its obvious effects, "We have still to learn its causes, its objects, its methods. . . . Be it bad faith, be it uncommon ignorance, the Revolution has been confused from the beginning by a great number of histories and an even greater number of memoirs based on it or written in its defense."[9] He singles out the *Collection des mémoirs,* and chides Mignet for "muddling the Revolution, seeking perpetually to justify it."[10]

Cottu registers the Conservative shock at how far the apologists of the Revolution have gone by 1829: "The notorious July Days, and the Terror itself, have they not their apologists today? Shall I say more? The greatest crime of the Revolution, the one which even under the Empire drove the guilty into the shadows, does it not inspire less horror with every passing day? . . . Is not it, too, ready to find its admirers?"[11]

This amazement at the temerity of the Liberal historians is matched by a growing awareness of what the Liberals are really trying to do, of what is at stake, and of the urgency of a Conservative rejoinder. Bonald, in a savage review of Mme de Staël's work, singles out her attempt to establish a tradition of resistance to authority:

> Mme de Staël, and in general all the writers of the same school, who look in all centuries for opposition or active resistance to authority, . . . do not sufficiently recognize that in those far-off times the nobles shared the country in the sense that they shared the territory, but not in the sense that they shared the power. No matter how one tortures our history, one will still find that the kings have commanded and that the people have obeyed, and that if it had been otherwise, there would have been no France.

So much for the Liberals' careful effort to locate a revolutionary tradition.

Bonald goes further, offering a psychological interpretation of this Liberal fascination with history: "The new . . . is so suspect that one wishes always to find an ancient origin for it, and the political innovators are, in this respect, like the leading heretics who ransacked the remotest centuries to find some precedent for their doctrine."

Up to a point Bonald seems to fully understand the new Liberal history as presented by Mme de Staël. In analyzing this search for precedents, he believes he has uncovered a basic contradiction in the Liberal position: "It is certainly strange, and a denial of the dogma of progress of the human spirit and of infinite perfectibility, to look for exact definitions of the ancient French constitution in the time of Dagobert or Charles the Bald, rather than in the time of Louis XII, Henry IV, or Louis XIV."[12]

Here, in fact, Bonald has isolated something important. The eighteenth-century ideal of progress which fathered the Revolution is contrary to the nineteenth-century Liberal glorification of the past. The appeal to history is something new that has been added to the revolutionary position. The eighteenth-century Liberals talked of the future; the Restoration Liberals sought out the past because, as Mme de Staël taught, liberty was ancient.

Throughout his review, Bonald reveals a testy impatience with the Liberals for "torturing our history." This annoyance, shared by others, is an interesting barometer of the Liberals' success. Maistre, in a letter to a friend in 1819, complains: "They have foraged history in order to discover facts which occurred a thousand years ago, and which have become more foreign to us than the Trojan War."[13]

A brilliant parallel to Bonald's review of Mme de Staël is P.L.B.'s anonymous answer to Guizot's manipulation of history. P.L.B. echoes Bonald's theme, calls for extreme care in interpreting history. History should not be used to reopen old wounds or provoke new controversy. Sympathy for the past, yes—but let us reject those who strain themselves to revive old ideas and suit them to their own."[14]

P.L.B. specifically accuses Guizot of speciously reviving the time-honored Franks *vs.* Gauls question: i.e., of making a deliberate effort to seek out and magnify the element of conflict in French history, with a view to exposing the Old Regime, accounting for the Revolution, and constructing a Liberal tradition of protest. Here the dilemma for the Royalist historian is a real one. The eighteenth century had more or less accepted this version of conflict and had chosen sides. Boulainvilliers had taken the Frankish conquest of the Gauls as the basis for aristocratic supremacy, and aristocratic historians like Chateaubriand and Montlosier were keeping this tradition alive in the Restoration. Liberal historians welcomed this version, happy to identify themselves with the defeated Gauls, who now, according to Guizot, have emerged triumphant with the Revolution. The Royalist apologist for the Restoration cannot take sides; to do so would be to admit that the deep chasm in French life could be traced beyond the Revolution to the beginnings of French history. And the Royalist historian is looking for something more substantial—and respectable—than a conquest for the origins of the French monarchy.

The Royalist historian of the Restoration, determined to preserve the fiction of a stable and peaceful past interrupted by the Revolution, denies any basic conflict in French history. According to P.L.B., the Franks conquered not the Gauls but the Romans, and their victory was actually a blessing for the Gauls. He proceeds to argue for the mixing of Frank and Gaul, demonstrating that the eighteenth-century notions of victor and vanquished are the products of party spirit, not historic fact: "Where, I ask, are these two peoples, the one exclusively Frank, the other exclusively Gaul? Miserable and meager invention of the passion for system and the spirit of subversion!" He counters this version of French history conceived in conflict by painting a picture of a happy blending of the three forces, Frank, Gaul, and Roman.[15]

This is the theme of the Monarchist historians of the Restoration—one big happy French family. Where Guizot had argued that unequal social situations were the product of an original feudal conquest, P.L.B. sees inequality as the general condition of human society. He willingly acknowledges the growth in French history of representative government, but he denies that this growth is the result of a struggle between rival classes:

It has been the result of the growth of institutions, of industry, of riches, of the tempering of customs by the mutual concurrence of all classes. . . . You need only read the pages of our history attentively and without prejudice. You will see that our kings have never ceased to work for the improvement of social conditions, and that the aristocracy not only has not always opposed such improvements, but has at times strongly supported them.[16]

The coronation of 1825 inspired Clausel de Coussergues, a Conservative leader in the Chamber of Deputies, to an equally determined defense of the fourteen centuries of French monarchy. In his Introduction to his historical work on the coronation ceremony, he notes the necessity of replying to the Liberal re-writing of French history:

Ten years ago, in order to justify the French Revolution, there was invented a system which travestied our history and denatured all our ancient legislation. This fiction, published in various obscure works, has since been taken up and developed by men of talent. One sought to show the "character of a nation originally founded on force and conquest, and whose first law had been a sharp distinction between the conquering barbarian and the degraded conquered." Another said . . . , "The revolution of the fourteenth century, that of the kings and the aristocracy against the people, has just been supplanted by the revolution of the nineteenth century, that of the people against the aristocracy and the kings." I believe that one could not write on the coronation of our kings . . . without demonstrating that all the pages of our history reject this vain theory, . . . without making it clear that the baptism of Clovis formed the most perfect union between Franks and Gauls.[17]

The attempt to establish the absence of conflict in French history is one aspect of the general Restoration effort to glorify the French monarchy. The Royalist historian takes his place alongside the Royalist poet, playwright, and artist in vying to resurrect ancient glories. The plays of the early Restoration celebrating the great monarchs of the past, the odes and hymns of the young Royalist poets Lamartine and Hugo, the statue of Henry IV, the canvases of Devéria—all this activity reveals the will of the returning Royalist, the disillusioned Revolutionary, and a tired France to recall past glories and bask in future hopes.

There is, in addition, a practical issue at stake. The name of the Bourbons had been calumnied during the Revolution, neglected under the Empire.[18] The calumnies had to be exposed, the Bourbon name restored along with the Bourbon person. The discourses of Frayssinous are samples of the early Restoration fervor. In 1814, citing the glory of the Royal house, he says: "For us old Frenchmen who were born and lived under the paternal regime of the Bourbons, the love of the king is not only a duty, it is a sentiment of filial piety. Those of you who are too young to remember will learn to love our king . . . and, as we do, you will feel that in a French heart, love of king is inseparable from love of country." Again in 1816: "The throne . . . founded by Clovis, fortified by the power of Charlemagne, illuminated by the wisdom of Saint Louis, and which a succession of kings has rendered august and honorable"—this throne will not perish.[19]

The return from exile, the assassination of the Duc de Berry in 1820, and the coronation of Charles X in 1825 were all opportunities to remind the Restoration of the greatness and glory of the Bourbons. The death of Berry was peculiarly suitable for an outpouring of loyalty, since it recalled to France that other royal martyr. Typical of the funeral orations was that of Archbishop Quélen, in which the Bourbons are extolled as "a family chosen by its good fortune and its glory, a privileged race. . . . There is nothing under the sun which surpasses the greatness of this most Christian house of France." The Revolution, he remembers with horror, called these Bourbons enemies of France: "Enemies of France! Who? This Saint Louis, the most perfect model that history offers? . . . This good Henry? . . . This Louis XI, full of justice, this Louis the Great who gave his name to so fine a century? . . . What, this Louis the Beloved? . . . The Bourbon tyrants of France!"[20] Chateaubriand published a life of Berry, in which the heir to the throne is seen as the summation of all the virtues of the family —"all this the Revolution delivered to Louvel's knife."[21]

The Restoration's extreme sensitivity about the reputation of the French monarchy can be seen in the frequent trials in which the central charge is "offense toward the person of the king." The Rioust affair has been treated in Chapter II. Even more sensational were the prosecutions of Béranger, the most famous poet of the day, and Paul Louis Courier, the most popular essayist. The Béranger and Courier trials were celebrated because the accused were distinguished partisans of the Left. Perhaps even more revelatory of the Conservatives' "religion of Royalty" and of their determination to treat the Bourbons *en bloc* was the trial of Fiévée in 1818. Fiévée was himself an ardent Royalist who devoted his widely circulated *Correspondance politique et administrative* to attacking the drift toward constitutional monarchy. He isolated as the apparent basis for the Liberal-Royalist alliance the notion that kings need to be popular. He attacks this notion as a ridiculous convention, as so much "sentimental hypocrisy." Calling for political realism, he holds that "in general men do not like those who command them," and that it is all but impossible to base policy upon affection. Most kings, he points out, have not in fact been popular, and those who have been have met disaster: "They adored and killed Louis XVI."[22]

This is accurate history, but in the Restoration the popularity of the French monarchy is high dogma, not to be questioned. His work suspended, Fiévée is brought to trial, whereupon he compounds his offense with a historical review of the French monarchs, rating them according to their popularity. He concludes that most of the Bourbons were not popular, and that the few popular Bourbons were unsuccessful. But Prosecutor Marchangy speaks for the official Restoration when he says: "To win the affection of the people was a paramount and innate policy of the Bourbons.[23] Fiévée is convicted despite his acknowledged loyalty to the monarchy.*

Another example of this Restoration piety for monarchs, past and present, can be found in the Chambers. In 1819 General Foy attempts to have the Restoration recognize the Legions of Honor granted by Napoleon. He argues that the source of the decorations is immaterial, pointing out that in the past such orders have been founded by "unpopular princes." He is immediately interrupted by Villèle: "The only unpopular monarch we recognize is Napoleon." Stung, Foy repeats, "These orders were founded by very unpopular kings, Louis XI and Louis XIV"—but he can get no further.[24]

One phase of this general glorification was the attempt to rehabilitate Louis XIV in the face of persistent Restoration attack. Clausel de Montals notes a widespread depreciation of the French past, "particularly the century of Louis XIV, the finest age since the time of Francis I."[25]

In 1820, Frayssinous, Bishop of Hermopolis and the king's Minister of Correction, takes up this question of the reputation of Louis XIV: "The vain detractors will pass, and the glory remains. Louis XIV gave his name to his century forever, and posterity will never cease to speak of the century of Louis XIV as, after two thousand years, we still speak of the century of Augustus. . . . I am happy to take this solemn occasion to avenge the memory of Louis XIV."[26] Elected to the Académie Française in 1822, Frayssinous returns to the curious Restoration denigration of Louis in an elegant apostrophe:

Why is it that your name still has enemies? Some errors of policy, some bursts of ambition, faults for which you had the noble courage to reproach yourself, ought not all that to be effaced before fifty years of glory and prosperity? . . . In our frenzied days, you have been misunderstood, your ashes profaned, your memory insulted; but you have remained victor over these impious outrages."[27]

* Fiévée acts throughout like a man anxious for the king to act in a fashion that he has apparently rejected in exile. It would be easy to characterize Fiévée as an Ultra, except for his complex attitude on the Revolution; he is simply a "pure" monarchist. "The first truth of a state of twenty-five million inhabitants, which has existed for fourteen centuries under laws and monarchical institutions, is the monarchy." (*Correspondance*, III, No. 12, p. 8.) Finally, Fiévée defends the right of the Restoration to suppress his work, since the Revolution has proved the danger of unlimited freedom!

Frayssinous's concern over the treatment given Louis XIV reveals one of the major difficulties of the Conservative defense of the French past. Louis is attacked not only by Liberals like Mme de Staël, Sainte-Aulaire, and Lemontey as a symbol of despotism, but by aristocrats like Chateaubriand and Jouffroy as the seducer of the French nobility, and by Ultramontanists like Lamennais and Maistre for his aggrandizement of the Gallican Church.[28] Thus the defense of Louis is in the hands of a small group of Royalist Gallicans like Frayssinous, Roche, and Clausel de Montals.

This division of sentiment is the clue to the Conservative dilemma. The Liberals, in their efforts to defend the French Revolution, have distorted the national past; the defense of this past should be the point of departure for the Conservative historian, but which past? Chateaubriand, Montlosier, and the aristocratic school defend the role of the aristocracy, including their Frankish ancestors. Lamennais and Bonald seek to defend the League. Others leap to defend the Concordat of the sixteenth century, the Estates of the seventeenth century, or the parlements of the eighteenth. Frayssinous defends Gallican liberties, Jouffroy glorifies aristocratic liberties, while Maistre attacks them both. A defense of the French past thus means a return to all the ancient quarrels, a reopening of all the divisions that are inherent in the Restoration coalition of monarchy, aristocracy, and clergy.

Clearly a study of the past could only divide the Conservatives, but where they could coalesce, could find historical unity, was where they had in fact found political unity—in the Revolution. The monarchist, the aristocrat, the priest, however at odds historically, could unite to defend their role in the Revolution, to refute the Liberal criticism of their conduct, to insist upon their innocence. After all, as Clausel de Coussergues had pointed out, the purpose of this new history was "to justify the French Revolution";[29] the Conservative, in his zeal to defend the French past, must not be distracted from the major issue. The indictment of the past needs a reply, but of more immediacy are the charges leveled against the Conservatives' conduct during the Revolution itself.

Carnot in 1814 had been the first to challenge the historic record of the newly returned aristocrats, charging that they had deserted Louis XVI.[30] This drew immediate fire from Chateaubriand. The émigrés had to leave, he wrote; it was a question of honor as well as one of survival. What had the nobility done for the king? Chateaubriand cites the record: "It shed its blood for him at Haguenau, at Wissembourg, at Quiberon."[31] He is equally specific in defending the role of the clergy, recalling the Vendée. Guillot, a year later, produces a fuller refutation of Carnot:

We never soiled our hands, either with the blood of brothers or with the blood of kings; we were never seated in the assemblies of sanscullottism. . . . According to you, our perfidious counsels were the undoing of Louis XVI. . . . But do you forget, M. Carnot, that, on the contrary, it is because our counsels were not followed that Louis finished his career so deplorably? . . . You ask what the Notables, the clergy, the nobility, did for the king; they did everything. You wanted their property, they yielded it up to you; you wanted the Revolution, it has taken place; you wanted their blood, you have been soaked in it. . . . Is any more proof of their sacrifices necessary?[32]

In 1818, in the pages of the *Conservateur,* Saint-Marcelin undertakes a defense of the Royalist army during the Revolution. He takes as his thesis "that a single party wished to arrogate to itself the exclusive privilege of high morale and of bravery." He gives us a remarkable picture of the Liberals' efforts to remind France of her revolutionary glories:

As for the valor of the victors of the Jemappes and the vanquished of Waterloo, there is no need for the lithographic profusion of great deeds which lines the booths of our printsellers, nor for the deluge of couplets in which *gloire* and *victoire, succès* and *Français* are ceaselessly rehashed for the ornament of our vaudevilles. On the other hand, there are some people who cannot be made to understand that it is possible for a royal bodyguard to have as much courage as a sergeant of the *braves.*

The neglect or denigration of the Royalist army "brands as incapable of directing our administration and commanding our regiments those who believed that one could have spirit, talent, and courage without being republican or Bonapartist."[33]

The Liberals had taken some pains to develop a technique of blaming all the misfortunes of the Revolution on domestic resistance or foreign provocation. The historian Riambourg offers a point-by-point refutation of this thesis. Varennes, he reminds us, was a flight, not a battle. The Vendée did not erupt until *after* the king's execution. As for the foreign wars, they were declared by the Revolution. On the whole question of the resistance, he adopts the common-sense approach—one could not really expect people to be murdered in their beds without resistance—and he stresses the ineffectual and hopeless nature of this opposition.[34]

The sensitivity of the Royalists to their performance during the Revolution can be seen in the trial of Jouy, the popular Liberal editor of *Minerve,* in 1820. In a sketch, Jouy had taken exception to an inscription he had noticed in the city of Toulon, "Fidélité de '93." The inscription was to commemorate the city's going Royalist in '93 and delivering itself to the English and Spaniards as representatives of the exiled Bourbons. By asking "Faithful to whom?" Jouy reopens the old question of the moral *vs.* the geographic France. He is accused of defamation, of slandering the "loyal" citizens of Toulon—and convicted.[35]

In 1824 Madrolle anonymously writes *De la Révolution dans ses rapports avec ses victimes et particulièrement avec les émigrés* as a campaign document in the struggle for indemnities. The first half of the work is devoted to a historical defense. Every possible historical analogy is trotted out, from

Louis XIV's reception of the Stuarts to the way in which the Liberals welcome *their* émigrés—the revolutionaries of Restoration Europe. Louis XVI, he argues, was an "émigré" himself; his misfortune was that he was not free to act as one—and thus the charge of disloyalty or desertion is absurd. Insisting that "where legitimacy was, France was," he rejects the revolutionary "politics of soil." Indeed, he argues that if we are to accept the notion that the country belongs to those who occupy it, then Joan of Arc should have joined the English![36]

The debate on the indemnities proposal of 1825 produces the fullest defense of the émigrés as part of a reexamination of the French Revolution. The émigrés base their claims for restitution on the justice of their conduct during the Revolution. Speaking to the Chamber of Peers, Conny de la Fay states the case for the Frenchmen who left: "Emigration was a duty, because it was prescribed by honor."[37]

The successful fight for indemnities vindicates the role of the émigrés, but they must wait until 1828 for their full scholarly apologia. In that year Antoine de Saint-Gervais's two-volume *Histoire des émigrés Français* appears, the theme of which is that "the French nobility, born defender of the throne, did not recognize any sovereign other than the king."[38] The emigration found its historian in Antoine de Saint-Gervais, and its poet in Delille:

> Emigrés, your virtues will triumph over fate;
> Noble children banished from a cherished land . . .
> *Console yourselves, you are immortal!*[39]

The Restoration Conservative echoes Burke and Maistre in viewing the Revolution as a decisive break with the past. In 1817 a Conservative pamphlet takes note of the Liberal habit of citing alleged parallels in French history which suggest that the Revolution is in the best French tradition. The pamphleteer decisively rejects any such casual parallels; for him the Revolution is so new that even the people are different:

> In vain one searches among the Frenchmen of today for the people of Henry IV and Louis the Great—all is changed. In those times, in the midst of civil dissensions and the disorder of religious wars, despite the tumult of arms, the fury of parties and excesses of all kinds, the French nation clung to the ancient customs that had made it great, and preserved a sacred respect for throne and altar.

Such disturbances as there were are not to be compared with the Revolution because they were not fundamental assaults upon society:

> The spirit of rebellion had not corrupted the mass of people. It was the same under Louis XIV. The League and the Fronde no more resembled our Revolution than an insect does an elephant. The League, to be sure, did commit great crimes, but it only misled men's minds; it did not corrupt their morals. The ambitious princes of the House of Guise were different from the Mirabeaus, the Talleyrands, the Robespierres, the Barras, the Bonapartes, the Carnots. The Fronde was only

a childish, ridiculous war of some who were discontented with the Ministry. Never, in these divisions, did people dream of overthrowing the monarchy, of destroying morals. Also, these troubles were soon settled. People easily returned to their former habits, and France rose up again stronger and more powerful.[40]

The Marquis d'Herbouville, a Royalist general, is even more precise on this distinction between a mere quarrel with abuses and a fundamental attack upon society: "Was it the clergy that the Revolution sought to destroy? No, it was Religion. . . . Was it the privileges of the nobility that it sought to suppress? No, it was the Nobility. . . . Was it the judicial order that it sought to change? No, they sought to destroy Justice itself."[41] It is ironic that this Conservative view—that a new race produced 1789, that the Revolution is something different than and separate from the French past—comes close to the original revolutionaries' view of themselves.

The Liberals have made every effort to read themselves back into French history; for the Conservatives, the Revolution is not only out of harmony with the French past, but positively destructive of that past. This is a restatement of Burke's thesis, but it has special weight in the Restoration because of the activities of the Liberal historians. Clausel de Coussergues reminds the revolutionaries that they stand self-convicted of physically destroying the past. Foreigners scattered the ashes of Joan of Arc, but "the *philanthropes* of 1789 have at least had the honor of overthrowing her statues."[42] He calls for the Restoration to reconstruct this past, and notes with satisfaction that the city of Orléans has already rebuilt one of the monuments.

Three years earlier, in 1822, this same author exposed still another method by which the Liberal historians sought to sink roots—the Liberal tradition. Defining Liberals as people who have "viewed the return of the Bourbons with repugnance," and observing that no such hatred existed before 1789 (a point the Liberals would be quick to agree upon), Clausel de Coussergues comes to the conclusion that Liberalism had no existence before 1789: "One will not find its origin before the Revolution. The soil of France nourished a nation renowned for its attachment to its kings."[43] Thus he denies the Liberals even the solace of their own tradition. Other Conservatives, however, are willing to grant the Liberals their tradition—a tradition of revolt stemming from the Protestant Reformation. Singling out the parlements as the source of the Revolution, Maistre in 1818 describes these representative bodies as "Protestant in the sixteenth century, *frondeur* and Jansenist in the seventeenth century, *philosophe* finally, and republican in their last years."[44]

The Liberal notion of the French Revolution as inevitable and popular is consistently met and contradicted by the Conservative description of it as accidental and unpopular. Translated into historical details, the Revolution becomes, not the natural product of European circumstance, but a measurable conspiracy. In the words of one critic, the Revolution "did not come from the force of things because things themselves do not have force. It does not come from nature. . . . At the risk of absurdity, it must be said that the Revolution is the result and the work of men. Men made the Revolution; when men act, it is because they want to act."[45]

The conception of the inevitability of the Revolution is singled out for thorough refutation by Bonald in his review of Mme de Staël: "I believe that the Revolution was no more inevitable in France than it now is in Austria. . . . It is true that once the three orders of the Estates were confused in the same assembly, and with a single vote, the Revolution was inevitable, for the excellent reason that it was accomplished."[46] The reference to contemporary Austria reminds his audience that in the eyes of the eighteenth century, France was the least likely country to have a revolution—a fact embarrassing to the Liberal historian.

With his customary insight, Bonald seizes upon the principle that underlies the Liberal insistence upon inevitability, *viz.*: "The Revolution was inevitable because the French people were the most unfortunate and oppressed people on earth." This is indeed a basic issue, and Bonald devotes the greater part of his review to an examination of the various "oppressions"—tax system, methods of justice, military service, the lack of a constitution—on each count comparing France under the Old Regime with Mme de Staël's beloved England. The English pay more taxes than the French, the English use impressment, the English Constitution has made the English morose, grumbling, discontented, and egotistical. He insists that there was more "true political liberty and equality in France than in any other state in Europe—not excepting England," noting sarcastically that it was in "oppressed and unhappy France" that even the richest Englishmen came to seek pleasure and health.

As a parting thrust at the Liberal notion of a France groaning under the burden of intolerable oppressions, Bonald asks: If the Revolution can be explained by oppression, wouldn't one expect those areas most oppressed to be most active in their demands for change? He raises in evidence the troubling vision of the Vendée: "Was it happier than the other parts of the kingdom? Did it pay less than the others of the *dîme* and feudal dues? Was it not the most feudal of our provinces?" This is a fundamental challenge to the whole Liberal Revolution, made on the grounds of sheer historical fact. The Revolution claims to be the response to oppression. Why are those most oppressed least revolutionary? The Revolution claims to represent the interests of the nation. Why have significant portions of that nation fought it savagely? In his dissent on oppression Bonald anticipates the modern realization that it is not poverty but pauperization that leads to revolution.

Bonald drives his point home by citing a contemporary example—Spain.

"Spain, according to our Liberals, trembles under oppression. . . . Spain, which is unfortunate enough to have neither juries nor liberty of the press: Why has it refused the benefits of the Revolution? And foreigner for foreigner, why has it preferred the foreigners who come to fight the Revolution to the foreigners who come to make Spain a present of it?"

Thus the Revolution is challenged on what appears to be its indispensable claim for recognition—popular support. Bonald is among the first of the nineteenth-century Conservatives to challenge the Liberals' assumption that they represent the people. This contradiction of the Liberal claim to popularity becomes part of the Conservative ritual. Chateaubriand holds the majority of Frenchmen to be Royalists.[47] Castelbajac, attacking Guizot's equation of France and the Revolution, identifies the revolutionaries as a "factious minority to which alone can be attributed the misfortunes that victimized the mass of France."[48] For Clausel de Coussergues, it was a "turbulent minority" which disturbed an essentially loyal France.[49]

If the Revolution was not the product of inevitable circumstance, of compelling oppression, if it did not represent the desire of France, how then did it come about?

In countering the Liberal thesis of the Revolution's inevitability, some Conservatives emphasize its purely "accidental" quality. Riambourg, for example, sees it as the product of many conflicting interests, each wanting some change: "Thus the calling of the States-General was a measure whose results were not sufficiently reckoned in advance."[50] Theologians speak of "the spirit of wrong."[51] Still others try to isolate some specific quality which can be assigned as *the* cause, usually cupidity or excessive self-interest;[52] or some specific villain like Necker.[53] But the most commonly offered explanation and the clearest contradiction of the Liberal conception of circumstance was the Conservative theory of a plot directed against society. This is not original with the Restoration Conservative, for in exile, side by side with Maistre's notion of the total guilt of the French people, there had emerged the contrary notion, classically stated by Abbé Barruel, of the planned and executed conspiracy.[54]

D'Herbouville, who sat in prison throughout the Terror, restates the plot theory of revolution succinctly for the Restoration. He picks up a key concept from the Liberal Guizot, that the throne has perished "accidentally."

If the fifth and sixth of October, the twentieth of June, the tenth of August, the twenty-first of January, the sixteenth of October, appear to certain people as simple accidents, it is not in such terms that Royalists will speak of them. . . . It will always be evident that the plot, long directed against royalty, became apparent on October 5 and 6, 1789, that it was completed on August 10, 1792, and that the assassinations of January 21 and October 16, 1793, were the final result of the plot. The throne perished, not "accidentally," but because they wished it to perish. It perished because it was deprived of its legitimate supports. It perished because the Constitution of 1791 was democratic and democracy can never ally itself with royalty. Charles I perished when the English Presbyterians wanted to found a republic. Louis XVI perished when the French demagogues seized authority. Such are the lessons of History; it has traced them in ineradicable letters of blood.[55]

The plot theory is perfectly consistent with the total Conservative thesis. As a conspiracy, the Revolution is a violation of French history; as a conspiracy it is the work of a discontented minority directed against a satisfied nation. One large question remains: Who are the conspirators? To a member of the refractory clergy like Abbé Barruel in 1797, this question presented no difficulty. He could lump together Jacobins, Freemasons, *Illuminati, Philosophes*; for him it was the illicit, underground character of these groups that indicted the Revolution. For the Conservative of the Restoration, the identification of the plotters could not be met so simply. There were no groups calling themselves by those dreaded names; though the Conservative pamphleteers might try to resurrect them officially, they did not exist. Indeed, the Liberals were making strenuous efforts to divorce themselves from any such revolutionary extremists. But there was a group with which the Restoration Liberals did proudly identify themselves, the *philosophes*; a golden age they did genuflect to, the eighteenth century. And for Restoration Conservatism, the eighteenth century is an ideal target, the *philosophe* a perfect scapegoat.

Basically, holding the Enlightenment responsible for the Revolution has two advantages for the Conservative. First, the Enlightenment provided a convenient common enemy for the three forces that returned together in 1814, upon whose unity the fate of the Restoration rested. Monarchy, aristocracy, and clergy all had deep grievances against the age of reason; exile had taught them its true meaning. And by blaming the *philosophes,* they expiate guilt their own "guilt," their own participation in the spirit of the century.

Second, attacking the Enlightenment is a convenient way of attacking Liberal activities in the Restoration, for the program has not changed radically since the Revolution. It is the ideas of the Enlightenment that are the basis of the Restoration Liberal demands, and these demands can be rejected in the nineteenth century if they can be shown historically to have produced the Revolution of the eighteenth century.

For the Conservative historian of the Restoration, the guilt of the eighteenth century is more an article of faith than a debatable historical proposition; it is an unassailable assumption demanding, not proof, but the widest circulation.[56] As a backdrop to his *Histoire des révolutions de France* (1817), Chaillot emphasizes the corrosive quality of the century: "The philosophy of the eighteenth century had so corrupted most of those who held the first rank in the social order that the court, the parlements, even the bishops, blushed at the religion of Racine and Fénelon."[57]

A pamphlet published in the same year begins with this simple proposition:

The Philosophy of the eighteenth century and the disciples of this impious sect produced the Revolution and all the crimes which accompanied it. The *philosophes*, the Jacobins, the propagators of Liberal ideas, are and always will be the enemies of monarchy; they secretly direct their attacks against throne and altar. . . . The Revolution owes its origin principally to the *philosophes*; they began it; they were the authors of all its crimes, of all the excesses which accompanied it. . . . In all this one must judge the future by the past.[58]

In 1820 Jouffroy singles out as the dangerous quality of the Enlightenment its theoretical aspect. Whereas other revolutions have had elements of accident and chance, "it remained for the Revolution of the eighteenth century to add an unforgettable example to the annals of the world: that of a general revolution executed by virtue of a positive theory."[59]

In 1829 a work appears entitled *Tableau des trois époques, ou les Philosophes avant, pendant, et après la Révolution,* in which an entire section is devoted to Voltaire's contributions to the Revolution. Discussing the confiscation of the property of the Church, the author notes that the plan the Assembly followed came from the pen of Voltaire. Another part of the work is devoted to attacking Cousin's glorification of the eighteenth century from the rostrum of the university. The Enlightenment should be judged by its results—the Revolution: "It is evident that during this Revolution there was no progress in civilization and the arts, but only vandalism and brutality."[60]

An interesting confrontation on this issue is the reply of Clausel de Montals to the Liberal Abbé de Pradt's *Les Quatre Concordats,* which in typical Restoration fashion comes around to a consideration of the French Revolution. Pradt argues that you cannot blame great movements on men, for that is to confuse cause and effect: "Philosophy did not produce the changes that led to the Revolution: the Revolution which erupted in 1789 had been brewing for three hundred years." Philosophy itself is seen by the Liberal as a blind pawn of centuries of uncorrected abuse: "Has it not been produced by vapors arising from the muck of the Regency, from fifteen years of humiliations brought to France by Louis XIV, from the sixty years of wars which filled his reign?"[61]

Pradt goes on to separate philosophy from revolutionary excess: "The excesses of the newborn philosophy were merely the consequence of excesses with which humanity was afflicted in general, and which, once they had come into habitual use, gave the Revolution its character." Finally, Pradt argues that you should never judge a movement by its excesses:

What can one think when one hears Robespierre and Danton called *philosophes*? . . . When one hears shameful and disastrous epochs cited as a part of and the direct outcome of philosophy? As if philosophy and revolution had been concentrated in these men and these times! We might as soon judge religion by St. Bartholomew's Day, and religious men by the perpetrators of the Dragonnades. . . . We might as soon judge monarchy by Nero, Henry VIII, or Philip II.[62]

Here Pradt defends the eighteenth century, using the same tactics as the Liberal historian defending the Revolution: you cannot blame the Revolution for producing the Terror.

Clausel de Montals, *prédicateur* to the king, begins by characterizing Abbé de Pradt's work as "a continual hymn to the honor of the Revolution."[63] He sums up Pradt's defense: "If he is to be believed, the *philosophes* have been the cause of nothing, and only wicked or limited minds can attribute to them some part in our disasters." Whereas for Clausel de Montals: "It is truly easy to demonstrate in their works the violent provocation to all the excesses and all the crimes which have so disfigured our Revolution; and their recommendations, if transformed into fact, would form a complete history in advance of this terrible catastrophe."[64]

Clausel's real contribution is his realization that there are two questions at stake. First is the degree of responsibility of the *philosophes*. This, he realizes, is only the minor question; the basic question is one's attitude toward revolution. Granted that the *philosophes* did not know where their arguments would lead: why, then, in view of the results produced, continue to eulogize them? If we really regard the Revolution as wrong, then at best we can forgive the *philosophes*; we cannot absolve them. Here Clausel has seized upon the fundamentals of the debate. The defense of the *philosophes* can only be based upon a larger commitment to the Revolution itself. Clausel has caught Pradt in the typical Restoration dilemma—the attempt of the Liberal to defend the Revolution without actually saying so: "What is decisive against his clients is that not a single voice was raised, from the heart of the sect, to disavow those abominable desires, and to prevent their publication and their results."[65]

The guilt or innocence of the *philosophes* has remained a live question from the days of the Revolution down into our own times, which have seen Barruel's charges revived by the brilliant Augustin Cochin. For the Restoration the question has a peculiar relevance: If the eighteenth-century *philosophes* are guilty of the Revolution and the large problem of the Restoration is to prevent further revolution, it is necessary to proceed against the Restoration counterpart of this Enlightenment elite—the journalists, historians, and lawyers of the Liberal opposition. But if the *philosophes* were not guilty, if they only represented an advance guard of an inevitable revolution, then their descendants can be allowed to exist, even flourish.

The attack upon the eighteenth century centered around its two giants—Rousseau and Voltaire. The Liberal pattern of defense of the Enlightenment is similar to the larger defense of the Revolution—first to deny the responsibility of the *philosophes*, then to defend them as men essentially right although betrayed and distorted by their interpreters. Toward this end the Liberals combined with the extreme Left, which had never ceased fighting the eighteenth-century battle of *philosophe vs.* cleric. Their chief weapon in this struggle was the works of the *philosophes* themselves. The Restoration was inundated with works of the eighteenth century; in 1825 the *Ami de la Religion* reported that more than 2,700,000 volumes of such authors had been published in the previous seven years. One publisher, Touquet, made it an industry, producing twelve editions of Voltaire and thirteen of Rousseau.[66]

Throughout the Restoration the Conservatives met, and fought with every weapon, the attempt to extend the influence of the eighteenth century into the nineteenth. In 1817, Clausel de Montals takes up the question of the "Complete Works" of Voltaire and Rousseau; he takes as epigraph for his pamphlet the words of Louis XVI: "These two men have ruined France." For Clausel de Montals the issue is: Does society have the right "to place under the sacred guarantee of law an enterprise whose immediate result is to propagate writings and principles which openly tend to society's dissolution and ruin"? He describes the tendency of the Restoration as "a wish to palliate all, to excuse everything in these celebrated men, even their most monstrous excesses."[67] He attempts to indict Rousseau and Voltaire by the judgments of their contemporaries, but basically it is *their* Revolution which indicts their principles: "But do we need to search for other witnesses in order to demonstrate that the so-called philosophic principles of Voltaire and Rousseau led to the dissolution of the social order and to anarchy, after the French Revolution furnished us with the facts which prove this truth so clearly?"

The Revolution is proof enough, but he notes that the Liberals have sought to dissociate their saints from sin: "It is useless for our incorrigible amateurs of the revolution to affirm with imperturbable audacity that those two oracles of incredulity counted for nothing in our calamities and in the outburst of outrages and crimes which marred the recent past. No one believes them." To prove responsibility he offers two kinds of evidence. First he cites the verdict of contemporaries; "Voltaire, Rousseau, and Diderot . . . have perverted youth" (Louis XVI) and "Voltaire did not see all that he did, but he did all that we see" (Laharpe). Then Clausel turns to the Revolution and finds damning evidence in the testimony of the Convention itself: "What names do the *Conventionnels* mingle in their cries and in their decrees? From whom did they borrow their cynical maxims or their cruel axioms? Whom have they apotheosized? . . . Who can know better than the revolutionaries themselves the influences under which they acted?"

As *chef d'œuvre,* Clausel offers Lakanal's proposal of a national day to commemorate Rousseau. Thus the attack upon the eighteenth century cuts both ways: the Revolution is self-condemned as the product of an age of impiety; the *philosophes* stand convicted by the Revolution they fathered. However, this is no mere quarrel with history; the Conservative critic tries to convince the Restoration that the men who upended the Old Regime are capable of doing it again. As a cleric, Clausel de Montals is particularly careful to label the *philosophes* a fundamental threat to monarchy as well as to religion. He denies Voltaire's attachment to monarchy, and after quoting Rousseau on the "provisional" character of monarchy, he observes:

> If all true Frenchmen are *indignant* at reading these seditious lines, how sad a thing that the books which include them are offered to the young and to all classes as a precious gift, and that the interest in these works, increased by their appearance and . . . the respect attached to new publications, will plant in men's minds the seeds of worry and revolt.

And this latest sedition is again reminiscent of the pattern; Clausel reminds us of the "quantities of infamous books to which the Revolution gave birth. Did there not appear, in those frenzied times, writings entitled *Les Crimes des rois, Les Crimes des reines,* etc., etc.? Were not collections of calumnies published against the most unfortunate of monarchs?"

In 1817 there also appeared *Vie politique, littéraire, et morale de Voltaire où on réfute Condorcet et ses autres historiens.* Its author, Lepan, sees his work as an answer to other biographies which have merely been "eulogies of the eighteenth-century philosophy of which he was chief spokesman." "Those who preceded us wished to propagate what they called Philosophy; we would like, on the contrary, to halt its distressing effects. . . . We have the unhappy advantage that events have proved their manner of interpreting things erroneous."[68] Lepan concludes his three-hundred-page exposé with a bibliography listing the refutations of Voltaire's works.

The continued flood of these works brought into the arena, in 1821, Bishop Boulogne of Troyes. His pastoral letter begins somberly: "Of all the scandals . . . which have afflicted religion and virtue, there is none more alarming in its results, more compromising to the safety of souls, and more likely to bring fresh calamities to France than the printing of the many impious writings that are circulating today." The conspiratorial, as opposed to the philosophical, character of the works is insisted upon:

> These are no light strokes escaping from an inconsiderate pen; it is a plan of attack followed with as much perfidy as audacity against Throne and Altar. . . . Here are the Complete Works, in which the legions of all the *Libertins*, all the amateurs of innovation and revolution, steep themselves.[69]

Boulogne also is alert to the Liberal line of defense. He asks rhetorically: Have these men perhaps been misunderstood?

> The captains who steered the bark of revolution . . . were they ignorant of the *philosophes*? Have we not, on the contrary, proof of their skill and competence? And these men of science, these cunning men, did they not pay honor to the horrible success of our two *coryphées* of philosophy? Did they not chant

hymns to their glory among the chants of death, did they not carry them in triumph and install them . . . among the Gods or demons of the Temple of *Great Men*?[70]

The bishop of Troyes does not neglect any weapon in his effort to discredit the *philosophes,* even to employing them against themselves, citing Voltaire's attack upon Rousseau and Rousseau's general attack upon the Enlightenment. He concludes with a series of "Gardez-vous de ces Œuvres Complètes," in which the works are pictured as capable of bringing about another revolution if this warning goes unheeded.[71]

The years 1822–27 marked the low point of Liberal influence in government, but in opposition the Liberals continued to reprint their long-range weapons, the writings of the *philosophes.* Clausel de Coussergues takes time from his celebration of the coronation to note the continuing infiltration of the eighteenth-century into the Restoration:

In the twenty-nine years which passed between the printing of the edition of Voltaire at Kell and 1814, there was only one edition of this writer. There have been at least sixteen since the Restoration. Rousseau, Diderot, Dupuis, Volney, and all the other impious authors have been multiplied in the same proportions. It would be impossible if, in such a state of affairs, the monarchy did not perish a second time. In order to deny this, it would be necessary to deny that like causes produced like results; it would be necessary to deny divine justice.[72]

Thus, by conceiving the Revolution as a plot and identifying its plotters, the Conservative theoreticians reduce it to its essential quality—crime. The Conservatives entered the Restoration assuming that this characterization would stick. But the first shock of the Liberal defense made them realize that the New France was not prepared to accept the facile equation, Revolution equals wrong; the new generation was in need of periodic reminders that the Revolution really was the "spirit of immorality," the *philosophes* "hordes of tigers."[73] Exhibit A was, of course, the regicide, but the September Days, the Noyades, the Convention, were almost as convincing.

In the first years of the Restoration, the magazine *Le Conservateur* becomes a clearinghouse for this right wing and its eagerness to prevent France from forgetting.[74] Writing in 1818, La Rochefoucauld is plainly irritated at the Liberals, now talking of moderation: "Considering all that was done when all that was necessary was the reform of a few abuses, how dare they still vaunt the results?"[75] This is a typical Conservative use of the Revolution—you had your chance and look what you did. The periodical devoted eight pages to a statistical summary of the Revolution, including everything from men lost to money spent, concluding with this comment: "Reduce this résumé to half its size and it is still the equivalent of ten centuries of calamities. Indeed, it seems that for thirty years the French have experienced all the scourges: civil and foreign wars, fires, proscriptions, plagues, famines, invasions . . ."[76]

This task of reminding France of the worst aspects of the Revolution falls largely to the extreme wings of the aristocratic and clerical parties. As groups, they had suffered most at the hands of the Revolution, and had regained least by the Restoration. Though the Royalists of the Restoration were committed to regarding the Revolution as criminal, they were even more committed to making the Restoration work—and in practice this often meant accepting the men and compromising with the principles of the Revolution.

In 1819, at the height of Liberal penetration of the Restoration, Vicomte Conny de la Fay addresses a work to Louis XVIII entitled *De la Nécessité pour les rois des souvenirs de la Révolution.* Alarmed at the Liberals' boldness and the recuperative powers of the revolutionary ideal, he warns: "France seems to march to the somber gleam of those fires whose pale glow illuminated the funeral of the king and all the outrages contained in the horribly concise words *French Revolution.*" Noting that history is the lesson of kings, he proceeds to offer a solution:

It would be a good custom to place a citizen near the throne who would be charged with constantly recalling to sovereigns the most memorable events of this great and terrible catastrophe. . . . The citizen assigned this austere and saintly task would ceaselessly din into the ears of the king the forever lamentable history of the execrable revolution of March 20. . . . He would present to his king the shameful and indescribable moments which raised crime triumphant.[77]

This absurd suggestion is significant on two counts. First, it is an insight into what the Conservative hopes to make of the Revolution in the Restoration—a morality play in which the devil can be summoned up, displayed, and slain. Second, it indicates the extreme Right's view of the Restoration monarchy—that it has come perilously close to embracing the Revolution and has betrayed the very reason for its existence.

Another long catalog of the crimes of the Revolution is found in Lespinasse de Langeac's *Journal de l'anarchie, de la terreur et du despotisme* (1821).[78] The author does feel some qualms about the reopening of old sores, but firmly consoles himself with a quotation from Chénier: "It is not true that disastrous events ought to be effaced from the memory of men. . . . On the contrary, they should lodge there forever, that they may continually inspire new horror and arm humanity against these plagues."

As we have seen, the Liberals countered this Conservative gambit with their own catalog of crimes. Carnot had been an early Liberal practitioner of this comparative criminology; borrowing the accumulating evidence of the eighteenth-century attack upon religious abuses, he sought to remind the Restoration that the Revolution did not introduce injustice into French history. Guillot does not allow Carnot these eighteenth-century tactics. He is astonished that "they still dare to speak of the Sicilian Vespers, of the Crusades, of St. Bartholomew and the Inquisition." The Conservatives seek to prevent the introduction of these stalking horses of the Enlightenment, and Guillot puts their case as:

When they have justified to humanity, to reason, to their contemporaries and posterity, the horrible September massacres; the frightful sentences of the Tribunal of Blood where the revolutionaries sat; the assassinations committed under Robespierre; the drownings of a Charrier [*sic*]; the *glacières* of Avignon; the cruel atrocities proclaimed and executed at Lyons, at Rheims, at Meaux, at Versailles, at Nîmes, at Nantes, by patriots, by agents of an assembly which called itself national, by monsters honored with the title of representatives of the people when they were no better than executioners—when, I say, they have justified so many misdeeds and so many crimes, superstition will have long since been pardoned.

Guillot does not deny past crimes, but he is perfectly willing to match them against the record of the Revolution: "The old prejudices with which the people were imbued, the weaknesses of our kings, the supposed tyranny of nobles, the alleged rapacity of the clergy . . . are all very feeble grievances after what we have seen in a revolution."[79]

The Liberals never do abandon their attempt to mitigate the crimes of the Revolution with a vigorous presentation of the "facts" of French history. The crimes of religion are particularly popular, and the burden of defense falls to the religious interests. Boyer offers a standard reply to these eighteenth-century "calumnies." St. Bartholomew's Day was a political purge, the Sicilian Vespers a common assassination, the Spanish Inquisition established by secular princes.[80] Here again we see the Conservative problem: in defending the clergy from the attacks of the Liberal historians, Boyer (a cleric) throws the burden of guilt onto the secular political leaders.

Crimes of French history *vs.* crimes of the Revolution—this is the Restoration struggle in microcosm. The Liberal indicts the past as crime in order to justify the Revolution; the Conservative replies that the crimes of the Revolution are greater and fresher.

In 1817 there appeared in the *Journal du commerce* a typical Liberal effort to resurrect the specter of religious crimes of the past, which noted that the "Inquisitor only burned several heretics from time to time to keep in practice." A Conservative reply, in the form of a dialogue, appeared in the *Conservateur*—a dialogue which reveals Conservative impatience at the Liberals' use of history to screen their own criminal record:[81]

LIBERAL: You must have seen [in the *Journal du Commerce*] that an Inquisitor named Torquemada had the satisfaction of burning 10,220 heretics in eighteen years . . . ?

CONSERVATIVE: And why does the *Journal* print these tragic stories?

LIBERAL: In order to make you see the results of religious fanaticism and the services rendered to humanity by philosophy. . . .

CONSERVATIVE: I have read . . . of this Torquemada . . . but I had not heard that he burned ten thousand heretics, and I suspect . . . the *Journal du Commerce* of having embroidered upon the text for its particular satisfaction and for the honor of philosophy. . . . Ten thousand people in eighteen years! Why, that's nothing! In our time, the great Fouquier-Tinville dispatched thirty thousand people in less than a year for certain political heresies surely less serious, after all, than those of the Moors. At Nantes the great Carrier killed off more than twenty thousand in the *bateaux à soupape*, a device that surpasses the *San Benito* in inventiveness. . . . That is what took place under the eyes of a triumphant philosophy, and I have been wrong to deny our progress.

LIBERAL: . . . You are confusing epochs and circumstances. In Spain the Inquisition was wrong, but in France the revolutionary tribunals were right. "If you are not bereft of all good sense, it is time for you to realize that the murders, robberies, and fires are in no sense the results of revolutionary ideas, but of despotism's dogged resistance to the irresistible torrent. . . ."[82]

CONSERVATIVE: What Torquemada said that? . . . But how long ago did those ten thousand heretics burn? You told us earlier yourself: in the fifteenth century. Ah well, sir, it seems to me a great deal easier to forget what happened in Spain in the fifteenth century than what happened in France in the eighteenth.

The conception of the French Revolution as conspiracy and crime is central to an understanding of Restoration politics. In broadest terms, it is the French manifestation of that nineteenth-century revulsion toward the eighteenth, theological in tone, intransigent in action. It is the belief of men who see the Revolution as an insurrection against God and history, a decade of crime as the logical outcome of a century of evil. These men want a return to the past—the most fundamental and utopian of all revolutions.

And it is this conception that is the identifying mark of that political animal of the Restoration, the Ultra. Convinced that the Revolution is a crime, political or religious, the Ultra conceives of the Restoration as a judgment on that crime. He enters the Restoration with a holy mission: the Revolution must be punished and history reversed. It was the Ultras who ruled France in the first year of the Second Restoration, and they made this year a black example; fifteen years later the threat of a return to this period drove France into revolution. Deposed in 1816, the Ultra party spends the next four years as His Majesty's most savage opposition. Under the leadership of Chateaubriand and in the columns of the *Conservateur*, it hacked away at the Decazes regime, the first of the Restoration efforts to unite historical France with the France of the Revolution. The Ultra greeted all the compromising legislation of these years—the Law of Recruitment, the Law of Elections—as betrayal of his Restoration.

The assassination of the Duc de Berry in 1820 destroys the Liberal-Royalist alliance, and from that point on, the Ultras are to play the decisive role. Villèle (1822–27) is not himself an Ultra, and although he rejects the alliance of the Liberals, he too seeks to bury the issue of the Revolution by successful foreign policy and sound economic measures. But the Ultras in the Chamber and the press refuse to forget; under their constant pressure,

Villèle is forced to introduce measure after measure whose sole purpose is to humiliate the Revolution, to endanger its supporters, to prosecute the past. The legislation of the 1820's—the Law of Sacrilege and Love, the Law of Eldest, the attack on the National Guard, the indemnities proposal—cannot be explained on grounds of logic or interest.[83]

Listen to Conny de la Fay: "Seated amidst the ruins of the Revolution, it [legitimate power] took on the job of repairing all that was reparable."[84] Or as Saint-Roman simply put it: "I hate the Revolution."[85] Or Chateaubriand's characterization of the debate over sacrilege: "You depart from the customs of the century in order to return to those times which we no longer recognize."[86]

The Ultras succeed only in splitting Restoration France and threatening normally loyal and peaceful interests. Further, this legislation plays right into the hands of the Liberals, justifying all their fears and propaganda: Privileges gained by the Revolution were to be swept away, feudalism was on the march. The men of the Center—the Royalists trying to make the Restoration work—were aware of the disasters inherent in this policy, but the Ultras persisted. Why did they persist? Because, as Thureau-Dangin pointed out, they were men of principle and they saw their role in the Restoration as *Ecrasez l'infâme.* Why did they resurrect dead issues? For the same reason the English Restoration dug up the body of Oliver Cromwell—the beast must be slain, twenty-five years of French history obliterated and atoned for.[87]

Throughout the Restoration there runs a kind of minority report in the Conservative tradition, a middle-of-the-road view that contrasts with the intransigence of the Ultras. It lacks the consistency and virulence of the Ultra view because it is an effort at uneasy compromise; its authors are men who, in theory, are opposed to the Revolution but, in practice, are willing to compromise in the best interests of the Bourbon Restoration. These are the men scornfully labeled by the Ultras as "Ministerials." Instead of seeing the Revolution as crime, they see it as history; recognizing that the Revolution is at the gate, they seek to tame and assimilate it.

Montlosier, the Liberal aristocrat, expresses a view characteristic of the optimism of the First Restoration. He does not believe in revolutions, but the Revolution has been accomplished: "I believe that it is wise to fall in with it, to adjust to it, to approach it in the spirit of forgetfulness, condescension, sacrifice."[88] A critic later refers to Montlosier's efforts scornfully: "He believed he had found the means of rendering French, the Revolution of 1789."[89]

Another example of this early Restoration desire to compromise is Billecocq's denial of any wish to turn back the clock, "to return France to the twelfth century and reestablish the *dîme* and feudalism." Billecocq is caught in the paradox that is to make the Center Royalist position so difficult—the

Revolution was a dreadful mistake, but it did produce some magnificent results.[90]

The tortured quality of this Center position is best revealed in Frayssinous, who, as a responsible minister and Gallican, is caught between the fire of the Liberal Abbé de Pradt and the Ultras, Maistre and Lamennais. As early as 1814, Frayssinous, in exile with Louis XVIII, had worked out the position toward the Revolution that was to identify the Center Royalists, make possible their alliance with Liberals, and alienate them from the Ultras. Frayssinous remembered that in 1795 Louis had called for a return of the old regime. Eager to defend the king's attitudes, past and present, he finds this particular attitude understandable in 1795 because the Old Regime was still a living memory after only six years. But after twenty years, new institutions, a rejuvenated clergy, and military glory had created a New France: "For a very great number of Frenchmen the Old Regime existed only in history."[91]

Appointed Royal Censor in 1814, Frayssinous delivered three discourses on the French Revolution. He blames philosophy and attacks Voltaire, but he is careful to point out that philosophy infected all of society.[92] The total guilt of France is stressed; the audience is urged to remember Louis XVI but "to dispense with all thoughts of hatred and revenge."[93] Throughout the Restoration, Frayssinous serves the cause of moderation and compromise with the New France which is symbolized by his master. The death of Louis XVIII in 1824 is the occasion to elevate this policy into a principle. The Ultras have singled out Louis for the most violent abuse; Frayssinous defends partial recognition of the Revolution as historically dictated: "France presented herself to Louis not as he had left her but as the Revolution made her, as a house ruined by time and ravaged by fire appears to its old master." He hastens to add that he does not mean to reject the past or to call for the spirit of innovation, but

> I also know that we are often forced to respect the ravages of time, that it is not within the power of the living to recall the dead . . . , and that after a long series of shocks and devastations in the religious and political order, it becomes as impossible to reconstruct the previous social order as it would be callous to preserve none of it.

Frayssinous, one of the great orators of the Restoration, movingly portrays Louis XVIII as a king who rose above the confinements of his background to lead France in the only direction she could possibly go—the middle way.

> What would Louis do? Would he be exclusively guided by the doctrines, habits, customs, in which he had been brought up . . . or would he be an innovator and depart from the way of monarchy? . . . He would do neither one nor the other. He would not try to rebuild the ancient edifice in its entirety; most of the stones which composed it were scattered, many no more than dust. . . . He espoused the cause of rejuvenating the antique monarchy.

This view, of course, was perilously close to the Liberals' claim that they had won, that the Revolution was accepted, that no surgery could eliminate it from the French body. Indeed, after 1824 the Center Royalists take the pessimistic view that the Revolution is winning and its ultimate triumph is inevitable. The Royalists take the tone of defenders of a lost cause. Cottu in 1829 gloomily notes: "Revolutionary prejudices are too deeply rooted in France to hope to triumph over them. . . . Our destiny is not to see royalty depart triumphant from its battle against anarchy, but to die like Achilles under the walls of Troy."[94] And in 1830, this pessimism becomes desperation. Cottu attempts to argue that a new revolution is unnecessary since the Revolution has won: "Frenchmen, be just toward your king, as he has been generous toward you. All that we wanted in 1789, we have obtained."[95]

In February 1830, in a letter to the Marquis de Clermont-Tonnerre, Frayssinous speaks for the Royalist generation that has been convinced by the logic of the Royalist position, the propaganda of the Liberals, and the events of the Restoration:

The new doctrines, the new systems, have struck deep roots. Children have sucked another milk than their fathers sucked. A revolution in ideas has been accomplished; it is a tree which bears and will bear fruit. It is no longer only a question of fixing limits and not permitting them to be crossed. . . . It is, then, true that the experiences of fathers are lost upon their sons.*

But it was the Ultra view that prevailed, the determination to blacken the Revolution in the mind of the Restoration, to catalog its crimes, and to insist that they were deliberate in conception and unmatched in savagery. The Liberals countered this version with their tactic of dissociation: the crimes were one thing, the Revolution another. To this the Conservatives replied with a concept of the Revolution that has since been part of the Conservative repertory—that the Revolution was, from conception to execution, a single thing.

Riambourg defines Liberals as "those who seek to separate the doctrines of the Revolution from the crimes it produced."[96] Specifically, the Liberals had identified themselves with the Revolution's Constitutional phase, equating the Constituent Assembly with the Revolution and regarding what followed as degradation and betrayal. Specifically, the Conservative response is to deny any such distinction, indeed to hold the Constituent Assembly responsible for what followed.

Charles de Lacretelle, the author of a two-volume history of the Constitu-

* Henrion, *Vie de Frayssinous,* II, 662–63, in a letter from Frayssinous to the Marquis de Clermont-Tonnerre. Also, Talleyrand writes to Barante, "We march toward an unknown world without pilot and without compass; only one thing is certain, that everything will end in a shipwreck. . . . The Revolution in England lasted for more than half a century. Ours is only in its fortieth year." Quoted in Barante, *Souvenirs,* III, 550–51.

ent Assembly, charts the Revolution's progress thus: "After having begun . . . majestically with the Constituent Assembly, it soon yielded, under the Convention, to the most violent and bloody dictatorship which has yet afflicted mankind."[97] For Marchangy, the connection is even more certain than the event: "Few persons have understood '89, but what human heart has not trembled at the crimes of '93, which were merely its immediate consequences?"[98] Pierre Chaillot blames the Constituent Assembly for being unable to halt the drift into the Terror:

If the Constituent Assembly, after having destroyed ancient laws, instead of dissolving, had had the courage to remain in session as the king requested; . . . if, instead of being frightened by the maneuvers of the demagogues, it had openly fought them; . . . if, instead of abandoning a tottering throne whose foundations it had itself undermined, it had sincerely united with the virtuous Louis XVI, . . . perhaps it could have healed the wounds of the country, made it forget the frightful hardships. . . . But a just and inevitable history proclaims its guilt, . . . and though it numbered men of great talent, . . . our unhappy country owes to it all the incalculable evils that afflict us still.[99]

Chaillot's judgment is echoed by Riambourg: "The crimes of the Revolution are the bitter fruit of the errors of the Constituent Assembly." And further: "At the same time it prepared the triumph of unbelief, the Constituent Assembly assured the triumph of democracy." Riambourg is loath to grant the Assembly any virtues: "doctrines of independence . . . usually prepare the way for greater usurpations"; even freedom of religion is seen, not as a friendly gesture to Protestants, but as "an expression of hatred . . . for the dominant religion."[100]

The Duc de Fitz-James, another discovery of the *Conservateur*, reviewing Mme de Staël's *Considérations*, flatly contradicts her version of this disputed period: "For Mme de Staël, the finest epoch of the history of France is unquestionably the one beginning the fourteenth of July and ending the tenth of August."[101] He grimly quotes her words—"happy time . . . when the heady air more freely swelled our lungs"—and comments: "No air more freely swelled the lungs of those aristocrats who were attached so gaily to the lampposts to the joyous cries of *Ça ira*." Mme de Staël had claimed that "the bloody scenes were promptly put down after the fourteenth of July." Fitz-James denies this: "The bloody scenes continued without interruption all over France, until the tenth of August, when the judicial murders began." He refuses to distinguish, sees no break in the Revolution. Mme de Staël, he argues, knows that things were bad under the Constituent Assembly; but she pretends they were not, so as "to avoid reproaching the soldiers of freedom for not having punished the crimes while power was still in their hands."

It is upon the other favorites of the Liberals—the Moderates—that Fitz-James pours his heaviest fire. These men were in control:

They were immensely popular, in control of the administration, in command of the army; and yet, as soon as lightning struck, they fled, without daring to try to help their unfortunate leader, who was delivered by them, bound hand and foot, to his executioners. They can congratulate themselves upon having prepared the way for the execution of Louis XVI.

Another effective answer to Liberal dissociation is to argue that, whatever the intentions of the Assembly, it set in motion an inevitable revolutionary process. Indeed, in the late stages of the Restoration, this argument is used to frighten the Liberals themselves, to remind them of the threat from below. In 1829 Cottu challenges the Doctrinaires on this count:

Let us assume they have become masters of the government, as a result of the ignorance and vanity of the middle classes. What resistance would they offer to the brutal energy of the Jacobins when these last, with the *Rights of Man* in their hands and the red cap on their heads, categorically demand the immediate reallocation of all property? . . . Would they not . . . like the Constituent Assembly and the Girondins, . . . be forced to abandon France to the experiments of a Robespierre or a Babeuf?[102]

The Revolution was guilty—the whole Revolution—this was the Ultra thesis. Whether through weakness, stupidity, design, or inevitable sequence, 1789 produced 1793. The Revolution is a crime; among its perpetrators, and as guilty as any, were the *philosophes* of the Enlightenment and the Moderates of the Constituent Assembly. There remains one final operation which will effectively cut off the Liberal efforts to sell the Revolution and reap maximum political advantage—to keep the specter of this age of crime before the eyes of the Restoration as stark reality.

Using the Charter to good advantage, the Liberals had insisted that the Revolution was over, that history had profoundly altered their status, and that they were the true Royalists of the Restoration. The Conservative reply to this bold maneuver is first to establish the existence of a revolutionary threat, and then, by a series of damaging parallels, to expose the links between Restoration Liberalism and revolutionary crime. This line of attack is at once an expression of a real fear and a major political asset.

Fitz-James sees more at stake in Mme de Staël's work on the Revolution than the distortion of history: "It is circumstantial, emotional, designed not so much to portray the past as to lead astray the judgment of the public. It is a catechism for young revolutionaries, for those who must be taught how to think and speak about the past twenty-five years and how to conduct themselves in the years to come."[103] To Fitz-James, Mme de Staël's *Considérations* are nothing less than a revolutionary handbook, dangerous in arming a generation already disposed to revolution.

Throughout the four uneasy years of the Liberal-Royalist alliance (1816–20), there are rumblings of this sort from the extreme Right, but Liberal participation in the government keeps the cry of "revolutionary" to a minimum. In 1821, however, after the assassination of the Duc de Berry, the discovery of the Carbonari plots (which implicated certain Liberals), and the subsequent elimination of the Liberals from responsibility, the stage is set for the Conservative charge that is to carry the greatest weight for the remainder of the Restoration. The Comte de Serre's speech of 1820, three months after Louvel's blow, signals official recognition of the existence of a revolutionary party:

The existence of this revolutionary faction, this irreligious faction, the enemy of all legitimate authority and of all safeguards, has been pointed out; it speaks out in the newspapers; it has its headquarters in the steering committees. . . . My convictions on this score spring not only from my conscience but also from what I have observed in my official position."[104]

With the evidence of actual revolutionary activity in hand, the Conservatives have their issue.[105]

The publications of Lombard de Langres, who had served under the Directory, offer an interesting barometer of Conservative feeling. In 1819, in his *Histoire des sociétés secrètes,* he gloomily predicts that in a hundred years there will not be a throne standing. In 1820, in a volume called *Les Jacobins depuis 1789 jusqu'à ce jour,* he presents fresh evidence of Jacobin activity. In 1822 he brings this 1820 volume up to date, and in this edition he revises his original prediction—barring decisive action, not a throne will be standing in ten years.[106]

The activities of the European revolutionaries throughout the Restoration were grist for the Conservative mill. Clausel de Coussergues, who had successfully led the fight in 1820 to oust the Decazes regime on the grounds of softness to the Revolution, sought to expose its international connections. "The Revolution, before which the ministry would raise all barriers, keeps advancing year after year. Soon, as in 1792, it will be solidly established in France; it will be able to send its doctrines, and, even more, its subsidies, to the revolutionaries of Spain, Naples, and Piedmont."[107]

In the same year (1822), Marchangy, prosecuting the case against the Four Sergeants of La Rochelle, sees the French conspiracy as part of a general European phenomenon: "That is why Naples . . . repeats word for word the language of the veterans of our civil disorders; that is why Spain . . . is harassed by a gang of troublemakers who are avid for regicide and eager to duplicate point for point the excesses of '93."[108]

The years 1822–27, the years of the Villèle administration, are an era of good feelings for the Ultras. The Liberals are out; the Conservatives are in complete command. The point of political friction has shifted to a struggle between Ultra and Royalist; the threat of Liberal revolution seems remote. But the return of the Liberals with the Martignac administration in 1827, and legislation which is a clear rejection of the Ultra pattern in the Restoration, resurrect Conservative fears. This Conservative concern is mirrored in a pamphlet, *Preuves frappantes de l'imminence d'une seconde révolution,* which lists as symptoms of the coming revolution everything from the millions of books printed to the growing crime rate, from the growth of secret societies to the state of religion. The writer finds 1789 mild in comparison with 1827; above all "Liberalism alone commands the affection of the people."[109]

In 1829 the situation is even worse for the Ultra. In the *Tableau des trois époques,* the history of the Restoration is pictured as one of steady Liberal penetration: "No more Revolution, these . . . impostors incessantly cry, and revolutions are their element." The author demonstrates the Liberals' revolutionary intentions by a series of comparisons, one page devoted to 1789–91 and a facing page summarizing the situation in 1829. The parallels are impressive: threats to the king while pretending hypocritical admiration, attacks against the ministers, hatred for the Catholic religion, zeal for lowering taxes, and so on. In each category the author makes out a strong case for finding the present dangerous, and it is significant to note that this late in the Restoration the specter of the past Revolution is being raised to prevent any future uprising: "The progress of the Revolution is the same in 1829 as in 1789, '90, and '91; this second revolution is now as advanced as the first was in 1792." The author concludes with a series of "Faut-il rappeler" in which the horrors of the Revolution are summoned up, including a list of twenty-five names at the mention of which "Europe still trembles."[110]

By 1830 the Royalist fear of a second revolution has hardened into a conviction. The fear has become a panic, yet the assumption remains that if France can only realize that the French Revolution is at the gate, it will rouse itself to action. Revolution is in the air. In January 1830, the *Journal du nord* states: "It is a palpable truth that a revolution is imminent, that it is directed against the Catholic religion and the throne of the Bourbons." The following day, it asks it readers to reflect on whether "the moral circumstances which prepared the French Revolution are not duplicated, in frightening fashion, in our present situation."[111] During the months leading up to July, the Conservative press adopts as its refrain the imminence of the revolution and the parallels with the France of 1789 or the England on the eve of 1688.

The Conservatives had long sought to relate the activities of the Restoration Liberals to those of their revolutionary predecessors, to find in the Liberal political program and procedures the pale imitation of the Revolution, to prove that the Liberals had learned nothing and forgotten nothing.

Frénilly, viewing the progress of the Liberals in 1818, sees their basic objective, a "plan reviewed and corrected from '93," unchanging but with a subtler approach: "Not a cry, not a drop of blood, because the path will be so easy, the transition so imperceptible, that we will awake in a republic without even having had our sleep troubled; we will have arrived there by law, in the name of the Charter, under the royal sanction, in the fullness of peace and legitimacy." Once the Liberals are successful, their real goals will be asserted: "having become independent, then perfected as democrats, they will finally be fulfilled as Jacobins." To prove his point Frénilly suggests a reading of the *Moniteur* of 1790:

If, then, someone is seduced by this bed of roses and this laughing future, let him reread the *Moniteur*. He will find there that in 1790, honest thinkers also wished for a monarchical republic, they preached it, and they even made it. Soon, since republic and monarchy are two contradictory entities, there arose in their midst others, who, reasoning more logically, sought to make the republic republican.

Throughout the Restoration, the Conservative willingly grants that the attitude of the Jacobin is more consistent than that of the Liberal; he tries to drive the Liberal into the camp of the extremist.

The Liberal historian is certainly not in any position to deny the sad facts of the revolutionary experience; at best he can deny their relevance to the Restoration. Frénilly cleverly evokes the Liberals' situation: "They are compelled, at each stage of this second revolution, to distinguish it from the first, out of pride or out of shame." He mimics the Liberals: " 'This is not the same thing; it is something new. They were wrong and we are right; they destroyed and we build, they killed and we regenerate.' " Frénilly's rebuttal is simple: "The forms differ, but the principles and their immediate consequences do not."[112] The Liberal belief in the inevitability of the Revolution is matched by the Conservative faith in the inevitability of the revolutionary process.

In the same issue of the *Conservateur*, another voice of the far Right, Boisbertrand, draws the noose of historical parallel even tighter, exposing the claim made famous by Guizot in 1818—that the Liberals are not a revolutionary faction: "To hear them talk, there is no longer a revolutionary faction in France." Subjecting this to examination, Boisbertrand finds little real difference in the behavior of the Liberals of 1789 and 1818: "What are we to conclude but that, if time has borne away some, others have taken their places, and that the same faction still troubles France?"

Boisbertrand comes to the heart of the Liberals' difficulty: the necessity of defending a Revolution whose results they deplore. How, he asks, can they ask us to return to a political doctrine which they admit led to disaster? For the Ultra, the purity of the intentions is worse than irrelevant; it supports his conviction that there is some relation between the moral earnestness of the reformer and the savagery of the reforms. Good intentions only remind him of the first fine flush of the Revolution:

Our intentions are pure, cry the propagators of this doctrine. . . . But those who spoke as you do twenty-seven years ago [1789], haven't they the same right to boast to us of the purity of their intentions? I see only one difference between you and them; their system had not yet covered France with mourning and destruction.

Again the appeal to experience, to the Revolution: in 1789 men had the right to be optimistic, but we—"with our eternal monuments of grief . . . to the most deplorable of all errors"—we have had our warning.

Indeed, for the Conservative the similarity of intentions between the eighteenth- and nineteenth-century Liberals is striking—and damning:

As you do, and perhaps even more than you, they believed that one could with impunity strip the royal authority of its most indispensable prerogatives. . . . As you do, they believed that the people would be happier with a more decisive influence in affairs, and better governed when they could choose their own magistrates; that deputies elected in the spirit of revolution would better appreciate and defend their constituents' rights; and finally that the army would be no more national when some of its leaders were no longer chosen by the sovereign.[113]

The Conservatives do not confine themselves to general parallels; they scour the Revolution, seeking an analogue for every Liberal action, every desire and demand; the Liberals are enclosed in a web of history. The attacks upon loyal members of the government, the widely circulated Liberal charge of a conspiracy emanating from the Right, the anticlericalism—everything is 1789 all over again. Or worse than 1789: "Who does not recognize that it is the Jacobinism of the Revolution which reappears in its entirety under the name of Liberalism?" They share the "same associations, same principles, same language, same passions, same means, same end."[114] Among the proofs offered are the parallels between the Jacobin and Liberal clubs—both have international connections. They are also indissolubly linked by their principles: irreligion, belief in the sovereignty of the people, and insurrection.

In trying to establish the guilt of the conspirators of La Rochelle, Marchangy takes up the defense argument that these men were patriots who meant only the best for France. Though few Liberals would defend the prisoners in the dock for their abortive revolution, Marchangy takes the occasion to strike a blow at the Liberals. He recalls that speaking in the name of one's country is not new. Mirabeau, "who wished to overthrow society to satisfy his spite," also spoke in the name of his country when he promised Louis XVI the protection of twenty-five million loyal Frenchmen. Lurking behind the façade of the defense argument, Marchangy finds the Liberal apology—events are to be judged by their intentions. He concludes his plea by characterizing the Liberal argument: "To the errors of the past we join the scorn of experience and the ability to forget the most memorable lessons."[115]

The grim parallel of Liberal activity in Revolution and Restoration was no mere idle speculation for the Conservative. This belief was basic to his politics, for it enabled him to conceive of the Restoration as a heaven-sent second chance to correct the mistakes of the previous generation. The belief that Liberalism was inevitably following the course laid down by its parent revolution was a comforting one, providing the Conservative with a blueprint for conduct in the Restoration. One had only to single out some Liberal activity, properly match it with its revolutionary precedent, recall the dire outcome, and crusade against it as a historically demonstrated error.

One by one the favorite Liberal stratagems of the Restoration are exposed by tracing them to their revolutionary origins. One of the crucial Liberal objectives is to drive a wedge between the clergy and the monarchy by suggesting their historical divisions. This effort culminates in Montlosier's attack on the Jesuits in 1826. Madrolle, in a reply to Montlosier, refutes the charges by identifying their ancestry; it has always been the task "of Philosophy, the great master of the theories of revolutions, to separate the king and the clergy."[116] He reasons that if the Jesuits were attacked in the eighteenth century, this should be sufficient proof of their innocence. And Madrolle turns around and offers as a basis for the Restoration alliance of clergy and monarchy the tragic parallel of the revolutionary experience. "Religion and monarchy have been condemned and even destroyed in this century. . . . When did the clergy ever serve as accomplice in the fall of kings? Open the true universal history of revolutions, and you will read there on every page that they have always risen, that they have always been weakened, that they have always fallen, with kings."[117] This is the positive side of the Conservatives' willingness to make use of the lessons of the Revolution—not only to deter Liberal action, but to guide their own policy.

Indeed, at the very heart of the Conservative drive to "reconvert" France is the lesson of the Revolution: religion is a buttress to monarchy; remove it, and monarchy is doomed. One could give innumerable examples of the Conservative appeal to the Revolution as the final oracle. We have seen that Liberal historians were fond of resurrecting the crimes of French religion—St. Bartholomew's Day, for instance—in an effort to make one forget the revolutionary "days." Clausel de Coussergues exposes this as an old tactic of the Enlightenment, a particular favorite of Voltaire's.[118] The equally persistent Liberal device of blaming the aristocracy is riddled by Conny de la Fay's reminder that death to the aristocracy was the constant cry of the Revolution.[119] D'Herbouville is also aware of this device: "Wherever revolutions have been plotted, there have been furious cries against the nobility. It is the bait that one hurls to the crowd to drive them toward the goal, . . . the profits of which the leaders have reserved for themselves. . . . They attack today what they attacked in 1789."[120] Even the familiar claim of the Restoration Liberal that the Revolution is over is found to have a revolutionary analogue: "After the promulgation of the Constitution of 1791, its admirers, defying the future, cried, "Ah, we can consider the Revolution over. . . . What can upset an order so perfect, an equilibrium so wisely established?' The year had not run its course before the Republic was proclaimed."[121]

In their campaign to sell the Revolution, the Liberals of the Restoration had discovered history, and history had paid off handsomely, providing them with a streamlined, spick-and-span revolution built for wear in the Restoration. But this revolutionary "new look" is not solely the result of a fresh historical version of the Revolution. As we saw in Chapter II, the Liberals relied heavily upon the Charter of 1814 in staking their claim for acceptance by the Restoration. Briefly summarized, the Liberal argument is that the Charter wrung from Louis XVIII embodies the basic liberties won by the Revolution and previously denied by a despotic monarchy. As such, it "proves" the essential justice of the revolutionary cause. As presented by the Liberals, the Charter is a triumph over the French past and a clear directive for the future. This is the challenge to Restoration Conservatives: they must both reject the version of the Charter as a verdict rendered on the French past and deny its significance for the future.

From the very proclamation of the Charter, the Conservatives were aware of the threats implicit in it. By 1816 there was an imposing body of Conservative literature on the Charter. The Conservative is sensible enough to realize that the Charter is a compromise, marking as it does the end of the revolutionary era and the beginning of the Restoration. To the degree that the Charter recognizes the Revolution, it is dangerous; for recognition can be taken to imply justification. Indeed, the Conservatives are uneasy with the Charter from the very beginning—almost as if they foresee its future use by the Liberals. The Ultras are frankly hostile, and Chateaubriand (at this point the voice of Restoration Royalism) devotes a good part of his *Réflexions politiques* to answering their objections. In 1814 the Ultras are suspicious of any constitution; for these émigrés, constitutionalism has an unfortunate pedigree. It was the cry of the hated "Lumières"; it is imitation of the English, which has proved so disastrous to France; it recalls visions of 1791; it is synonymous with revolution. Chateaubriand's task is to remove these negative associations from the word, and for the author of *Génie du Christianisme,* the inevitable means is history: a brief, brilliant foray into the French past to establish that constitutionalism is not something dreamed up by the Enlightenment, copied from the English, and imposed by the Revolution, but a basic French tradition, honored by age and previous experience:

> If it is true that France has a parliamentary tradition, what we would be doing by adopting constitutionalism today would only be, like the English, reinstating the government of our fathers; but whether this tradition came from our Frankish forefathers, from the Christian religion, or from both these sources, it is certain that it suits our present habits, that it does not contradict them in the least, and that it is not at all a foreign product in our midst.[122]

In a wild search through the French past, seeking precedents for the constitutional tradition, the aristocrat Chateaubriand has selected the parlement. He argues that, thanks to the Charter, the aristocracy can look forward to playing the same decisive role in French affairs that it formerly played in the age of parlements: "The Charter will guarantee you all that was essential in your former existence." "Thus the Charter, which restores to the *gentilshommes* their ancient role in government, will restore the original spirit of their order."[123] In his frantic efforts to appease the aristocratic faction, Chateaubriand comes up with a Conservative reevaluation of the French past, discovering that the *ancien régime* can be given a Liberal reading; indeed, he spends the entire Restoration trying to convince his fellow aristocrats that they are the true source of French liberties. Though unsuccessful in his task—the Ultras are absolutists and unsympathetic to any reminder of their past indiscretions—he does formulate a view of the French past which becomes part of the Conservative reply to the Liberal defense of the Revolution.

In defending the French Revolution, the Liberals were necessarily driven to attack the Old Regime as lacking these basic liberties which the Revolution demanded and won. They conceived of the Charter as their great triumph because it was the recognition—for the first time—of these liberties won by the Revolution. But here, at the dawn of the Restoration, in response to Liberal claims for the Charter, there emerges a Conservative history which first denies the revolutionary portrait of the Old Regime, and then denies the Charter any special distinction by placing it in a constitutional tradition. Broadly speaking, these Conservative historians maintained that the basic advance for which the Revolution claimed credit was illusory—that liberty and equality had existed in the Old Regime. This broad question was reduced by the controversy over the Charter to a more specific one: Did France of the Old Regime have a Constitution? The Liberals insisted with Mme de Staël that "France has been governed by custom, often by caprice, and never by law."[124] They held that constitutions were specific written guarantees of liberties, and that it was the absence of such a document that led to the Revolution.* Though the debate raged on these relatively narrow lines, the larger question—judgment of the entire French past—was never far out of sight.

Chateaubriand, writing in the First Restoration, reflects on what appeared to be the political problem of the return of the Bourbons—how to

* For the classic statement of this position, see Lanjuinais: "But this constitution which is alleged to go back thirteen or fourteen centuries is nothing but a chimerical hypothesis. Never, before 1791, did France have a constitutional code; and, if one calls any distribution of public power a constitution, there were actually in France, in the course of thirteen centuries, a multitude of different constitutions, each more informal, absurd, unjust, and deadly than the others. Which are we to choose? Which is to be perfected or modified? None of them could be tolerated today." Lanjuinais, *Constitutions de la nation française* (1819), II, 23.

hold the Ultras in check. But Agoult, an émigré, a bishop who had returned after 1801, writing in the midst of the Hundred Days, sees the failure of the First Restoration as the failure to properly sell the Charter to the New France. The Charter should not have been "graciously proclaimed" because the rights it guaranteed "were no more than the expression of our national liberties of old, to which all the monuments of our history attest."[125] Agoult admits that the "habit of assembly" had been lost for a few centuries, but it has been a basic error of both Right and Left to forget that these liberties *did* exist:

Such is our . . . ignorance that, on the one hand, our modern constitution makers do not suspect that the little they have done for civil liberty is merely an imperfect copy of our ancient institutions; and that, on the other hand, men of good will, while detesting the horrors of the Revolution, nevertheless believe that they owe the Revolution some thanks for abolishing the privileges of the nobility and clergy. The truth is that the ancient French constitution accorded no privileges whatever to the first two orders over the third.

He proceeds to document this claim with a survey of French history involving a legalistic defense of feudalism. He concludes: "The ancient constitutions establish a perfect and inviolate equality between the Third Estate and the first two orders." It was the "alleged privileges of the first orders that served as pretext for despoiling, proscribing, and executing them." The Revolution has been guilty of a giant distortion of the past, which Agoult spends twenty-four pages trying to redress by defending the clergy and nobility:

They . . . have never claimed to have constitutionally any political rights other than those they hold in common with the Third Estate. We deem it important to establish the truth of this last proposition, since the agitators are so strenuously seeking to arouse resentment in the people against the nobility and clergy.

As proof, Agoult offers an extract from the Estates of Foix dated February 9, 1789, affirming the equality of the orders. He regrets that "our Constituents had less sense than the smallest and most remote of our provinces." And Agoult clinches his case for the essential good will of the French system by citing the calling of the States-General: "It is certain, by the single fact of the convocation of the States-General . . . that the ancient constitution of our state was fully reestablished and the most perfect equality between the three orders reaffirmed." This defense of the French past, as essentially anticipating all the advantages of the Revolution, of course does not allow the Royalist to take a very strong stand against the original demands of this Revolution: "We did not need the Revolution to preserve this liberty and equality among us forever; we had only to provide for the periodic convocation of the States-General."

The Revolution was not really necessary—this is considerably different from the revolution-is-crime school of Ultras. It is apparent that this attempt to undercut the claims of the Revolution by arguing for the existence of equality in French history is characteristic of the Moderate Royalists. Agoult's conclusion is typical of this school—it is a plea not to allow the Revolution to steal the tradition of constitutional liberty away from the monarchy:

We must acknowledge, then, from all the foregoing, one great truth, that those articles of the Royal Charter which are truly constitutional, those which essentially define our national liberties, are only the expression of our ancient institutions. Let us not allow, to the eternal shame of France, the perpetrators of the drownings of Nantes, the massacres of Lyon, the *glacières* of Avignon, and so many other horrors to boast of having been the founders . . . of our civil liberties. The honor for this rightly belongs to the forever dear and venerated memory of the unfortunate Louis XVI, who, in convoking the States-General, reestablished all our rights.

The basic proposition presented by Agoult—that liberty is ancient—is one that might be expected to win the approval of the Liberal Mme de Staël. But Agoult uses the fact of ancient liberties to sanction, not a Liberal tradition which will justify the Revolution, but a tradition of ancient liberties which would eliminate the presumed cause of the Revolution. Indeed, the next step is to hold the Revolution responsible for the destruction of this ancient tradition.

In 1815 Delbare sees his task as "exposing the criminal, violent maneuvers by which the ancient constitution of royalty was destroyed." He hopes to do this by examining the tradition of the States-General:

It will not be useless to trace rapidly here the history of our States-General. We will show that they were established during the infancy of the monarchy, and that those who in 1789 dared to state publicly that France never had a constitution uttered an absurdity. A state which grew, prospered, and expanded for fourteen centuries, which acquired all manner of glory without having had a constitution, would present a phenomenon so extraordinary, so miraculous, that one must deny its existence and even its possibility.[126]

This debate, Delbare reminds us, is a restatement of the controversy of 1789 itself. Delbare has adopted Burke's thesis that, by definition, a nation has a constitution—if it didn't, it wouldn't have survived. The arguments have not changed since 1790, but their significance has. In 1790 the monarchy is threatened, but in 1815 the Revolution has had twenty-five years in which to make its point, to equate the Old Regime with tyranny. The granting of the Charter is the opportunity to redress the record, to salvage the French past from two decades of a bad press. And the resurrection of such a past, in its full glory and honor, seems to offer the Royalist a valuable underpinning for the successful return of this monarchy. In 1814, Ducanel had traced the eight unwritten provisions of the French Constitution through French history, a Burkean enterprise: not history as a giant abstraction with which to flay the Revolution, but an immersion into history itself to establish that France was constitutional.[127] Delbare sees the Champ de Mars and the Champ de Mai as the first constituent assemblies, which would locate the origin of the Estates prior to Charlemagne or Philip the Fair. Willing to admit that the assemblies have had a stormy and interrupted career, he nevertheless takes the optimistic view that "the French monarchy tends imperceptibly to return to its ancient constitutions." The clue can be found in the following key passage, which follows a discussion of the fourteenth-century assemblies:

> From this time on, the States-General assembled under different reigns and at irregular intervals. Despite the storms which were stirred up at their assemblies, from 1350 on, by factious enemies of the country, Charles VII, Charles VIII, Charles IX, and Henry III were not afraid to have recourse to them. Their long neglect under Louis XIII, Louis XIV, and Louis XV did not prevent the nation from recognizing, in 1789, their existence and necessity. Louis XVI, the most disinterested of kings, the least jealous of his authority, put himself in their hands with confidence. . . . It was demonstrated, then, by the example of this virtuous and unfortunate monarch, . . . that France had a constitution and perhaps the finest of constitutions.[128]

Where the Liberals tended to emphasize the uncertainties of the States-General, their long silence, their historic impotence, Delbare stresses their continuity if only as a presence. For Delbare it is not their 175-year silence that is significant, but that they could be resurrected with ease.

A book by the famous jurist Henrion de Pansey takes much the same view. According to Henrion, Louis XVIII has clearly modeled his Charter upon the institutions of ancient France: "Our ancient constitution is the best commentary on the new. If we are to understand the spirit of the Charter, if we are to define precisely the nature and limits of the powers it establishes . . . , we must refer to the former order of things."

Henrion, too, assigns an essentially constitutional character to the beginnings of French history. He goes further than Delbare in admitting that the initial liberties were quickly lost, but, like Delbare, he emphasizes that there was a tradition: "Our constitutional Charter restores to the nation the right to tax itself, a right in truth suspended for ten centuries, but which the sovereign courts had preserved by frequent protest. . . . Hence this provision of the Charter is not a concession but a confirmation."[129]

The details of French history are embarrassing for the Conservatives who are trying to establish a vigorous constitutional tradition, but they persist. If positive evidence is skimpy, one can shift the burden of proof—how could France have done so well if she had not had a constitution? As Bonald testily remarks: "The constitution of a people is the mode of their existence; to ask a people who have lived for fourteen centuries if they have a constitution is to ask a man eighty years old if he is constituted to live."[130] Henrion de Pansey gives us the clue to Conservative intentions—if the new generation has been trained to associate greatness with constitutions, why then of course France has one:

If France had not had a constitution, how could she have raised herself to the highest degree of civilization?

How could she have been such a great factor in the European balance of power?

How could she have carried the glory of her arms so far?

How could she have had the finest judiciary that ever existed?

How in the fields of science, of letters, of arts, could she have so frequently led other nations?

If France had not had a constitution, how could she have presented such a magnificent spectacle of ever-increasing prosperity for ten centuries?

. . . If she had not had a constitution, how could Machiavelli ever have said that "France holds the first rank among well-governed states?"[131]

Here the Conservative historian opposes the revolutionary caricature of the French past with a favorable portrait of Old Regime France. Such a France indicts the Revolution for having destroyed it; such a France is a model and inspiration for a Restoration.

The coronation of Charles X in 1825 and the discussion over whether he should also swear allegiance to the Charter is another opportunity to place the Charter in the context of French history. Clausel de Coussergues defends the idea of the coronation and feels that there is no reason to eliminate the twelve-hundred-year-old ceremony, since nothing has changed in the State. True, France is constitutional—but only in the sense that she has always been:

We must remember that Louis XVIII changed none of the principles of our ancient monarchy; and that our government is constitutional, as it has been from the time of the early parlements assembled annually under the first two of our kings, as it has been since the consent of the States-General became necessary for the imposition of taxes, and as it has been shown to be in our own time, when laws must be registered by Parliament before they can be promulgated.

Clausel attacks the Liberal version of the Charter as a great emancipating document: "His Majesty Louis XVIII in granting his Charter . . . thought not of creating new rights, but of reaffirming the old ones and regulating their exercise. It would be easy to point out provisions in our old ordinances which correspond to the diverse articles of the Charter." For example, Article 3 of the Charter—"Frenchmen are equal before the law"—which "has been celebrated for ten years as the triumph of the Revolution, . . . the great victory of the Gauls over the Franks, of the people over the privileged classes," is old stuff: witness the French bishops who ascended from the lowest orders, and the equality of the French military tradition—Gauls served as heads of the Frankish armies, and marshals rose from the ranks under Louis XIV. To Guizot's remark, "In giving the Charter to France, the king adopted the Revolution," Clausel replies, "No, the king of France did not adopt the Revolution in granting the Charter; he is a constitutional king, like Charlemagne and Saint Louis. . . . The Charter has added nothing new to the principles of the monarchy."[132]

This defense of the monarchy as constitutional loses its force as the Restoration wears on; it is produced on special occasions like the coronation when the past is rolled out for inspection. Two factors account for the shift to a more positive attack on the Liberal version of the Charter. First, as the years roll on, the Conservatives are more and more obliged to defend their political record, and have less and less time for the fourteen centuries of French history. Second, the Liberals' success in claiming the Charter as theirs results in the Conservatives' abandoning their own claims.

The most disturbing of these arguments—the one that offered the greatest threat to the Conservative historian—was the argument that the Liberals, thanks to the Charter, were the true Royalists of the Restoration. It is one of the oddities of Restoration history that both Liberals and Ultras insist that they are the true Royalists. The Ultra bases his claim upon the past, a hereditary loyalty, and a hated exile. The Liberal has a solid piece of contemporary evidence to establish his claim—the Charter in Louis's own hand. The Conservative can no more accept this Liberal reading of the Charter than he can the Liberal version of the Revolution.

This Liberal line, as we have seen, was most eloquently argued in Guizot's article of 1818. The Ultras are alarmed, particularly since the article is given a kind of official sanction by being reprinted in the *Moniteur*. Castelbajac counters in the *Conservateur*, and his point is a simple one: "I cannot admit the alliance of royalty and the Revolution for the simple reason that the latter abolished the former. . . . The Revolution began in France with the destruction of legitimate authority; it ended with the single fact of the return of this authority." He denies the transforming quality of the Charter; for him this document is "freely and entirely the work of the royal will; Louis XVIII did not owe his throne to a compromise with the Revolution." For the Ultra the attempt to wed the Revolution to the monarchy is blasphemy—there was nothing accidental in the death of the king; the Revolution consummated by the execution of the king has been defeated by the counterrevolution which returns the king. How, he asks, can the Revolution be said to be the basis for royal power, for any power?[133]

Guizot had reiterated his basic position in 1820; that is, that 1814 was the alliance of king and Revolution. P.L.B. ridicules this: "The Revolution has been an unfortunate deviation from the path of liberty, a horrible political aberration. How can a man of sense believe and say that the king, by giving the Charter to France, adopts the Revolution?"[134] P.L.B. debunks this Liberal claim by an examination of the text itself. The Revolution presumably wanted equality, yet provision after provision limits it. The

Charter, insists P.L.B., does not adopt the "system of absolute equality" that the Revolution affected. Guizot has argued that the new interests were no longer revolutionary; P.L.B. denies this:

Doesn't it make sense to wonder if the Revolution, which has overthrown the legitimate throne once, will seek to overthrow it again? Revolution and legitimacy are two clearly antipathetic things. To reconcile them is impossible; to readjust them, scarcely less so. And what absurdity it would be to admit that the Revolution is compatible with the Charter; has not the Charter condemned this Revolution and pronounced its judgment in reestablishing . . . royalty and the aristocracy?

Thus there are three points at issue: first, the actual circumstances surrounding the granting of the Charter; second, the actual, literal meaning of the Charter; third, and most important, the question of ownership—who is the party of the Charter, who *really* believes in its principles?

P.L.B. does not consider the Charter the product of thirty years of Liberal demands. Look to the Constitution of 1791, he says; there is the revolutionary program, not representative monarchy but democratic equality. As P.L.B. reads the Charter, the Liberals cannot possibly be sincere in their professions; they can only "aspire to the overthrow of a Charter proclaimed by a Bourbon king, a Charter which establishes a hereditary peerage, restricts the electoral function to fewer than 100,000 persons, and worst of all, recognizes two nobilities and a state religion." P.L.B.'s Royalist Charter is just as logical as the Liberals' revolutionary Charter, and Conservatives cling to it. Even P.L.B. must recognize, however, that whatever the justice of the case, it is the Liberals and not the Conservatives who made of the Charter the "political *noli me tangere* of our days, the holy ark which it is impossible to enter."

One explanation of the Liberals' success in capturing the Charter is the deeply held suspicion that, whereas the Conservatives accept the Charter *because* it is the king's will, the Liberals' allegiance to it is due to its having been torn from a reluctant king. The Conservatives fear that the Liberals really believe in the Charter and only the Charter, while their own primary loyalty is to the king. This difference emerges in the exchanges in the parliament. In 1820, General Foy defends a demonstration of young students by noting that they cried, "Vive la Charte! Vive la Charte!" Castelbajac interrupts: "They cried 'Vive la Charte sans le Roi!' "[135]

In another exchange defending the youth of the nation, Foy lauds them as "devoted to the government of the country as defined by the Charter."

A DROITE: Au roi! Au roi!
FOY: A la monarchie constitutionnelle!
A DROITE: Au roi! Au roi!
FOY: A la monarchie constitutionnelle!
A DROITE: Au roi! Au roi![136]

In the first part of the Restoration, the Conservatives battle for possession of the Charter, but they have nothing to match the Charter worship of the Liberals. Bonald is prophetic in writing to Maistre in 1819: "We perish to the cries of 'Vive le Roi et la Charte.' "[137]

In 1822, Clausel de Coussergues flatly labels the Charter as conceived by the Liberals a threat to the existence of monarchy: "The cries of *Vive la Charte* are opposed to the cries of *Vive le Roi.*" He warns his fellow Conservatives that the Charter is no proper base for monarchy: "People who cry *Vive la Charte*—can they not cry at the same time, *Vive l'Empereur, Vive la République?*"[138] As Clausel sees it, the Liberals are trying to whittle away the monarchy and convert the monarch into a constitutional king, which he emphatically is not. The explanation for this break with the Conservative tradition of stressing the constitutional character of the French past is the threat of revolution in 1822. The Liberal alliance has produced only the assassination of the Duc de Berry. European revolutionary parties are constitutional; if the king is constitutional, then logically he should support the European revolution in 1822.

But Clausel goes even further. The Liberals, searching for parallels to strengthen their claims for a constitutional monarchy, had argued that this was the expressed wish of Louis XVI as well as of Louis XVIII. Clausel emphatically denies this:

> Here let us note well that these words constitutional throne, constitutional king, were never found in any language before the Declaration of the Rights of Man in 1789. Louis XVI no more wanted to become a constitutional king than Louis XI, Charles VIII, and Louis XII, when they convoked the first, second, and third States-General of Tours; or than Henry II and his sons, when they convoked the States-General of Paris, Orléans, and Blois; or than Louis XIII, when he convoked the last States-General in 1614.
>
> It is the Declaration of the Rights of Man, and the dogma of the sovereignty of the people, that introduced the words constitutional king; this means a king whom several factions, which are called the sovereign people, can appoint, dismiss, judge, deport, or kill, according to their liking.[139]

Cottu, in a pamphlet of 1830 entitled *De la Nécessité d'une dictature,* justifies proposed radical changes in the Charter by the Conservative version of its origins. He attacks the idea that it was a negotiated contract: "No! I appeal to all France. That is not what happened in 1814. Louis XVIII did not find himself facing an armed nation, fearing to be rejected, and consequently having to listen and weigh their proposals. He had been established on his throne by the general will of a nation tired of the tyranny of Bonaparte."[140]

As 1830 approaches, the Charter becomes—for the Conservative—the rejection of the Revolution. The Royalist attitude toward the Charter in the final days of the Restoration is mirrored in one of Conny's speeches to the

Chamber. The Charter is a counterrevolutionary document and Conny glories in it:

The counterrevolution was made in France the day when the old family of our kings was returned to us. We are therefore counterrevolutionary because we blessed this happy return; we are counterrevolutionary, and in expressing this thought we are the organs of France, for all France is counterrevolutionary! Never accuse France of the crimes which sully our annals; she submitted to the yoke of the Revolution, but she detests this Revolution; she vows eternal disgrace to those who made it.[141]

The old notion, the defense of the French past by denying the Charter's originality, is still there.

We are too French ever to insult the great memories of our country; we refuse to believe that under the ancient laws of the monarchy our fathers were slaves. No, they were free; liberty is the essence of our French customs; all our historical monuments, these living expressions of our national character, attest to this; they teach all the world that France was free under the titular authority of her kings.

The Charter is accepted, then, not because it is consistent with a Liberal past, but rather because it is the work of the king: "We accept the new forms of our government; the Charter is the work of our king, and by this sacred right it has earned our loyalty; we bow before it because it is a royal emanation. Every conspiracy against royalty is an attempt upon the Charter."

CHAPTER V

Gallican Liberties and Ultramontanist Pretensions

They came back together in 1814—monarchy, aristocracy, and clergy. Broken and exiled by the Revolution, these three forces found unity, for the first time, in their common fate. French history had been the story of the conflicts of these antagonists: monarchy *vs.* clergy, monarchy *vs.* aristocracy, arstocracy *vs.* clergy. Confronted by the New France that had made the Revolution, the Old France, restored, had learned its lesson: monarchy, aristocracy, and clergy must forget their historic differences, must uphold their unity found in disaster. Never had there been such a formidable combination of forces.

The unity of this coalition presented the great problem for the Restoration Liberal. In the eighteenth century and in the first phases of the Revolution, there had been no such problem. There had been a Liberal aristocracy, a Liberal clergy; Louis XVI himself was a kind of slow-witted *philosophe*. In the eighteenth century the Liberals did not have to create divisions; they were already there. In 1762 the Jesuits were tried by the aristocrats and in 1764 they were sentenced by the king. It was a revolt of the aristocratic parlements which forced the calling of the States-General.

But all this has changed with the Restoration. The Enlightenment is discredited, and the reaction to twenty-five years of revolution has produced the political and theological Ultra. The Jesuits are the first to be restored, and the aristocratic party boasts of being "more royalist than the king."

Faced with this coalition, the Liberals probe for a soft spot. In 1816, Chateaubriand had argued in a pamphlet that there was nothing particularly new about this happy Restoration association of throne, nobility, and altar. This argument was attacked as poor history by Jubé de la Perrelle, a Napoleonic general who held a position as historian at the Ministry of War.

History, whose stern lessons will not be lost upon the present, shows us some princes of the blood about the throne; but it reveals them constantly misled by the ambitions of the lords, overwhelmed by the kindnesses of their sovereign. The people were never guilty of the rebellion of the Constable of Burgundy, of the Duc d'Alençon, of Gaston d'Orléans.

The friendship of aristocracy and monarchy is, for Jubé de la Perrelle, only another pipe dream of Chateaubriand's. As for the clergy:

Kings, Monsieur le Vicomte, no less than the people, have had to complain of the usurped powers of the clergy. . . . The annals of our history attest to the turbulence, ambition, ingratitude, and criminal rebellions of the clergy. Their tracts have always fed the flames of our civil wars; their decrees have caused assassins' daggers to be raised against our kings; and they compose frightening diatribes against the rights of the sovereign. Can you deny that under Louis the Meek, Robert the Devout, Charles VI, Henry III, and Henry IV, the clergy was steeped in all the prejudices of the day?[1]

This early attack upon the Conservatives' conception of the unity of French history reveals the function of history in the Liberals' war against the coalition. Unfortunately for the Liberals, the coalition is based upon the realities of the Restoration. The giant dislocation produced by the Revolution having united these previously irreconcilable forces, it is in the best interest of all three that they remain united. Lacking any persuasive political arguments to split them apart on contemporary issues, the Liberals turn to history. History is called upon to give the lie to this artificial unity, to remind each faction of former differences. It is even hoped that history may reawaken these differences.

The Liberals seek any opening that will allow them to recall these traditional divisions. Occasionally they get a windfall. In 1817, Bonald, in a volume of *Pensées,* jots down a brief defense of the League. In Bonald's view:

The League has been attacked, from Henry IV to the *philosophes,* because it prevented democratic Calvinism from establishing itself, because it made the religion of the state a necessary condition of royalty. . . . When religion was attacked, it could not be separated from royalty. . . . France wanted then, as she wants today, a royalty consecrated by religion, affirmed by legitimacy. The object is the same though the motives are different; the Leaguers of that time would be Royalists today.[2]

Bonald's defense of the League is complex, but it is based upon sound Restoration politics. He defends the League as the representative of the true interests of legitimacy and religion, which may at times be forced to oppose the king himself. From the point of view of the political-theological Ultra, the Protestant Henry IV was an example of a king who failed to recognize his own interest, and the vacillating Louis XVIII may well be another. Bonald is willing to risk the identification: "We who call ourselves Royalists want royalty to be affirmed by legitimacy; if, then, we begin to act somewhat like Leaguers, we must be excused—even praised—since it is because we think that royalty is being opposed to legitimacy, and that we are right to serve it [royalty] against itself."[3]

Bonald is here seeing history through the eyes of the Restoration coalition. It is not only a deposed monarch that has returned in 1814, but the principles of legitimacy and religion as well. These three are indissoluble in the early years of the Restoration; the Catholic religion and the French nobility are essential to the throne. Bonald finds the parallel convincing: Just as the League could attack the monarchy in the name of religion, the Restoration Ultra could attack royalty in the name of legitimacy.

Bonald had boldly seized upon a sensitive area of French history, and the Liberal *Archives* lost no time in exploiting his choice. An article expresses surprise at a Royalist's identification with a group that plainly stands convicted of treason. Reviewing the evidence against the League, it comes to the conclusion that the League was a sixteenth-century phase in the permanent struggle of the nobility against the crown. "After a great deal of shifty maneuvering, the resentful and jealous nobles firmly took their stand under the banners of the two religions." The Liberal magazine welcomes Bonald's parallel on all counts. It is happy to become the defender of monarchy, past and present, and to brand the League as a conspiracy, a state within a state: "One of the first results of the spirit of the League was the assassination of the king." Bonald's praise of the League for rejecting one king and assassinating another is an opportunity for the Liberals to insert a wedge into the coalition. Bonald has justified the League's refusal to recognize Henry IV; the article in the *Archives* replies, "This League, which could not separate royalty from religion, continued the war against royalty and religion."[4]

The proposal of a concordat between pope and monarch in 1817 raises the first of the crises upon which the coalition is to founder. Ultramontanism is the question. The Liberals realize that the unity of clergy and monarchy can be broken on precisely the same issue that divided the two historically—the pretensions of Rome *vs.* the French monarchy. Though clergy and monarchy were united in 1817, the proposal to strengthen their bonds by a formal treaty reopens a whole network of problems surrounding the relations of Church and State. The controversy over the proposed concordat is indeed a godsend to the Liberal cause, for it shifts the battleground from politics to history. The historical question rises naturally out of the proposal; the Conservatives base their demand for a new concordat on the tradition of such agreements, dating back to the Concordat of 1516. The Liberals call for an investigation of the circumstances of the three most recent concordats, which revives the ancient struggles between monarchy and clergy. Best of all for the Liberals, it resurrects the Gallican question. Whether dealt with by histories of concordats or by essays on Gallican liberties, the opportunity is the same: to reveal that the coalition is founded upon historical absurdity, and to reopen and intensify the divisions of the past, in the interest of destroying the unity of the present.

Typical of the Liberal campaign against the concordat was *De la Liberté des cultes et du Concordat* of Benoît, a writer for the *Bibliothèque historique.* Writing in 1818, the year following his release from prison, Benoît launches an attack upon the most fundamental assumption of the concordat, "that in all times there existed a filial alliance between the pope and France."[5] The concordat expressed the desire of the Restoration Conservatives to slur over past differences, to read the amity of the present back into the past, but the Liberals' reading of history recalls an even older and more suggestive alliance:

> Before this alliance [between the pope and France], which dates only from the sixteenth century, history offers us numerous examples of very different alliances. If it is absolutely necessary that the present imitate the past, Louis IX declared himself protector of the Gallican Church, . . . Charles VI renewed this edict a hundred and fifty years later, and finally, Charles VII gave the seal of his authority to the Pragmatic Sanction.

This is historic Gallicanism, which, as Benoît reminds us, existed before "Louis XI, who sacrificed the independence of the Church to the insistence of two popes, or Francis I, who made the same sacrifice for the sake of his designs on Italy." Thus, the Conservative supporters of the latest concordat are accused of distorting history by conveniently selecting as models Louis XI and Francis I, whose traffic with Rome, rightly viewed, stands opposed to an older and more fundamental tradition of Gallicanism.

Upon this anvil is forged one of the decisive alliances of the Restoration—Liberals and Gallicans—the one battling for political liberties, the other for religious liberties. For the duration of the Restoration, the Liberals become Gallicans and, as such, seek to drive the "true" Gallicans within the Church into collision with the Ultramontanists. Historical Ultramontanism is the specter that will frighten and divide the coalition. And Benoît offers evidence that the specter is quite real:

> Pope Pius V renovated the bull *In Coena Domini.* . . . Gregory XIII approved the plan of the League. Sixtus V anathematized the king of Navarre and the prince of Condé, who considered himself superior to all the kings of the earth. Gregory XIV excommunicated Henry IV, and made war on France. Clement VIII ordered the French to choose a Catholic king, and the great Henry had to support his right to the throne with an abjuration. Urban VIII did not accord to Louis XIII the title of king of Navarre. Innocent XI condemned the celebrated Four Articles of 1682 and refused to confirm the bishops named by Louis XIV.

This is the record of papal pretension; as for the kings: "From Charlemagne to Henry IV, thirteen kings of France, otherwise of irreproachable faith (Henry IV excepted), were subject to ecclesiastical censure. Almost all had to neglect affairs of state for Church quarrels, which they often bequeathed to their successors." Benoît's recital of the conflicts between Rome and Paris is recognizable as a narrower version of the Liberal crimes-of-French-history tactic, here confined to the actions of the papacy.

After attacking Ultramontanism in the name of Gallicanism, Benoît concedes that, historically, there can be no separating of politics and religion. But this very concession is a subtler form of the historical argument. Formerly, he implies, under absolutism, religion was a necessary adjunct to political power. But history has produced significant changes; "the political doctrines which were good for absolutism are no longer applicable." The argument can be summarized briefly: the age of religion is over, and with it the age of concordats. Formerly, kings held the piety of their subjects to be one of their responsibilities; conversely, respect for the king was a function of one's belief in God. But Benoît insists that this has all been changed: "Religion returns to its primitive domain; it is no more now than it was before the conversion of princes." Further, "our obedience to law and our respect for the prince no longer have their source in the fear of hell."

In effect, Benoît grants the Conservative view of the past only to insist upon the giant changes consummated by history and the Revolution. What has produced these changes? The shift from absolute to constitutional monarchy—"We cannot have both the Charter and the concordat."

This typical attack upon the concordat is ultimately directed against Ultramontanism, the common enemy of the two audiences to which the Liberal appeal is addressed—the monarchists and the surviving Gallicans of the French clergy. The king is reminded of his past difficulties with the papacy and assured that his dependence upon religion is no longer necessary. The Gallicans are also summoned to remember their past tormentors: "Rome has her maxims, the Church of France has hers. The Ultramontanists will not become Gallicans, nor the Gallicans Ultramontanists." Thus, Benoît suggests the formation of a natural alliance between believers in constitutional monarchy and a free Gallican clergy. The opposition to this Liberal coalition—Ultras and Ultramontanists—is already formed. "Who would not be frightened at the league of political Ultramontanists and religious Ultramontanists? The absolute powers of the prince and the supremacy of the pope are supported with equal zeal by both."

In 1817 Baillot published a series of relevant source materials dealing with this latest threat to the Gallican Church.[6] Among the documents included are the Declaration of the Assembly of 1682, and résumés of the works of the great Gallicans—Bossuet, Fleury, Fénelon. This is a pattern we shall observe again and again in the religious controversy of the Restoration—the summoning of voices from the past to legislate for the present.[7] It had taken some ingenuity to find favorable historical precedents for the Revolution, but no such difficulty is encountered in the quest for religious traditions. Be it espousing the Gallicans or attacking the papacy, or siding with kings against Rome, the Liberals find the French past teeming with corroborating evidence, precedents, and a large supporting cast.

Baillot's clever enlistment of the French monarchy in a pamphlet entitled *Dialogue entre François I, Louis XI, Charles VII, et Louis XII sur le nouveau concordat* is an excellent case in point. The form of the dialogue is simple: The three older monarchs take Francis I to task for having granted the first concordat in 1516. This concordat is the center of a long and continuing debate, for proponents of the concordat of 1817 naturally see in it both precedent and legal justification for arrangements between the French monarchy and the papacy. The older monarchs throw all the historic charges—taken from Mézeray—against Francis: that all France was opposed to this concordat, that it was a purely political arrangement, that France was humiliated, and so on. Francis is not exactly a straw man; he attempts to turn the tables on the other three by attacking the earlier Pragmatic Sanction as unacceptable to the Church and by insisting that the Council of Basel was schismatic. Charles VII defends both the Councils of Constance and of Basel as "a very necessary brake on the constantly increasing pretensions of the court of Rome."[8] The battle surges back and forth across the French past. The charges against Francis mount in frenzy; the concordat was not simply unjust *per se*, but unjust to the future for which it legislated:

> Tremble, O Francis I, at the thought of having paved the way for the return of the religious wars which bloodied Europe for so long. Does not the concordat . . . contain the same elements of religious intolerance, and sacred proscription as the butcheries of the Inquisition, the massacres of Mérindol, the outrages of St. Bartholomew, and the parricides committed on three of our successors?

Here, in the mouth of Charles VII, Baillot has delivered the Restoration indictment of this first concordat, holding it responsible for three centuries of religious crimes. The Concordat of 1516 is the fountainhead of all error, an obvious warning to those now considering a new concordat. And Baillot makes it perfectly clear that the papacy was responsible for the abuses in question, and indeed for all the calamities of European history. Louis XI delivers Baillot's "analysis" of the history of the Church:

> It was by the scandalous traffic in indulgences that Leo X paved the way for the triumphs of Luther and Calvin; it was by the abuse of spiritual weapons . . . that Gustavus Vasa introduced Lutheranism into his states. The impolitic scruples of a pope separated England from the Roman communion; Clement VIII, by refusing to absolve Henry IV after his abjuration, set France and Europe aflame, as of old; and had it not been for the hatred fomented by sophistical theologian, perhaps the Turks would never have entered Constantinople.

Having pronounced the judgment of history, the monarchs then apply its lessons to the Restoration and to this proposed concordat. Louis XII declares that the proposal of 1817 is "rejuvenating the Concordat of 1516 for the French of the nineteenth century." Charles VII hopes that in such an advanced century it is not necessary to revive a law which was not popular in the sixteenth. Louis XII is given Lanjuinais's contemporary description of the concordat as "an act incompatible with the honor of religion, with national independence, with the safety of the people and the throne."

To all this, Francis replies that he had the right to do what he thought best, even in the face of the opposition of the nation. It is the reply of a despot. Louis XII observes that the secret of a good king is the ability to unite all the elements in society, and that this secret is "the only one that counts in the nineteenth century." As a parting shot, Louis reminds Francis that whereas Francis is known to his courtiers as *le roi des gentilshommes,* Louis was known to all France as *le père du peuple.* The lesson is clearly intended for Louis XVIII. The Concordat of 1516 stands indicted by three of his greatest predecessors, and the policy of papal control and interference with monarchy stands condemned as disastrous.

Perhaps the strongest attack on Ultramontanism—and the clearest example of the politics of history—is to be found in Abbé de Pradt's three-volume work of 1818. Pradt, one of the storm centers of the Restoration, was himself wonderfully situated in this debate. A controversial figure out of the religious struggles of the Revolution, he had been, as archbishop of Malines, Napoleon's chief religious adviser and architect of the proposed concordat of 1813. A staunch Liberal, he remained to haunt the Restoration as a perfect symbol of the alliance of political Liberalism and royal Gallicanism.

Pradt defines Ultramontanism as (1) the subordination of the temporal power to the spiritual, and (2) the monopoly of ecclesiastical powers in the hands of the pope. The Ultramontanists believe that the pope, "who is infallible, can dispose of all Church property; he is accountable only to God; he judges everyone but is judged by no one, . . . it follows that a pope can also dispose of crowns."[9] Ultramontanism is indeed an enormously effective scapegoat for the Restoration Liberal, for it can be shown to threaten both the sovereignty of the French monarchy and the freedom of the French Church.

To Pradt, the proposed concordat raises basic questions about the validity of all concordats, and the legality of arrangements between kings and popes. This is an important consideration, for by challenging the philosophy of concordats, Pradt attacks the Restoration assumption of the union of politics and religion.

Pradt's objections to any concordat are shrewdly made. The pope, he says, has no right to negotiate for the French clergy: "The keystone of religious order is the episcopacy, of which the concordat renders the pope complete master."[10] Moreover, he objects to the very idea of a diplomatic arrangement; he stresses the spiritual character of the papacy. He finds the old pragmatics infinitely preferable to the concordats.

But it is not only that the notion of concordats is morally abhorrent; the concordats themselves are historically demonstrable mistakes. Pradt launches into an examination of the historical circumstances surrounding the first concordat, and the misfortunes stemming from it. Having attacked the idea of concordats as "political," he finds the document of 1516 purely political. Politically necessary, yes; "but it is not the task of religion to repair the faults of politics." Politically useful? In the short run, no; it was "rejected by the nation." And in the long run? "Not at all, . . . it has given popes an immense advantage over kings."[11]

Surprisingly, Pradt does not linger over 1682, the favorite haunt of all Gallicans. The reason becomes apparent: he quotes in full the retracting letter of Louis XIV, thereby accepting the non-Gallican view that the results of 1682 are vitiated by this letter of 1693. Even here, however, Pradt loses no chance to widen the breach between the monarchy and the papacy. He adopts as his theme, "See the mighty Louis, and see how easily three weak popes vanquish him." Indeed, the "surrender" of Louis XIV to the papacy, in the form of the discovered letter, has had the most unfortunate reverberations. "From this time on, Rome kept the letter of the French monarch as a trophy; she displayed it as a monument to her victory."[12] And Pradt remembers that when the pope came to France in 1801 to conclude the second concordat, he brought this letter as proof of papal supremacy.

In his second volume, Pradt takes up the role of the clergy during the Revolution. Having done his best in his first volume to reopen the old wounds between kings and popes, he now drives still another wedge into the coalition. He explains the unpopularity of the clergy before and during the Revolution as a result of the close relations between clergy and nobility:

> At the time of the Assembly, the clergy and the nobility had come to share in the same misfortunes; the future presented dangers common to both. . . . However, by becoming a partner to the loyalties and aims of the nobility, the clergy condemned itself to sharing the hatred directed at the nobles. . . . It thus assumed the odium which attached to the others. After the emigration of the nobles, the deportation of the clergy was inevitable; the one was the natural consequence of the other.[13]

This analysis is peculiarly designed for Restoration ears, for Pradt recognizes the "cruel but inevitable alliance" in adversity which is the hallmark of the Restoration coalition. The clergy and nobility had been driven together by their revolutionary experience, a shared disaster which is the link that binds them in the Restoration. But speaking to the clergy, Pradt suggests that this alliance was not only unfortunate, but unnecessary; that the clergy had unjustly paid for the resistance of the nobility.[14] The experience of the Revolution should have taught the French clergy the danger of allying with the nobility, of confusing the spiritual and the temporal. The lessons of history are that popes are the enemies of kings, and aristocrats the enemies of priests.

Moving on from the lessons offered by the Revolution, Pradt considers the Napoleonic Concordat, which, in his view, only served to squander the second great opportunity to clearly separate the interests of Church and State. He examines the 1801 concordat as minutely as he has examined its precursor. Was it necessary? Only if you consider the mixing of the temporal and the spiritual necessary. Was it national? No, because again it introduced a nonnational element into the state. Was it useful? Perhaps, like the 1516 concordat, it can be considered as meeting the political necessities of the moment (the need to unite France and to convince Europe of her stability), but ultimately its effects are disastrous: religion in France has been a political football ever since. Pradt's point is clear: that those who accuse Napoleon of making religion an instrument of politics are trying to do the same thing in 1817—only the politics are different.

Another incident in Napoleon's stormy relations with the papacy—his excommunication in 1809—is dredged up by Pradt as relevant to the Restoration. Here, citing the papal bull of Pius VII, Pradt seeks to convince France that Ultramontanism is no historical specter summoned up for political purposes, but a threat as recent as 1809. After quoting at length from the bull, he points out: "This is from Gregory VII and from Boniface VIII. Here are the ancient pretensions of the court of Rome in all their naked haughtiness."[15] Even the inglorious captivity of the pope by Napoleon reminds Pradt of a similar occasion in the French past: Charles V and Clement VII. Throughout Pradt's treatment of the religious history of the Empire, he is in the best tradition of the Liberal historians; he stresses the continuity of French history, viewing Napoleon's conflict with the papacy as only the most recent engagement in a past dominated by struggle.

After having invoked history, Pradt analyzes, in his third volume, the religious situation of the Restoration in an effort to determine what is at the heart of the demand for a concordat. Essentially an eighteenth-century cleric, he finds that the Revolution has produced a new breed, with a most dangerous opinion: that "France must be regenerated by the clergy, to which end the clergy must be greatly increased, the young must be returned to its hands, and a great share of political influence must be allotted to it. . . . They would make the clergy the base of everything, . . . the instrument for the regeneration of France."[16]

In treating the proposed concordat itself, Pradt rests his case upon his historical analysis. He summarizes current objections to the Concordat of 1817 as: (1) fear of Rome, (2) concern for the loss of Gallican liberties, and (3) belief that the concordat is a backward step. In his words: "For a long time Rome will remain an object of distrust for the French, and it must be admitted, in view of all that has happened, that this is not surprising." Basically, 1817 stands accused of resurrecting 1516: "The Concordat of 1817 abolished that of 1801 and re-established the Concordat of 1516. . . . How far will we be swept by thoughtlessness and infatuation with the past?" Subjecting the 1817 concordat to analysis, Pradt finds that it contains all the fatal weaknesses and misconceptions of its predecessors: it is unnecessary, it is not a religious document, it does not preserve equality between pope and king. How, Pradt wonders, in the light of the experiences of Francis I and Napoleon, can such mistakes be repeated?[17]

Returning to the Ultramontanist conception of the concordat as an essential part of a general return to religion, Pradt points out that despite all the cries for expiation and restitution, religion did not fare so badly during the Revolution. From his own intimate acquaintance with the revolutionary clergy, Pradt argues that religion—true religion—prospered during the Revolution, and particularly under the Empire. He notes the surprise of the émigrés at the soundness of France: they did not find the chaos they expected. Further, Pradt portrays the present fears of the coalition as groundless, for the French Church is flourishing: "Since the Restoration, France is the only country in Europe in which the clergy is treated justly. . . . Never was France more religious than at the present time."

By denying that any threat to religion exists, Pradt seeks to remove another prop from the Restoration coalition. This effort recalls the Liberals' attempt to deny the existence of any threat to the monarchy. To establish the relative well-being of the French Church, he compares the state of religion in the age of Louis XIV with the state of religion in the Restoration.

Much is at stake in this comparison. Pradt seeks to undercut the Conservative belief that irreligion and revolution have marched hand in hand throughout history, that these hostile forces emerging out of the French Revolution are the major threats to the Restoration. To counteract this view, Pradt traces irreligion to the *grand siècle*, the age of Louis XIV:

> Under Louis XIV, aside from Fénelon and Bossuet, there was no true religion, no true religious feeling; there was pomp, the propensity to dogmatize, to dispute, . . . there was theology, a political religion in opposition to Protestantism and Jansenism; there was hatred for other religions, an absolute ignorance of tolerance; but there was no true religious feeling. Since the Reformation, religion had only been an instrument of politics. . . .
>
> Louis XIV and the men of his time regarded religion exclusively as a positive, legal thing, created to oppose the heretics of the day.

Then Pradt launches into the comparative approach so dear to the Liberal historian. Louis XIV's disregard for religion is as flagrant as any outburst of irreligion during the Revolution or under Napoleon: "Louis XIV treated the pope . . . almost as badly as Napoleon treated Pius VII;

he was going to send an army into Italy to occupy Rome. . . . Did Napoleon do anything to match the revocation of the Edict of Nantes and the war of the Cevennes?"

The charges against Louis XIV and the indictment of his century reveal the Liberal intention. Pradt denounces the Conservative attempt to date the attack on religion from the age of disbelief; the seventeenth century is shown to be less religious than the Restoration. The source of this state of affairs is found in the confusion of the temporal and spiritual that was so characteristic of the age of Louis XIV: "Was it truly religious, this era with its record of outrageous disorders from the monarch down to the least of his subjects, this era in which dissoluteness, duelling, frenzied gambling, heavy drinking, and pillaging by the tax collectors formed the usual state of society? . . . Our much maligned age has produced nothing to equal this."

This appeal is directed at genuinely religious Conservatives who feel that religion has suffered as the handmaiden of politics. Although Pradt is careful to center his attack on Ultramontanism, as the more immediate threat and the easier rallying cry, he is, in fact, also opposed to Gallicanism. Gallicanism, too, is the confusion of temporal and spiritual: it is as bad for the king to control the clergy as for the papacy to dominate the king. Gallicanism has been useful to the Liberal cause, and it does appeal to a wing of the religious party. Ultimately, however, the Liberals want the exact opposite of Gallicanism—what today would be called the separation of Church and State. Yet Gallicanism is too important a weapon to be abandoned, and the anti-Gallican aspect is subordinated to attacking the clergy in politics.

Pradt is forced to conclude that the French clergy of the Restoration has not learned the lessons of history. Instead of realizing the necessity of abstaining from politics, it has interfered in temporal matters, in direct opposition to the spirit of the new France. Pradt is capable of understanding that this wrong choice is historically motivated, that training and associations have made the clergy anti-Liberal; but that the clergy should fight philosophy, repudiate the Revolution, and try to reinstitute that old alliance with the party in power which has proved so disastrous to it in the past—this Pradt finds incomprehensible and unforgivable.

Two forthright embodiments of the Liberal-Gallican alliance growing out of the concordat are Lanjuinais and Abbé Grégoire. Lanjuinais sees the proposed concordat as an attempt to reestablish 1516 at the expense of the Four Articles of 1682: "The pope wants the retraction of these Four Articles, which constitute the safeguard of the people and the king and without which the pope would be free to depose princes."[18]

Grégoire, writing shortly after his unsuccessful effort to be seated in the Chamber, traces, in the two centuries preceding the Revolution, the struggles of Gallicanism against anti-Gallican forces within the Church: Jesuits, Ultramontanists, Jansenists. The French Revolution complicates the picture, but basically Grégoire views the Civil Constitution of the Clergy as a Gallican document: "A great number of priests . . . always considered the defense of the Four Articles and that of the Civil Constitution of the Clergy as two practically identical causes."[19]

Grégoire sees the whole question of the concordat as an excellent opportunity to defend those priests (like himself) who took the oath of loyalty in 1791. He relates French priests during the Revolution and after to two clear and separate traditions: historic Gallicanism, whose sympathizers took the oath in 1791 and opposed the concordats in 1801 and again in 1817; and historic Ultramontanism, whose exponents refused to take the oath, accepted Napoleon's concordat (even coming out of exile to do so), and are clamoring for the new concordat. "In 1789 we swore loyalty to the king; you followed the pope's wishes. Thus, in 1801 you were compelled to go along with the pope. We took the oath of 1791 to our legitimate king; you took the oath of 1801 to a government which had replaced the one you recognized as legitimate."[20] Grégoire is able to draw the implication, so dear to the Restoration Liberal, that Gallicanism and political loyalty to the king are two aspects of the same position; that Ultramontanism is consistent only in its devotion to the papacy.

There are two salient facts of the religious history of the Revolution that the Liberal-Gallican wants remembered: first, that those who refused to take the oath in 1791 were, in effect, refusing an oath to the king; second, that these same *insermentés,* the priests who refused loyalty to Louis XVI, later swore loyalty to Napoleon Bonaparte. Again the Liberal seeks to make capital out of this historical evidence, seeks to expose the villain Ultramontanism, the same Ultramontanism which is rearing its head in 1817. Among the interesting documents that Grégoire includes is a reported conversation with Napoleon in 1800, in which Napoleon had questioned him closely about the historical precedents for a concordat. Grégoire, in 1820, proudly records his reply—that concordats are documents in which "principles are always sacrificed to political calculations."[21]

No better proof of the powers of history can be found than the Conservative response to this Liberal sponsorship of Gallicanism. Once again the Conservatives are divided. Somehow they must defend their religious position, but how? There were three answers. First, there were those who proclaimed their own Gallicanism, defended the status quo, and insisted that the concordat was Gallican; these Gallicans defended the historical unity of Church and State, and supported the concordat as an expression of that unity. Second, there were those who frankly espoused Ultramontanism; these Conservatives found the concordat too Gallican. Third, there were those who accepted the Liberal analysis of the dangers of Ultramontanism to the state; these Royalists rejected the concordat as unnecessary.

The first position might be termed the official Restoration view. It is the view of the Gallican bishops who refuse to be "out-Gallicaned" by the Liberals. Yet these men are still determined to defend the proposed concordat. Abbé Frayssinous's *Vrais Principes de l'église gallicane* of 1818 is the classic statement of this center position. Frayssinous sees no real conflict in the history of the French Church. The Concordat of 1516 he defends as a necessary and mutually advantageous arrangement between Church and State. There was no betrayal, no pretension, no loss of rights. The Liberal apprehensions about the true meaning of the 1817 concordat are chimerical: "Never have our kings felt less the power of the court of Rome, never have they been freer from what is called 'ultramontanist pretensions,' than in the last three centuries."[22] Frayssinous skirts the line carefully—Gallican Liberties are staunchly upheld, Ultramontanist pretensions are duly noted, but the concordat is seen as a historically tested compromise for the solution of these "difficulties." The tone and spirit of the work—the spirit of the Restoration Center's attempt to avoid conflict—is captured in a paragraph: "Rome has its maxims and usages, which it will not renounce; the Ultramontanists will not become Gallicans. We too have our maxims and usages, to which we will remain attached; the Gallicans will not become Ultramontanists."[23]

This middle-of-the-road Gallicanism is to be buffeted from both sides throughout the Restoration.[24] Frayssinous is prevented by his official position as Inspector General of Studies from replying to his attackers; but a representative defense of his position is provided by an anonymous pamphlet of 1818 printed in *Le Publiciste.* Its title, *Des Livres et des pamphlets sur le concordat,* suggests that its intention is a summation of the literature of the controversy. Actually, it is a perfect reflection of the effort to be Gallican without falling in with the Liberal attack on Ultramontanism.

The author is impressed by the enormous amount of pro-Gallican literature and its curious origin: "Never has the Gallican Church been more militant. Everywhere volunteers arm themselves to defend it. The recruiting is immense, and although the recruits are by no means all members of the family, each presents himself as the firmest champion of the Church."[25] From the viewpoint of traditional Gallicanism, there is something suspicious in these parvenus, led by Abbé Grégoire, and in the issues that they are crying up: Ultramontanism and the Jesuits. Such issues, protests the author, are "mere phantoms": "I am certain that neither M. Grégoire nor the writers of the *Censeur européen* fear the resurrection of the Jesuits or the establishment of the Inquisition in France any more than I do." The best response to Liberal alarums is to deny that there is any threat from Rome, and to deny also that Gallicanism is losing ground: "The maxims of Bossuet and Louis XIV are not without credit in the Council of State, the Chamber of Deputies, and the Chamber of Peers." Gallican sentiment is clearly preponderant in the government and in the clergy, and the Liberal fears are unfounded.

Indeed, it seems that the whole Liberal effort rests upon the summoning of Ultramontanist ghosts, "the exhuming of Gregory VII or Alexander VI." Since the Liberals have raised the specter of Gregory VII, the author of *Des Livres* chooses to say a word in his behalf: "Gregory VII was, I am convinced, the true Bonaparte of the Church: a man of genius, a man who fully understood the spirit of his century, a man who aimed at universal domination. Fanaticism was for him what sovereignty of the people was for Napoleon—an immense lever to raise the passions of the multitude."

Thus, the Center Gallican condemns Ultramontanism but defends its chief practitioner. This defense is curiously reminiscent of the Liberal historians' defense of the Revolution: Gregory is wrong, but he must be understood as operating in his time, and so on. Though the pamphlet concedes the attempt at papal domination, it denies the success of Ultramontanism. Francis I was no more vassal to the pope than was Napoleon; the Four Articles were opposed but were established anyway; the power and independence of the French monarchy is recalled and reasserted. The author concludes that, notwithstanding "the concordats of 1516, 1801, and 1817, France has not become the domain of the pope."

As for Ultramontanism, the author admits its existence: "There still exist some fanatics in the fashion of Hildebrand. . . . These are the Bonapartists of the Church." (The author is captivated by his own historical analogy.) For these remnants, "who continue to treat Bossuet as a heretic" and who "predict that the concordat will push us into Calvinism," he recommends ridicule. The men who take this position—the followers of Lamennais and Maistre—are plainly an embarrassment to the Royal Gallicans, who insist that these are old ideas which have no meaning for the present.[26]

One of the difficulties of answering the Liberal attack on the Restoration coalition was that there were really two attacks. One was the Gallican attack against the Ultramontanists, designed to attract the Gallican clergy and its traditional friend, the French monarch. But beneath this formal espousal of Gallicanism—and closer to the true Liberal intention—we have noted the objection to any alliance between throne and altar. History here has served the Liberals, first by destroying the myth of any such previous unity between monarchy and clergy, and then by establishing the basic antagonism between them. Consequently, some Conservative energy was drained in replying to the Liberal-Gallican argument: Gallicans like Frayssinous denied the threat to Gallicanism, and Ultramontanists like Maistre attacked the decrees of 1682. Most Conservatives, however, recognized the Gallican argument as essentially diversionary and realized that it was more important to reply to the Liberal effort to separate throne and altar. As Chateaubriand put it in 1816: "The first step toward safety [is] to reunite the clergy with the monarchy."[27]

As early as 1817, Abbé Clausel de Montals, observing the Liberal tactics in the early Restoration, noted a significant departure from the attitude expressed during the French Revolution. Then the clergy had been charged with being the "flatterers of kings, the guilty supporters of their authority; today we are represented as the scourge of states and their bloody enemies."[28] Thus, Clausel refutes the Liberal charge of the conspiracy of the clergy by reminding the Liberals of what they were saying during the Revolution. In the Restoration, the Conservative would prefer to bear the burden of the original charge—that priests were too close to kings.

In 1819 Clausel de Montals undertakes a full refutation of Pradt.* He seizes upon the heart of Pradt's argument—the separation of spiritual and temporal. This doctrine, he asserts, is a product of the Revolution; its effect would be to place governments in a public and permanent state of atheism. As proof that the alliance of temporal and spiritual is necessary, he cites the English experience. (This is a common, and effective, Conservative gambit; the Liberals, who find their examples of constitutional monarchy in England, are always embarrassed by the Conservatives' use of England as the model religious society.) Clausel explains Pradt's opposition to the concordat as simply the result of Pradt's attitude toward the papacy: naturally a man like Pradt, who regards the pope as an alien, a foreign power, will be hostile to all such agreements. Clausel, however, rejects this hostility toward the papacy as un-Catholic: "The pope is *ours*, since we are Catholics."[29] As for the historical attack upon the Concordat of 1516, Clausel challenges Pradt with a general defense of the state of the French clergy for three hundred years: How could the French Church have flourished so, if 1516 had produced disaster? All the heroes of the Gallicans are then brought forth—Bossuet, Fénelon, *et al.*—to prove the vitality of the French Church.

Perhaps the clearest effort to answer the Liberal version of the historic conflict between Church and State was Kentzinger's essay of 1820.† Kentzinger feels that the present French State, unlike its most glorious predecessors, does not maintain sufficiently close relations with the Church: "Today French legislation refuses this solemn homage to religion, though the strongest considerations of public order call for it more powerfully than ever; forgetting the centuries of prosperity that France has enjoyed since

* Clausel de Montals was a close friend and supporter of Frayssinous, but his position is less forthrightly Gallican. He is even accused by Dillon of Ultramontanist tendencies. To the extreme Gallican wing, any effort to work out an arrangement with the pope was regarded as Ultramontanist.

† Kentzinger had emigrated in 1791, had served as Metternich's secretary at Radstadt, and had been rewarded in the Restoration by being named mayor of Strasbourg.

Clovis triumphed at Tolbiac under the banner of the faith, we banish religion from the French code of law."[30]

Kentzinger offers historic proofs of this unity of interests, in direct contrast to the Liberal charges. He cites parallel legislation to good effect, notably on the necessity for religious control of marriage laws, a question that found St. Thomas Aquinas, the edicts of 1629, the Declaration of 1698, and Montesquieu on the same side. Kentzinger further argues that, historically, states have always taken upon themselves the duty of protecting religion and suppressing its enemies. Here he lists an imposing array of French monarchs who have published ordinances punishing blasphemy.[31] Francis I's ordinance of 1536 is seen as only one highlight in a royal tradition stretching back to 1347, a tradition which culminated with Louis XIV.

Another form of evidence that religion has marched hand in hand with politics in France is direct testimony. Séguier is quoted: "Clergy and magistracy must unite in harmonious accord lest they fall victim to the criminal attacks that godless doctrines seek to unleash on throne and altar." Kentzinger contrasts this eighteenth-century call for unity with the revolutionary cry of Odilon Barrot: "Yes, the law in France is atheistic, and must be." Another voice from the past, raised to preserve the Restoration coalition, is a decree of the Parlement of Provence in 1732: "In the realm, Your Majesty holds the place of God Himself, of which he is the living image; the submission which is due him is a duty of religion."[32] Indeed, to demonstrate the historic allegiance of religion to monarchy, Kentzinger goes all the way back to Gregory of Tours' conversation with Chilpéric.

Having demonstrated that religious interests are inseparable from the State, Kentzinger turns to a consideration of French monarchs, a quick and altogether fantastic box score on French kings wherein is noted their particular piety, devotion, and energy in the cause of religion. Again he does not shirk the full story; he begins with Dagobert, Charlemagne, and Hugh Capet, and the declaration of Noyon in 987. Robert "found the most powerful resources in religion"; Philip Augustus was distinguished by "the repression of impiety"; Louis XI "employed no other means than those of religion." Kentzinger interrupts his catalog to inform us: "In these citations, we have no other object than to demonstrate that in France, in all times and in all situations, everything was said and done under divine auspices, and society was well off."[33]

The clash between Liberals and Conservatives on historical grounds is direct; their positions are clearly drawn. The Liberals remind Louis XVIII of the historic difficulties between Church and State; the Conservatives counter with the fundamental religious devotion of the French monarchy. In reply to the Liberal attempt to split altar and throne, numerous Conservative pamphleteers rose to insist upon unquestioning allegiance to the principle of unity. In Chateaubriand's words: "The regeneration of France will occur . . . when we restore to religion its rightful influence, . . . when the men favored with the confidence of the king . . . are the friends and protectors of religion."[34]

In 1822 Clausel de Coussergues, the elder brother of Clausel de Montals, writes: "It is with such doctrines that the Revolution prepares for war; it must be opposed zealously with the only doctrine that protects society."[35] In his 1825 book, he sets out "to show what our country owes to the unity of religion and royalty." There are two general ways of proceeding. One is to deny conflict, as Kentzinger does; the other is to admit religious outrages and attempt to explain them. It may seem particularly difficult to admit and explain away the League, where Catholicism seemed linked to the enemies of the monarchy, but Clausel finds a way: he suggests an analogy with England. Surely, he says, the League had as much right "to maintain the religion which had reigned in France since Clovis" as the English Parliament had to insist upon a Protestant line of succession.[36]

The inseparable nature of religion and monarchy is an article of faith for the Restoration Conservative. An expression of this faith can be found in a pamphlet of 1829: "It is only the spirit of the Virgin that can separate the cause of religion from that of royalty. All the great statesmen have sworn that Christianity is the most solid base for empires, and experience has only too often demonstrated that the overthrow of the altar leads to the fall of the throne." The experiences of the Revolution have confirmed the experiences of history: "Royalism, left to itself and finding no external support, degenerates into indifference; impiety spreads with the rapidity of gangrene; everywhere faith weakens and withers."[37]

The revival of Gallicanism and the attack on Ultramontanism brought into the arena two of the strongest voices in the Restoration, Félicité de Lamennais and Joseph de Maistre. Maistre entered the Restoration with a considerable reputation; long before his death in 1821, he had become, from far-off Saint Petersburg where he served as ambassador, the unofficial spokesman for politico-religious reaction. Lamennais entered the Restoration unknown, but his essay on religious indifference burst upon France in 1817, and from that point on he was the voice of Ultramontanism, as well as a focus of all the forces that saw the necessity of a return to religion. Maistre was influential among the political Ultras of the Chamber, and particularly with his close friend, Bonald. Lamennais was the idol of a whole wing of younger priests and seminary students.

Maistre's essay on the Gallican Church appeared in 1818. The first volume, devoted to a history of the French Church, is concerned primarily with flaying the Jansenists.* For Maistre, the Jansenists function as the Ultramontanists do for the Liberal historian; they are the real threat to

* "Jansenist" has missed out on the revival of older religious terms: Gallican, Ultramontanist, Jesuit, and so on. Yet it is heard occasionally—Lanjuinais is frequently referred to as a Jansenist—and it is a vague word of abuse used by Conservative clergymen.

monarchy, they have infected the parlements, they produced the Civil Constitution of the Clergy, and they are even blamed for the regicide.

Having freed Ultramontanism from these charges, Maistre turns in his second volume to a consideration of Gallicanism. In the central issue, the Declaration of 1682, Maistre finds himself in difficulty. He bitterly opposes the theological implications of 1682, the "liberties" of the Gallican Church; but in the age of Louis XVIII, he does not want to attack Louis XIV openly. He begins with an analysis of Louis XIV's character: "Never was a king more attached to the Catholic faith, but never did a king (since Philip the Fair) cause the pope more pain."[38] This is his way of resolving the difficulty—1682 was a disaster despite the king's good intentions.

In his attempt to destroy the Articles of 1682, the cornerstone of Gallican liberties, Maistre begins by attacking the very notion of an "ancient tradition of the Gallican Church" as separate from Catholic Christianity. Liberal historians had gone back to the forests of Gaul to suggest this tradition, but Maistre reminds his readers that, aside from "accidental and transitory opposition," the Gallican Church has always supported the mother Church.[39] Further, such statements of papal supremacy as that of 1626 were as solemn and binding as the Declaration of 1682.

He then turns to the infamous Articles themselves, attempting to undermine them by describing the circumstances surrounding their declaration. The prestige of the Articles rests upon the names attached to them, and Maistre points out that they stand condemned by their own authors. The Declaration was not the work of Bossuet, he was merely forced to defend it; Louis XIV is rather to be remembered as the author of the famous letter of retraction of 1693.* Perhaps the strongest of his historical arguments is his recording of the original reception of these Articles, the reactions of seventeenth-century Catholic and Protestant opinion. This is a telling stroke against those who are trying to defend 1682 as the summation of Catholic belief, for after the publication of the Articles the Catholic world is shown to be apprehensive and Protestants hopeful that the French are about to follow the English example of proclaiming a national church.

In Maistre's analysis of the content of Gallicanism, the divisions within the Restoration coalition emerge most clearly. Subjecting Gallican liberties to a Burkean analysis—in what precisely do these liberties consist?—he reduces the fundamental beliefs of the French clergy to Jansenism. Gallican liberties are seen as "parliamentary license . . . , slavery, with permission to call it liberty." He quotes Fénelon's judgment: "The effect of Gallican liberties is subservience to the king."[40] Actually this charge of

* Maistre also goes to great lengths to establish that the popes were ready to condemn these Articles, since their failure to do so was used as an argument for the Declaration. *De l'Eglise gallicane*, p. 128. Earlier (*ibid.*, p. 104), Maistre suggests Colbert as the evil genius of the Four Articles.

the clergy's subservience to the monarchy and its consequent loss of religious stature is basic to the attack on Gallicanism. Yet in the language of Restoration Liberalism, this Gallican subservience becomes "loyalty" to monarchy, as contrasted with Ultramontanist loyalty to the papacy. Thus, Maistre must somehow attack the Gallican clergy for its servility to authority without making it appear too attractive to Restoration monarchy and aristocracy.

Maistre resolves the difficulty by attacking Gallicanism as a revolt from the principle of authority within the Church. As such, it must inevitably lead to an attack upon the principle of authority within the State.[41] As if to leave no doubts about his own loyalty, he devotes a long hymn to the Bourbons: "We have seen all that Catholic unity owes to the House of France."[42] But if the monarchy is great and enduring, it is no thanks to the Declaration of 1682. Here, at the conclusion of his work, Maistre places himself in direct opposition to the official Gallicanism of the Restoration. He quotes Bossuet's paean to 1682 and replies:

> This same event is, to me, the greatest stain on the record of the French clergy; next to the formal schism, the most guilty act; the fecund source of the greatest evils of the Church; the cause of the visible and gradual weakening of that great body; a fatal and perhaps unique *mélange* of pride, thoughtlessness, audacity, and weakness; finally, the saddest example which has been given to peoples and kings in the Catholic world.[43]

Maistre believed that loyalty to the papacy was ultimately loyalty to the monarchy, that in the long run his Ultramontanism would prove a better prop for the monarchy than Gallicanism. In fact, he shared the faith of so many men of his generation—a faith based upon the experiences of the Revolution—that the interests of throne and altar were inseparable. Writing on the state of Christianity in Europe in 1819, he said: "One can say that all princes are dethroned in a sense, since there is not one who reigns as completely as his father or his grandfather did, and the sacred character of monarchy is effaced to the same degree that irreligious principles spread. . . . Thousands and thousands of times it has been said to sovereigns that the base of the throne is the altar."[44]

What separates Maistre from the Royal Gallicans is the *terms* of this rapprochement between politics and religion. Ultimately, Maistre sees his Ultramontanist attack on a Liberal-sponsored Gallicanism as in the best interests of the monarchy. He appeals to the Bourbons, in their own interests, to renounce their traditional Gallicanism and to form an unprecedented alliance with the papacy.*

* I have treated Maistre's Ultramontanism in the context of this one work, since it is a direct response to the Gallican issue. For the more positive and theologically oriented defense of Ultramontanism, there is, of course, Maistre's Restoration classic, *Du Pape* (1819).

When we turn to Lamennais's Ultramontanism, we are no longer considering an attempt to preserve the Restoration coalition. We have, instead, a historically presented Ultramontanism acting as a powerful corrosive, a logic so rigid that it will eventually drive Lamennais and his followers out of the Restoration coalition and into the Liberal opposition. No brief summary can do justice to the importance of Lamennais's attack upon the Restoration from the furthest extreme of religious Ultramontanism. Perhaps the best way to measure his influence is to observe that when, in 1830, he performed his amazing switch from fanatical Ultramontanism to social Catholicism, he took with him the greater part of young Catholic France.

The "Essay on Indifference" that made his reputation overnight in 1817 had, beneath its glittering prose and uncompromising logic, a simple message.[45] Indifference was no longer acceptable to the new generation; the Restoration was to be an age of faith. Through the years of the Liberal-Royalist alliance, Lamennais continued to be a storm center. The columns of the *Conservateur* were thrown open to him, and he took the opportunity to attack the government policy of indifference toward education, toward the Church, and so on.[46]

Lamennais was already a violent Ultramontanist in 1817, and as early as 1819 he is attacking the Declaration of 1682.[47] In 1823, when the Conservatives were congratulating themselves upon getting rid of the Liberal professors Guizot and Villemain, he accused Frayssinous and the University of moral anarchy. Both Lamennais and the *Drapeau Blanc*, which published his attack, were fined for this outburst.[48] In the same year, he attacked Chateaubriand's Spanish policy, but from assumptions that no Liberal could share. His real declaration of war against the political Restoration in the name of the religious Restoration was made in 1825, with the appearance of *De la Religion considerée dans ses rapports avec l'ordre politique et civil.* An examination of this work reveals how complete is the religious split within France. Consistent with his earlier attack upon the Royalist conception of the Restoration, Lamennais based his work on the assumption that France in 1825 is a democracy: "France is an assembly of thirty million individuals, among whom the law recognizes no distinctions other than in fortune." As for the king, he is no more than a "venerable memory of the past: the inscription of an old temple, which has been placed on the façade of a modern building."[49]

Because the Restoration is a democracy, says Lamennais, it comes into inevitable conflict with Christianity. Democracy rests upon the principle of mobility and change, whereas Christianity depends upon a fixed order of things. The democratic principle is acknowledged to have begun within the Church; it was in the form of Protestantism, however, that it spread to the states of Europe. Catholic France has witnessed the democratic principle in action with the French Revolution, which was a "rigorously precise application of the final consequences of Protestantism." With the triumph of the Revolution (and democracy), atheism has become the basis of the law: "It does not matter whether religion is true; what matters is whether it is national."[50] It is to this level that religion has been reduced. This is Gallicanism, the conception of a national church, the historical descendant of Protestantism and democracy.

Lamennais documents this charge in an attack on the Restoration's religious record, concluding that "religion in France is, in the eyes of the law, only a thing to be administered." As a result, a state of war exists between true religion and the State. The only consolation for Lamennais is that this war cannot last forever, for "either the State will become Christian, or it will abolish Christianity." This war of which he speaks sounds suspiciously akin to the irreconcilable conflict between religion and society which had been the motto of the radical *philosophe,* but for Lamennais it is a war directed against religion by the new State, an institution with rights and powers separate from the Church: "The State has its doctrines. . . . The Church has essentially opposite doctrines. . . . There is, then, between it and the State, a state of continual war."

Lamennais specifically scorns those who, in the face of "reality," try to preserve the coalition of throne and altar, those who fail to see that religion is merely tolerated in Restoration France, since its spirit is in absolute contradiction to the State. He is quite bitter about the place of religion—"it figures in the budget under the same heading as *beaux arts.*"

Accordingly, for Lamennais, the real threat to the Church emanates, not from the Revolution, but from the Bourbon Restoration which is trying to supplant it. In effect, while the Liberals are striving to convince the Gallicans that Ultramontanism is the enemy, Lamennais is telling the Ultramontanists that it is the *Gallicans* (those who are satisfied with the status quo) who are their most formidable foe. Lamennais is certain that the Restoration is aiming at the establishment of a national Church—for him, a contradiction in terms. "The destruction of Christianity in France, by the establishment of a national Church . . . this is being worked for tirelessly." Thus, he sees what few others can, in a Restoration rocked by cries of Gallican and Ultramontanist: that the real threat to the Church is the growth of a rival power which has come to fruition in the nineteenth century—the State. In Gallicanism statists have found the necessary historical excuse for the State's aggrandizement: "They needed a pretext; they found it in *Gallican liberties,* which has become the war cry of all enemies of Christianity. . . . They needed a name to oppose to Catholic authority: they profaned the name of Bossuet."[51]

What is most remarkable about Lamennais's analysis is that he addresses it not to the Liberals, but to those Royalists and Royal Gallicans who have accepted Liberal arguments. He is especially scornful of historians, who have a "dangerous mania for searching in the past for chimerical analogies with the present erring and false spirit."[52] But in order to clarify his own Ultramontanism, to slay Gallicanism, Lamennais himself must become a historian.

He devotes his sixth chapter to a defense of the papacy. Lashing out at the Gallican and the general Restoration tendency to glorify the French monarchy, he attacks kings as oppressors, and points to the papacy as the only check upon monarchical tyranny.[53] Whereas the Royal Gallicans understate controversy in French history and the "unionists" deny it altogether, Lamennais—the Ultramontanist—sides with the Liberals in conceiving of French history as one continual conflict. Indeed, Lamennais sees two struggles, nobility *vs.* throne and people *vs.* king, the first terminated by Louis XIV, the second by the Revolution. Why did these struggles occur? Because in the absence of papal authority, the law of the jungle operates in society: "Machiavelli was the lawmaker for this society of sovereigns who declared themselves independent of God."[54]

Thus, for the Ultramontanist as for the Liberal, history has its special message. The corruption of the French monarchy started when the king began to act independently of the Church, when he "substituted . . . for the immutable laws of justice, the unstable spirit of interests." Lamennais traces this shift from justice to interests—i.e., from spiritual to secular—back to the origin of the parlements and Estates, which he says were called into being by the kings as a weapon, "in order to give legality to their aggression against the spiritual power."[55] The culmination of this program was the Declaration of 1682. This Declaration is a Restoration totem; Liberals and Royal Gallicans outdid each other in devotions to it; but for Lamennais it is a deliberate conspiracy to separate the political from the religious, the monarchy from the papacy.

It is with the aid of this fanatically Ultramontanist prism employed by Lamennais that one important confusion of the religious conflict can be dispelled. Lamennais sees Gallicanism, whatever its platform, as the essential separation of Church and State—Church being defined, *à l'ultramontain,* as the papacy. From the vantage point of 1825, he can see that 1682 represented a victory of the temporal powers over the spiritual, and that this was a step in the general decline of religious strength. Oddly enough, then, it is Lamennais the Ultramontanist who gives us the best explanation of the appeal of Gallicanism to the Liberals: simply that historical Gallicanism, being aimed at the weakening of papal power, ultimately leads to the weakening of religion. The Liberals' "conversion" to Gallicanism is not puzzling to Lamennais, for Gallicanism is Protestantism, the principle of independence in religion. That it takes power away from the papacy and gives it to the monarchy is no objection for the Liberals, who have learned, during the Restoration, to regard the monarchy as their friend. Thus, the Liberals have instinctively and correctly chosen to identify themselves with a movement within the French Church which historically conforms to their own desires.

Lamennais concludes with a warning to the members of the Restoration coalition. He first tells the monarchy that it has chosen the wrong path, that by sponsoring Gallicanism it has introduced into society the spirit of disobedience. During the Revolution, the monarchy reaped the bitter harvest of this policy, but the revived Gallicanism of the Restoration indicates that the monarchy has not learned its lesson. Lamennais promises open warfare against any efforts to create a French Church. He then turns to the sincere Gallicans within the Church and, in a savage analysis of the Four Articles, reduces the Gallican credo to heresy. This, then, is the Ultramontanist reply to the Restoration revival of Gallicanism: war on the monarchy, anathema to the Gallican clergy.*

The Liberal-Gallican offensive succeeded in two respects. It drove Gallican Royalists like Frayssinous into vigorously affirming their Gallicanism, thus making the principles of 1682 an official part of the Restoration. This, in turn, drove the Ultramontanists into open opposition to official Gallicanism, producing a near schism within the French Church. Most significant of all, the historically directed attack on Ultramontanism and the resurrection of the old hostility between throne and altar had a natural and powerful appeal to the pure Royalists of the Restoration. These Royalists are prepared to accept the message of the Liberal history, *viz.*, the dangers of the alliance of Church and State. But, whereas the Liberal Pradt rejects this alliance as harmful to the clergy, and the Ultramontanist Lamennais denounces it in the name of true religion, the Royalist attacks it as detrimental to monarchy. At first this opposition to the alliance is not large—the union of throne and altar is a watchword of the Restoration in its early years. But as the Restoration progresses, the absolute monarchists and the old aristocrats come to see the Church as an albatross around the neck of the French monarchy, and seek to have the Bourbon political Restoration shed its burden of religious support and "go it alone."

The impact of the Gallican controversy upon these Royalists can best be seen in the case of Joseph Fiévée, whose volumes of political correspondence and parliamentary histories enlivened the first years of the Restoration. The debate over the proposed concordat of 1817 found Fiévée in a curious and special position. As a Royalist committed to the defense of the monarchy past and present, Fiévée resents the Liberal-Gallican attack upon Francis I and the Concordat of 1516. He offers an explanation of why French kings have been subservient to popes: "From Francis I up to and including Louis XIV, what rendered our kings so timid before the pretensions of the court of Rome . . . was the very legitimate fear that they would

* For the effects of Lamennais in action, see Chapter VII below.

see Protestantism increase at the expense of divisions between the temporal and spiritual powers."[56] Fiévée denies that Francis I surrendered to the pope for purely political reasons.[57]

In his defense of the Concordat of 1516 and its creator, Fiévée is close to the official Gallican position. Soon, however, he reveals that he has justified 1516 only to make his stand against 1817 clearer. The 1516 concordat was motivated by fear of the Protestants; no such motive exists in 1817. Indeed, the Charter proclaimed by Louis XVIII has officially recognized freedom of religion. Fiévée's analysis of the Concordat of 1817 is particularly damning since it comes from an acknowledged Royalist.* It draws fire from all sides.

In his *Histoire de la session de 1817,* Fiévée replies to his critics, strengthening and extending his original attack upon this concordat. He grants that concordats were once politically necessary—before sects were recognized, when the clergy was a united body—but he insists that the political need for such arrangements has disappeared. In short, he opposes the concordat of 1817 because of its assumption, once true but now false, that monarchy needs religion as a base.

Fiévée gives his reasons for believing that religion is no longer a force in political life:

> Religion has . . . been considered by temporal sovereigns as a means of strengthening their political power at the expense of their subjects. This concept, borrowed from the Stuarts, was very closely linked with the fate of that royal family. I believe it my duty to warn those who assert that the Royalist party can be established by the ascendancy of bishops . . . that, given the actual state of our administration, nothing is as ill-founded as this hope.

As a Royalist, Fiévée approves of the Stuarts and their tactics; as a realist, he finds such tactics obsolete. Since the king no longer opposes civil liberties, he no longer requires the official support of religion.

There is an additional practical reason why religion can no longer be useful to monarchy, namely, the great changes wrought by the eighteenth century and the Revolution:

> Let us not mix any religion into our plans, our political hopes. Do not forget that in a country where *Vive l'enfer* was shouted during the Hundred Days, where one hears the cry *A bas les prêtres* during elections, there are many who regard religion as a means of subjecting people to an ancient yoke, and who attack it violently and treacherously for this reason. What appears good to one party necessarily appears inimical to the opposing party; let us avoid this difficulty.[58]

Fiévée comes to the same conclusions as Lamennais for precisely the opposite reasons. For the cleric Lamennais, the Church can only soil itself

* The clearest indication of the purity of Fiévée's Royalist feelings is his remark that the king would still be king, even if he ceased to be Catholic.

by being involved with the throne; for the monarchist Fiévée, the throne can only damage itself by being linked to a historically defeated and unpopular party.

In 1818, Fiévée's advocacy of a monarchy independent of religious support is unpopular. But if his view is unrepresentative of Royalist sentiment during the early Restoration, it is inspired prophecy, for by 1826, more and more Royalists—under the pressure of the Liberal attack—have come to agree with him. Indicative of this Royalist concern is a pamphlet written by the magistrate Charles Cottu. Cottu begins by considering the possibilities of revolution in the year 1826. If revolutions had no cause other than excessive tyranny, he says, France would have nothing to worry about. But revolutions can stem from another source, from government's willfully ignoring the "customs, needs, and sentiments" of the people.[59] Cottu is no sentimental Royalist; he believes the Restoration occurred not because the people hated usurpers and loved Henry IV, but because they expected the Bourbons to set up institutions that would guarantee the welfare of France.

In the light of these realities, he examines what the Restoration monarch has done. It was a mistake to surround the monarch with the hated aristocracy; worse yet was the political use of the clergy. For Cottu, one political fact overshadows all others: "There exists in France today an insurmountable aversion to domination by the clergy."[60] Cottu is convinced that the Restoration has erred in ignoring public opinion; instead of discarding the clergy, it has offered them undiscriminating protection on their own terms and attempted to "introduce them as a new power among the other political powers." Cottu even supplies us with the source of this mistake: it is a new doctrine born of the Revolution, a doctrine "adopted with enthusiasm by the greater part of the clergy and by other young people destined for the ecclesiastical calling."[61] In a word, it is Ultramontanism. He sees the difficulties of the 1820's as stemming from the demands of the clergy for a greater participation in Restoration life, the right to teach youth, the right to an independent revenue, and the right to promulgate laws on sacrilege and religious marriage. From the viewpoint of a Royalist interested in the survival of the Restoration, these are useless provocations of a society already hostile.

For Cottu, there is nothing new in this hostility between clergy and society. A member of the magistracy, he has often found himself under clerical fire. "The clergy . . . , if only from memories of its great past, must be the natural enemy of our ancient institutions." If the Restoration clergy is determined, so must its old foes be determined: "Is it not the duty of the ministry, with Chamber, the magistracy, and generally of all citizens, to oppose with tireless perseverance all that might augment the clergy's political influence?"[62]

Cottu is a Gallican, but he is less concerned with the threat to "Gallican liberties" than with the threat to the king's power:

> It is enough that our kings have renounced the right they had under the first two lines, and which they held without contest for centuries, to name bishops of their kingdom without interference from the court of Rome, and that they thereby opened the way for all these subsequent claims. Convinced today, by sad experience, of the imprudence of this first concession, they must redouble their vigilance and must be on guard against other snares laid for their piety by papal ambition.[63]

Cottu analyzes all the mistakes of the Villèle administration, but concludes that it is the government's confusing of throne and altar, its coddling of Ultramontanists, that is the basic reason for its unpopularity.

We have seen the Conservative reaction to this Liberal Gallicanism. Some Conservatives were aware of its dangers and were quick to expose its maneuvers. One such Conservative was Joseph Bernardi, director of civil affairs in the Ministry of Justice. In a direct reply to Lanjuinais's attack on the concordat, Bernardi raises the question of the motivation for all this historical interest in Gallicanism: "They have compiled everything that our most commonplace histories have to say about the Parlement's opposition to Francis I's concordat; they have repeated all the accusations which were made in the time of Cardinal Duprat." Noting that the real focus of the attack is upon the relations of the pope and the French king, Bernardi writes: "What especially excites your fears and those of your canonists is that seven or eight centuries ago, popes sometimes excommunicated kings."[64] Thus, he reveals his understanding that the Liberals have embraced Gallicanism in an attempt to prove their loyalty to monarchy. This stratagem is reminiscent of the Liberals' desire to become more Royalist than the Royalists in defending and espousing the Charter granted by Louis XVIII.

The Conservatives are bewildered by this switching of roles; they are astonished to see the men who overthrew Louis XVI bidding to be the most loyal supporters of Louis XVIII; they can only rub their eyes and deny that it is happening. Summoning up memories of the Revolution, Bernardi finds the Liberals' solicitude for Louis XVIII laughable. How dare they pretend concern over the fate of kings, they who have "overthrown or shaken most of the thrones of Europe, after having led one of our best kings to the scaffold."[65] The Liberals are obviously trying to leap onto the Royalist bandwagon, and the only answer for the Conservatives is to refuse to let them on. How? By reminding France that these are not Gallicans but revolutionaries.

Bernardi also attempts to expose this nefarious Liberal Gallicanism by establishing the real motives behind its arguments. Lanjuinais, unlike Pradt and Grégoire, had defended Napoleon's concordat while attacking that of 1516. This enables Bernardi to charge: "Thus, according to you, what was illegitimate under our kings was rendered legal by Napoleon."[66] Everywhere he seeks to deny that the Liberals are truly taking the royal side of the question. He attempts to capitalize on the universal Liberal attack upon Francis I: "Why are you so bitter and blind about the Concordat of 1516? Is it because it was the work of one of our kings? I think it is." Totally spurious, according to Bernardi, is the Liberals' adoption of Gallicanism. If you are really Gallicans, he cries, how can you support the Concordat of 1801, which "many people regard as having greatly threatened the liberties and independence of the Gallican Church." Further, in attacking 1516, the Liberals reveal their true intentions, because this agreement marked the dawn of the most brilliant epoch of the French Church: "Never have its liberties—in which so many people, who do not know of what they consist, show such a hypocritical interest—been better known or defended." His indictment of the Liberals as false Gallicans is concluded by arguing that it was the Revolution which "destroyed this fine edifice built by our fathers." The concordat of 1817 is consequently, for Bernardi, the triumph of Gallican liberties—how consistent of the Liberals to oppose it!

We have seen that the Liberal-Gallican offensive against the Ultras and the concordat of 1817 seriously split Conservative ranks, ranging Royal Gallican against the Ultramontanist and pious Conservative against pure Royalist. Perhaps these divisions would have occurred if Gallicanism had not been revived by the Liberals. Yet, at the outset of the Restoration, there *was* internal religious unity and a Conservative determination, born of the Revolution, to remain united. Lamennais might still have raised his standard, Royalists might still have wanted to abandon religion, but on what grounds could the struggle have been fought? The fact is that it is the determination of the Liberals to convince the monarchy that they were its best friends, their subsequent conversion to Gallicanism, their fight against Ultramontanism and for separation of Church and State, that precipitated the religious quarrels of the Restoration.

CHAPTER VI

The Jesuits

The Society of Jesus has not lacked historians; most of the time they were enemies.

Joseph Burnichon

The concordat of 1817 dies a natural death, the victim of a revived Gallicanism and the fear of Ultramontanism. But more important than the immediate Liberal victory in preventing this concordat is the fact that these two forces are unleashed, for they are to do untold damage to the Conservative Restoration.

By 1820, the actual conflict over the concordat has petered out, but the issues it generated remain. In the years that follow, the Liberals, politically discredited by the assassination of the Duc de Berry and by their implication in the plots of 1821, turn more and more to the religious question. The debate in 1817 had raised the charge of Ultramontanism; from 1820 until the dénouement of 1830, the air is to be filled with charges of Ultramontanist, Jesuit, *parti prêtre*, Missions, Congregation. Histories, poems, plays, novels, the press—all combine in a vast Liberal effort to undo the alliance of throne and altar achieved by the Restoration.

After 1820, it is quite natural that the Liberals should turn their efforts to splitting this formidable alliance of throne and altar. In the years 1816–20, they had concentrated, with signal success, upon splitting the aristocracy from the throne. After the Duc de Berry's assassination, that policy can no longer be pursued; the Ultras have returned to the government, playing a decisive role in the Villèle administration. The accession of Charles X in 1824 made the chances of destroying that alliance even more remote. Moreover, during the eighteen twenties, a considerable body of Liberal aristocrats had grown up—men like Barante, Sainte-Aulaire, Broglie, Molé—men who were willing to maintain close and continuing relations with the Doctrinaire wing of the Liberal party. When the Ultras attempted to revive primogeniture, for example, it was the aristocrat Molé who led the successful opposition in the Chamber.

Another important factor in this shift of the aristocrats was Chateaubriand's break with the Villèle regime in 1824. From this point on, Chateaubriand and the *Journal des débats* became a nucleus around which Liberal aristocratic and dissident royalist sentiment could form.[1] Finally, it should be noted that the Chamber of Peers, composed as it was largely of peers created by the Empire, was always more Liberal than the Chamber of Deputies, which, owing to the narrow electorate, contained a nest of Ultras.*

Reason and circumstance, then, seemed to the Liberals to dictate a change of tactics after 1820, to shift their attack exclusively to the weak link of the coalition, the alliance of Church and State. There were other advantages: first, an assault upon undue religious influence in the government would be historically satisfying to all elements of the Liberal Left. With the Liberals virtually eliminated from the government after 1820 (they dropped to nineteen deputies at one point), the Liberals and the Left tended to come closer together, and the religious issue was one upon which they could agree. As for the coalition itself, it seemed to offer ample opportunities to sow disunion. Both the aristocracy and the monarchy had a host of historical grievances against the Church, and these fears could be fanned into suspicions. The religious forces, too, were ripe for dissension; the alliance of Church and State on Ultramontanist terms could rouse both the Gallicans and all who were genuinely convinced of the necessity for separation of Church and State. Finally, because the concordat of 1817 has made the religious question a burning one for three years, the Liberals have been able to establish their battle lines and assume their position for the showdown.

To the cries of Gallican and Ultramontanist which continue through the Restoration,[2] another is added after 1820—the cry of Jesuit. The Jesuits, expelled from France in 1764, had been dissolved as an order by Pope Clement XIV in 1773. In 1814, as part of the general European Restoration, they were reinstated by Pius VII, and returned to France. The papal condemnation of 1773 was thus rescinded, but the national expulsion of 1764 was not.

Before examining the role the Jesuits were to play in the Restoration, we must understand what Conservative France hoped to achieve by the return of an order that had been absent for fifty years. A petition to the king from the citizens of Aix-en-Provence for the reestablishment of the Jesuits in 1814 mirrored Conservative hopes.

> The designs of these innovators [of the Revolution] are known to Your Majesty. In order to overthrow the throne to which, in their blind fury, they had sworn implacable hatred, they attacked religion, its unshakable support. . . .
>
> The usefulness of each of the religious orders to the Church may be gauged

* As the Restoration rolls on, a general Liberalizing tendency seems to take place. Labourdonnaye, for example, whom we have met in the columns of the *Conservateur* in 1818, and in the Spanish debate, actually defends freedom of the press in the Chamber.

by their hatred; and there is no doubt but that they regarded the Society of Jesus as the one order which could best serve the throne and combat them.

> Sire, give back to the throne at least some of the sacred battalions which in all times have been dedicated to its service and defense—dedicated by the spirit of their calling, dedicated by their oaths.
>
> In these times of misfortune and of weakening faith, these auxiliary troops are as necessary to the throne as are its ministers.[3]

Thus, from the experiences of the Revolution, Conservative France has learned that the Jesuits were a prop to the throne, and that their dissolution was the first step toward dissolution of the monarchy. In part, therefore, the return of the Jesuits is expiation for sins of the past. But Conservatives are also looking to the future, and many are convinced that the Jesuit is the dike that stands between Catholic civilization and the forces of revolution. A letter from Bonald to Maistre accurately catches the spirit of the men who have lived through the French Revolution: "Those who sixty years ago destroyed this celebrated religious order which it was their duty to defend have become, almost without exception, the victims of this terrible vengeance [i.e., the Revolution]. . . . I believe . . . that it was the destruction of this order, an order so necessary to Christianity, which led Europe into the abyss."[4]

From the very moment the Jesuits returned, fears were expressed by Liberals and Liberal Gallicans.[5] Carnot refers to them in his memoir to the king, and Montlosier is worried about them as early as 1815. From 1814 to 1820 these fears form a minor though persistent current in the literature of the Left. In the columns of the *Minerve française*, the activities of the Jesuits are exposed and exaggerated.[6] For the readers of the radical press, no real analysis of the Jesuits is required; they are prepared to believe the worst of this ancient foe. To many of them, the very existence of this order in the Restoration is sufficient threat to Liberal France.

During these first years, however, Jesuit activities are on so small a scale that scant attention is paid to them. There are more immediate targets: the Liberal broadsides are reserved for the aristocrats, and the major religious issue is the concordat. In the attack upon Ultramontanism, the Jesuits are referred to, but only incidentally.[7]

The Jesuits do not become a major political issue until 1820. One factor in their sudden prominence is the defeat of the Liberals in 1820. Driven into opposition and thrown into closer alliance with the radical Left, the Liberals adopt some of the religious virulence of the Left, including something of the eighteenth-century attitude toward the Jesuits. This Liberal-Left alliance is willing to exploit the religious issues raised by the concordat, but since the concordat has failed, a new line is needed to keep the cry of Ultramontanism alive. An attack upon the Jesuits appears a natural and logical extension of the defense of Gallicanism.

But the most obvious explanation for this increased interest in the Jesuits would seem to be the expansion of the Jesuits themselves. The Liberal press points with horror to the establishment of Jesuit seminaries at Montrouge in 1818 and at Saint-Acheul, and the names Montrouge and Saint-Acheul become symbols of papist infiltration. But a modern Jesuit scholar, Joseph Burnichon, has carefully demonstrated that these charges were largely the products of the inflamed Liberal imagination rather than accurate descriptions of the state of affairs. The attacks on the seminaries would be believed by an audience trained in the arguments of the *philosophes*, but as a reasonable attempt to convince Restoration France of the Jesuits' influence, the charges lacked authority, even evidence. The simple truth is that the Jesuits were more of a Conservative hope than an actual power; their numbers, strength, and influence were, as Burnichon proves, infinitesimal. By 1826, at the height of anti-Jesuit agitation, there were eight seminaries, 130 Jesuit priests, and a total of 431 Jesuits of all grades.[8] This total cannot compare with the strength of the Gallicans, or even the number of young seminary students of Lamennais's persuasion. All things considered, the Jesuits supplied only a fraction of the religious strength and vitality of the Restoration.

Hard as the Liberals try, they can find little or no contemporary evidence to give substance to their attacks on the Jesuits. But there exists "evidence" which, in a sense, is beyond dispute, evidence that will sway Frenchmen who have no use for the attacks of the *philosophes*. That evidence is the evidence of history. The Jesuits have scarcely had a chance to take root since their restoration in 1814; they have had little time to commit "outrages." History can supplement the record, as well as suggest the true character of the movement.

Further, the Jesuits are now a loyal and trusted part of the returning coalition of monarchy, aristocracy, and clergy. Like the aristocrats who are now more Royalist than the king, like the absolute monarchists who have learned the wisdom of constitutional government, the Jesuits have learned their lesson in exile. However shadowy their past, their loyalty to the Restoration monarchy is blind and unquestioning.

But the Liberals, in their efforts to split the Restoration coalition, can ignore or falsify this loyalty to the Restoration monarchy, and can instead play up the historic role of the Jesuits, their quarrels with monarchy, aristocracy, and non-Jesuit clergy. History, judiciously arranged, can present the Jesuits as the assassins of kings, the enemies of the aristocracy, and the scourge of the Gallican wing of the French Church. The Jesuits are, in fact, an ideal means of reopening half a dozen basic controversies in the French past. The variety of their past struggles makes them a perfect target; at one time or another, every group in France had feared them, and every shade of Liberal, Bonapartist, and Republican sentiment could join with the Gallicans, aristocrats, and monarchists in this renewal of the eighteenth-century campaign. By recalling the Jesuit past, the Liberals are paying off an old enemy as well as destroying the effectiveness of this order in the Restoration.

Perhaps the first significant effort in this Liberal campaign to expose the Jesuit past was J. F. Goubeau de La Bilennerie's two-volume *Histoire abrégé des Jésuites* (1820), "wherein is proved that these *religieux* and all ecclesiastical corporations ruled by the Institute of the Society of Jesus are not to be tolerated in any civilized state."[9] Goubeau strikes all the themes that are to dominate the Restoration attack on the Jesuits. Indeed, it would seem that little ingenuity is needed by these hostile Restoration historians of the Jesuits—they have only to resurrect the indictments of two and a half centuries of critics. Goubeau selects as his epigraph an extract from an edict of Henry IV: "The Jesuits are . . . enemies of the State and Throne of France, corrupters of youth, disturbers of the peace."[10]

In his preface, Goubeau asks rhetorically: Why write a book on the Jesuits? Hasn't the story been told accurately and well by a host of celebrated historians? His answer reveals the role that histories of the Jesuits are to play in the Restoration:

> It is certain that men of our day are little disposed to occupy themselves with readings that have become so foreign to their minds, tastes, and habits; and it is still more certain that the new Jesuits, who have returned to France disguised as missionary fathers of the faith, . . . profit by this almost nation-wide ignorance—ignorance of the shameful conduct of their former *confrères* and of their dangerous system of association—to seduce men's minds anew. . . . Frightened by the thought that our glorious country may become the prey of the formidable children of Loyola . . . , we have tried to give our citizens a succinct but faithful exposé of the general history of the Jesuits.[11]

In all politically motivated histories it is assumed that history is a safe guide to present politics; in this instance it is assumed that one can legitimately indict the Jesuits of the present with the sins of their past. The Jesuits themselves confirm the validity of the historical approach by their behavior during the Restoration:

> When we see . . . the persecutions that follow their every step; when we see their lectures and teachings fomenting new divisions within the Church, their doctrines openly attacking our Gallican liberties; finally, when we read the flood of writings recalling the grim era of the League, we can no longer doubt the return of the Jesuits.[12]

Goubeau argues that it is particularly important for the Restoration critic of the Jesuits to speak out. In the past there were formidable groups arrayed against the Jesuits, an enormous natural opposition: "When they first appeared, . . . they had great difficulty in getting a foothold, because all the orders were against them, including this very clergy that we now see embracing their cause with such ardor."[13] But when they appear in the Restoration, this situation no longer exists; monarchy, aristocracy, and clergy, their ancient enemies, are now their strongest supporters. Goubeau seeks to reinvigorate some of the old opposition, and thereby to break up this historically false alliance. To this end, he reads the roll call of its historic opponents: "parlements, bishops, universities, *curés,* and a great number of scholars, among whom figure the illustrious names of Thou, Pasquier, Mézeray, Pascal, Arnauld, Nicole, and Saint-Cyran."[14]

Outlining the Liberal case against the Jesuits, Goubeau reminds his readers that the Jesuits are newly reestablished, that their return with the Restoration was a violation of the previous judgment of European society, including that of Rome itself. He carefully draws a parallel between their suppression in 1773 and their reestablishment in 1814, printing the decrees of Clement XIV and Pius VII in an appendix. Which of the popes was right, he asks; which was guided by divine wisdom? "Enlightened Christians will not hesitate to regard the brief of Clement XIV as the work of the most enlightened justice." Why, then, did Pius VII restore this discredited order? The answer is evident to the Liberal of 1820: "to spread Ultramontanist doctrines and, if possible, to recover the ancient powers that the popes had usurped from kings."[15]

The author sums up the historical record of the Jesuits as a society "which has stirred up trouble for two centuries, has conspired against kings, and has been convicted of a thousand other crimes, a society whose laws and regime are . . . openly in opposition to our Charter."[16] Goubeau's book is typical of the Restoration "histories" of the Jesuits in its embellishments and variations on this theme. After disposing of Loyola as a ridiculous figure, the author proceeds to the argument of Volume I, Jesuit treason against the monarchy. The Jesuits are called the soul of the League; Jacques Clément and Ravaillac, the assassins of Henry III and Henry IV, respectively, are linked to the order. It is this accusation that is to haunt the Jesuits throughout the Restoration; it is this telling reminder that must bring to their senses those who look to the Jesuits as a prop to monarchy: "Soon we see them audaciously attack the throne whose firmest support they claim to be. . . . They swear love and loyalty to kings at the very moment when they set in motion against them a Jacques Clément, a Jean Châtel, a Ravaillac."[17]

Châtel, Clément, Ravaillac—the names reverberate through the Restoration. There is indeed something ironic in the selection of this charge to bedevil the Jesuits of the Restoration, for it is clear that high treason—much less assassination of kings—is the last thing the men of Montrouge and Saint-Acheul contemplate. The new Jesuits and the old are different men, fundamentally different. Gone and forgotten—by the Jesuits themselves—are their historic quarrels; they are, as Lamennais pointed out then and as

Burnichon has shown since, fanatically Royalist—to a fault. That the Liberals should put stock in such nonsense is remarkable testimony to the relevance of history to the Restoration mind.

Having established the Jesuit connections of these early assassins, Goubeau in Volume II carries the story through the seventeenth and eighteenth centuries: a plot against Louis XIV, a conspiracy against Joseph I of Portugal, and so on. There is an exposé of the "missions," and suitable reflections on the "commerce and avarice" of the Jesuits. The whole work is a rich compendium of crimes and mementos, from purest history to rankest gossip.[18]

In a hymn to Clement XIV, the author notes the careful way that pope went about collecting evidence against the Jesuits before deciding to extinguish the order. He pays particular attention to this eighteenth-century climax of their career, which he regards as the accumulated judgment of history on their crimes. It was, after all, not a revolution, but a French monarch and a pope that destroyed the society. It is its condemnation by France in 1762 and its final dissolution in 1773 that the Liberals wish to recall. And Goubeau is furious at the Jesuits in 1820 for not coming out into the open, acknowledging their past, and requesting retrial and reversal of the eighteenth-century decision: "Why aren't the Jesuits, who assure us that France asks for them *with loud cries*, . . . the first to solicit *with loud cries* the reexamination of their case?"

It is the Liberals who are to insist upon the reopening of this eighteenth-century trial.* The Restoration Jesuits, Goubeau complains, "will not even blush at having been publicly indicted by one of the prosecutors of the Crown, found guilty by our sovereign courts, and placed under the most solemn condemnation. Thus, they will bear all this ignominy, without the slightest qualm, in the midst of the present generation." He finds the motivation for the Jesuits' silence apparent: they want to appear to be a new organization sprung from the Restoration in 1814. They even prefer to be known as "Fathers of the Faith" in order to lose the unfortunate historical associations of their name.

Goubeau does not stop at the eighteenth-century expulsion; he insists that the Jesuits acknowledge their entire past, that they not only justify their existence in the Restoration but defend their historical record:

> In a word, if the Jesuits want to appear innocent in our eyes, they must prove, in a public examination before the king and the Chambers, that they have never given and still do not give a private vow of obedience to the pope; they must make a clean breast of their secret and acknowledged credos; they must demonstrate that their system, so vaunted by their partisans, has always been and will continue to be in accord with our government and our Gallican liberties; . . . they must

* The Liberals are referring to the Chalotais trial of 1762, which, in condemning the Jesuits, prepared the way for their expulsion in 1764. See Chapter VII below.

prove that their morals have always been pure, their former conduct pacific, far from all intrigue, and beyond reproach from peoples or princes; they must demonstrate that the magistrates, bishops, and popes who condemned them were lying, ignorant, or *parvenu* judges.

In effect, the Jesuits stand indicted, not by their conduct in the Restoration, but by their historical record. It is this record, the Liberals insist, that the Jesuits must bear as a cross. The historical battleground will prove embarrassing for the champions of the Jesuits, for to defend the Jesuits historically is to attack those forces in French life—monarchy and aristocracy—the order now claims to defend.

In a final chapter, Goubeau deals with the reestablishment in 1814. Seeing the Jesuits as a pawn in the struggle of Pius VII to spread Ultramontanism, he notes that the pope finds certain maneuvers barred to him:

Our Holy Father Pius VII, despite his preference for reviving the pretensions of the Holy See, would not dare do today what his predecessors did—strike with his thunderbolt our kings of France. . . . He would not dare, for example, to anathematize Louis XVIII if this prince, acceding to the demands of a great nation, refused to give his signature to the concordat.

Therefore, the pope must find a "new" weapon: "He believed that, by reestablishing the Jesuits, . . . by putting this armed order on its feet, he could recover the ancient authority of popes over temporal powers." The support of papal authority had been a historic function of the Jesuits, and the Liberals find it sufficient explanation for the reestablishment of the Society in 1814.

The Restoration Conservatives, however, had their own version of this recall. They contended that, since the destruction of the Jesuit order had paved the way for the French Revolution, its return was the safest guarantee against future revolution. In a sense, the Restoration coalition forces regarded the Revolution as a judgment on its predecessors for having banished the Jesuits, and were determined to make amends.

The Liberals undercut this argument by denying that the Jesuits could have prevented the Revolution. Every Liberal account of the Jesuits sought to prove this thesis. Goubeau makes two points. First, the writings of the *philosophes,* which were presumably responsible for the Revolution, were in print long before the dissolution of the Jesuits in 1764; the Jesuits, therefore, were not a very effective check to their influence. Second, the Jesuits themselves were a vast revolutionary organization: "Didn't they always revolt when their ambitious projects were resisted?"[19] Moreover, they are accused of being responsible for the general decay of standards and the corruption of religion in the eighteenth century. Whatever the grounds, the Liberal historian seeks to suggest that the Jesuits are as unqualified to lead the counterrevolution as they are unsuitable associates of Restoration monarchy.

Goubeau concludes his work with a plea addressed to Louis XVIII, a remarkable example of the enlistment of history in the service of politics. He exhorts Louis to remember his ancestors and reject the support of his ancient enemies, to spurn his present political friends because they were the historic opponents of the Bourbons:

O Prince, wise and full of wisdom, you who have yourself studied in the school of misfortune, and whom the great events of the Revolution have given centuries of experience, you know too well the interests of France and of the throne . . . to permit elements of discord to be introduced anew. You will not permit them to afflict us with the burdens that our fathers could not bear. . . . You will reflect on the many whose crowns did not guarantee them protection from the blows of the society of regicides.[20]

Goubeau's work contains all the themes that are to be developed by a host of eager "historians," and suggests to his generation the weak points that are to be exploited. Clearly the eighteenth-century expulsion of the order would be a profitable mine to be worked. In 1823 Gilbert de Voisins, a Liberal member of the Chamber of Deputies, produces a record of the investigation and trial of 1761. Everything that can be said against the Jesuits was said then, and said by an authority the Restoration must accept—the Parlement of Paris. In his Introduction, Gilbert deals with two questions: Why did the Parlement of Paris institute proceedings against the Jesuits, and why is he, Gilbert, publishing an account of this trial? The first question is answered with a long quotation from Abbé Fleury to the effect that the Jesuits are a secret organization which considers itself beyond the law. As for the second:

It is the duty of a good citizen to place before the eyes of the public the motives which united against the Jesuits all the parlements of the realm, all the universities, a numerous portion of the clergy, and a host of men recommended by their religious and monarchical principles, because the dangers that would result from their present influence would be much greater than were the dangers at the time of their destruction.[21]

Gilbert then proceeds with the familiar argument—the power of the forces formerly ranged against the Jesuits, forces which are now complacent or compliant. The Liberals are particularly anxious to remind the Restoration aristocracy of the attitude of the eighteenth-century aristocracy: "The parlements, by noble and courageous resistance, rejected the new Ultramontanist doctrines which were supported by the Jesuits." The parlements, as protectors of Gallican liberties, could serve to summon latent Gallican feeling revived by the controversy of 1817. Finally, the opposition of the universities, archenemies of the Jesuits, suggests a parallel to the gloomy situation in 1823; for has not Frayssinous just driven the Liberal professors from the University?* Thus the parlements are gone, the universities are no longer independent, and even a part of the clergy has deserted the doctrines of Bossuet: "If, despite resistance from these sources, the Jesuits perpetrated such great evils, what could they not do today?" Gilbert summarizes the historical record of the Jesuits:

> Henry III was assassinated at their instigation. The repeated attempts on the person of Henry IV were their work. . . .
>
> The Gunpowder Plot in England, the massacre of St. Bartholomew's Day in France, the furies of the League, the proposed expulsion of the Bourbons, the religious disturbances at the end of Louis XIV's reign, and those which troubled the reign of Louis XV, were their work. . . .
>
> History, impartial history, will say that the Jesuits caused more misfortune to nations and the downfall of more kings, than the most violent of popular assemblies.

In this variety of comparative criminology, the Jesuits are as bad—and at least as disloyal to the king—as the Revolution. The disloyalty charge is usually linked to that of supporting the papal party—Ultramontanism—but Gilbert seeks to deny the Jesuits even the solace of papal support. He paraphrases a letter sent to Innocent X by Bishop Juan de Palafox in 1649, another document included in this collection: "The Jesuits serve governments and the Church when the Church and governments submit to them. But if the Church and governments do not please them, the Jesuits become their cruelest and most dangerous enemies." After this revealing introduction, there follows a 336-page summation of the 1761 trial.

Another remarkable example of the relevance of this eighteenth-century action to the campaign waged by Restoration Liberals is the publication of *La Galère Jésuitique* in 1826. "The Jesuit Galley" was a painting taken from a Jesuit college in 1762, by order of the Parlement of Paris, to be used as evidence against the Jesuits.† The painting is reproduced in the front of the volume and unfolds to a size of 15 by 23 inches. It is followed by 31 pages of text, consisting primarily of the "analysis" of the painting by the Parlement of Paris in 1762. The value of this painting as damning evidence is immediately apparent to the viewer. To describe it let us use the paraphrase of the Parlement's description given by the anonymous editor of 1826:

> In this picture . . . Religion is represented as a great vessel; on this vessel only monks of different orders are shown, and neither popes, bishops, nor secular priests are seen on it. . . . Saint Ignatius, holding in his hand the name of

* "The universities, with their liberties, their independence, their franchises, exist no more. A single university, at the head of which is a chancellor, subject to the Ministry of the Interior—that is all that exists today. What resistance can we expect?"

† Montlosier uses this as one of his *pièces justificatives* for his *Mémoire à consulter*. See Chapter VII below for the details of his trial.

Jesus, appears ahead of eight other founders of orders; *everywhere the Jesuits hold the first rank; the other monks appear to act only on their orders and as their subalterns.*

And this is not all:

But what especially scandalized the commissioners, what must excite general indignation, is to see *outside of the vessel of Religion*, relegated to small boats, *the pope, a cardinal*, a king of France, several crowned heads. . . . It is thus under the protection and with the aid of a Jesuit that the pope, kings, and bishops can approach the *vessel of Religion* to arrive at the *port of salvation.*[22]

All the historical calumnies against the Jesuits can be read into this painting; but to the eighteenth century, as to the nineteenth, the most serious and most effective charge was disrespect for the French monarchy, which bordered on treason. In "The Jesuit Galley" the investigating committee in 1762 found everything it expected to find. In the right center of the painting is the bark of the heretics; one figure in this bark is subjected to close perusal:

One especially is oddly shown; only a small part of his bust is seen. The face is painted upside down, in such a way that the hair is below and the beard on top. In considering this face closely, and looking at it in the natural direction, one could well believe that the artist sought to paint *a prince whose memory will always be dear to the French (Henry IV), whose portrait is graven in all hearts, and whom the League forced to conquer his own kingdom.*[23]

Henry IV—the great national hero, the founder of the Bourbon dynasty, virtually the only French king above historical discussion—is found in the bark of the heretics! What clearer indictment of the historical role of the Jesuits, what better proof of their lack of patriotism, than the vision of themselves given in *La Galère jésuitique.* They have had the temerity to commit two French kings to damnation, one as a heretic, and the other (Henry III) as an apostate; they are guilty of pride and of distorting Scripture. The eighteenth-century court reporter concludes the indictment by noting that "in this picture, there are very false and wicked interpretations of passages from Holy Scripture and the Fathers."[24]

Both the eighteenth-century aristocratic commission and the nineteenth-century Liberal propagandist are careful to link the Jesuits historically with the League, the antinational, antimonarchical force in French life. Indeed, the commission made a point of "dating" the painting and, after some research, asserted that it was painted during the period of the League. The Parlement of Paris concludes that the painting was "the fruit of the fermentation of the League and of the aid that the Jesuits lavished on the enemies of Henry IV."

Generally, the anonymous editor of 1826 is willing to let the famous men of 1762 speak for themselves, but to avoid any possible misunderstanding, he brings the indictment of the Jesuits up to date. The epigraph on his title page—"When they are chased out the door, they return through the window"—is a reference to 1814. The tenacity of the Jesuits in the face of the judgments of history is one of their most dangerous qualities: "Banished twenty times, at various times, and from various states of Europe, twenty times Jesuitism has been seen rising from the wreckage . . . despite the efforts of wise kings and courageous magistrates." Above all, the Jesuits are actually seditious, for "they occupy themselves with plots, and conspiracies, and they wish to dispose of the throne. Banished ignominiously for having assassinated two kings of France, they are not disconcerted."

Perhaps it is not really necessary to go back sixty-three years for anti-Jesuit ammunition, says the editor, since the essentials are in everyone's memory; but it is his duty nevertheless:

> Since no act of the present legislature has invalidated the decrees which banished the Jesuits and Jesuitism forever, any ciitzen, any true friend of the prince and the country, may legitimately try to prevent the return of a disease which could not be cured for a long time; and the best means of avoiding this disease is to make known all the dangers it presents. . . . Our only purpose at this time is to make known one of the most singular monuments to the insolent pride of the so-called Society of Jesus.

His purpose is accomplished by presenting to the France of 1826 a picture painted circa 1589 and judged in 1762. The painting, in the words of the 1826 advertisement, "was held in great veneration by these good Fathers, and deserved all the attention given it by the Parlement of Paris."[25] And in order to make this piece of Jesuit insolence clear to the Restoration reader, the editor translated the original Latin inscriptions in the painting into French.

The Liberals of the Restoration are not far behind the eighteenth-century prosecutors of the Jesuits. They too discover the technique of letting the Jesuits indict themselves.[26] In 1824 the first French translation of the *Monita Secreta* is printed, and in 1826 alone eight such translations are published.[27]

In 1824 Abbé Grégoire writes a somewhat oblique historical attack on the Jesuits, a history of royal confessors. For his theme, he takes the proposition that much damage has been done to France whenever her kings have been too pious or superstitious, and that the responsibility for such damage falls upon the kings' confessors. For three hundred pages, Grégoire hammers away at the undue influence exercised by fanatic confessors upon weak kings of the remote past. Arriving at the sixteenth century, he observes that "the leaders of the League . . . were always allied with the Jesuits, and had Jesuits for confessors."[28] And from Henry IV on, it is significant that Jesuits have been the confessors of kings, with the most baleful results. And yet Jesuits once again surround the throne: "Of what value are the records of the past, if they offer no lessons for the future?"[29]

Still another contribution to the Liberal attack is Abbé de Pradt's work of 1826, *Du Jésuitisme ancien et modern.* Having led the Liberal attack upon the concordat, Pradt turns his polemic against the Jesuits. As his title suggests, he takes a somewhat sophisticated approach, one befitting a clergyman. The Jesuits, he argues, had historical justification. They rose out of the reaction to the Protestant Reformation, out of the need for a militant, blindly loyal corps to conduct the Counter Reformation; moreover, they filled the need for missionaries: "Jesuitism said to Europe, I will exploit the new worlds which God has given you." For two centuries, the Jesuits had their uses, after which "Jesuitism was detached from the Christian world completely and without regrets."[30]

In the nineteenth century, there are no Luthers, no Calvins, no new worlds to win to the true faith. Not only are the Jesuits unnecessary to the Restoration, but they are a positive inconvenience to both the monarch and the Church. Pradt charges that Catholic emancipation is defeated in England because of fear of the Jesuits, and that the new society in France—with its Charter, its freedom of the press, and so on—simply has no room for an organization with their peculiar history and commitments. As to the claim that Restoration royalty needs them, Pradt reads the record: "You speak of your attachment to thrones; you begrudged Henry IV his throne; . . . you lost the Stuarts theirs."[31] In short, as Pradt sees it, the historical "virtues" of the Jesuits render them misfits for the Restoration. As his title-page epigraph has it: "Humanity is on the march, and the Jesuits can do nothing to stop it."

Another work, interesting because of its avowed effort to strike a balance, is the Liberal author Charles Laumier's *Résumé de l'histoire des Jésuites,* which also appeared in 1826.[32] In the previous year, Laumier had written a satirical novel, *L'Enfance du Jésuite,* but he insists that his later book is to be a serious effort to judge the Jesuits. Like Pradt, he adopts a historical approach, attempting to explain the present inadequacy of the Jesuits by an institutional analysis. Thanks to a series of sixteenth-century bulls, the Jesuits were exempted from the usual civil and ecclesiastical controls. In addition to specific powers, the Jesuits were granted all the powers of all other orders. Laumier concludes from this extraordinary situation that "it is impossible for a society composed of educated men, men for the most part ambitious for the greatness of their order, not to achieve excessive power when it is furnished with weapons that monarchs themselves are forced to respect. The most absolute humility could scarcely hold out against the desire to avail itself of these immense advantages."[33]

The theme of Laumier's work is that a great religious order has been perverted by time. He willingly concedes the original greatness of the Society, only to point up its historic corruption and degradation:

All the practices and laws that the founder of the order had conceived as necessary to lead its members to piety, humility, and self-abnegation were skillfully diverted and directed toward an end he never dreamt of. Regulations were modified, augmented, explicated; privileges succeeded privileges; humble men of religion became high and mighty *seigneurs*; the spirit of the order was completely inverted.[34]

Basically, however, he sees the Jesuits as victims of the privileges granted them by a host of popes and kings. These privileges were accorded in the century of the Jesuits' birth, a time when corruption was so prevalent that the idealism and devotion of the Jesuits were naturally rewarded. These privileges were disastrous because they produced pride: "Pride, as much as the doctrine of regicide, the original sin of the Society, was most injurious to them." Moreover, these privileges produced suspicion and jealousy among their natural friends: "Privileges . . . made them the eternal enemies of the other religious orders, of *curés,* of bishops, and of the universities." Most serious of all, these special rights created a desire on their part for additional power and domination, which Laumier sees as the real source of their unpopularity:

This thirst for power and money which consumed them; this insatiable thirst which made them regard all means to their ends as equally good; . . . this fanaticism which led them to interfere in secular affairs . . . in order to sow trouble, disorder, hatred, and dispute; . . . this perseverance in the pursuit and elimination of their enemies, has caused it to be said of them, more than of any other religious body, that there is nothing more formidable than the hatred of a priest.

Thus, all the traditional charges directed against the Jesuits—their Machiavellianism, their worldliness, their intolerance—are traced to this original granting of privilege.

In addition to this factor, Laumier finds another that is equally helpful in explaining the tragedy of the Jesuits. The falling away from the original purity of their intentions can be explained by their institutional structure. Chalotais, in the eighteenth-century analysis of the order which figured so prominently in their expulsion, had found the source of corruption in the Jesuit General, and specifically in his absolute power, which allowed the Generals succeeding Loyola to emulate the court of Rome and corrupt the Society from above. Laumier quotes five pages of Chalotais's analysis, and agrees that the totalitarian character of the organization has been its special strength and its peculiar weakness.[35]

Throughout his work, Laumier strengthens his position as an impartial historian by judiciously weighing the commonly circulated charges. He admits that the private lives of most Jesuits have been above reproach; as for regicides: "Yes, there have been regicides sponsored and defended by the Jesuits, but it is wrong to argue that all Jesuits are regicides. . . . If the

Society of Jesus had been composed of assassins and regicides, it would not have lasted fifty years." Yet he rejects the most intemperate of the charges only to strengthen the real case against the order:

The Jesuits have been reproached for causing demonstrations against the State. This reproach is better founded than all those we have recounted. It is true that their pride and their desire to dominate have occasioned great disorders and often troubled the public peace. For that alone, they might justly have been expelled from such tranquil kingdoms. There has scarcely been one tumultuous assembly without its Jesuit.

In his typical fashion, he softens this indictment: "However, to see them as authors or principal instigators of every conspiracy is to carry things too far."

In bringing his account down to the Restoration, Laumier is able to capitalize on his reasonable approach. The Jesuits cannot help themselves, he explains; they are the victims of their historical origin. They cannot be expected to compromise with the modern world, renounce their constitution, or change their character. To do so would be to lose the name of Jesuit. They are obliged to reappear in full historical character, with all their fatal flaws and errors. And in this form, Laumier warns his Restoration audience, "they will be dangerous to the Church and to civil society. Their appearance in the Christian world will cause a thousand worries, recall a thousand memories, and produce a thousand cries of alarm." This is, in fact, what had happened—as Laumier in 1826 well knew. And the advantage of his historical dissection is that it enables the reader—even the one who is inclined to be sympathetic to the Jesuits—to see that this reception is inevitable. Laumier seems to be saying that, though history has exaggerated the charges, the charges have been made, and a return of the Jesuits can only weaken the cause of true religion. It is interesting to see that, in concluding his argument, Laumier makes no effort to determine the accuracy of the charges made against the Jesuits during the Restoration. His argument for their removal from national life is that history has already passed judgment: "A given century will accept some institutions and reject others; our century is not favorable to the reestablishment of religious corporations, and the resurrection of the Jesuits . . . would openly go against all accepted ideas."

Except for an occasional Jesuit like Abbé Georgel,[36] the first decade of the Restoration finds few Conservatives eager to reply to the Liberal assault on the Society. For one thing, Jesuits have never been popular even within the Church. For another, a general defense of religion—with appeals to Gallican liberties, the union of throne and altar, or even the papacy—is considered more to the point. Until 1826, the defense of the Jesuits is merely incidental to this general defense. When the attack upon the Jesuits mounts in intensity, it becomes apparent that they are being used as the most vulnerable target of a Restoration antireligious campaign, and the Conservatives are then compelled to reply to the historical indictment.

Their first uncertain efforts are typified by Montfleury's reply to Abbé de Pradt. Montfleury attempts to argue that Pradt's concession of the original historical necessity of the Jesuits is proof of their true and present worth. It is particularly interesting to note the despair felt by this Conservative defender of the Jesuits at the histories being turned out. According to Montfleury, important lessons—the wisdom and justice of God—can be learned from history, but: "What is the object of almost all the histories, if not to denigrate kings and pontiffs, often by citing false or exaggerated facts, with a view to exciting the people to revolt and making them hate institutions which are necessary for social order."[37] Montfleury's display of hostility and disgust at this use of history is a familiar phenomenon, the first reaction of the Conservative to the Liberal manipulation of history.

With the Jesuits on trial before all France in the Chalotais and Montlosier affairs of 1826, a procession of Conservative pamphleteers—Bonald, Madrolle, Bellemare, Saint-Chamans*—attempt to clear up the distortions of Liberal history. But the most systematic defense—and the most remarkable example of history as the language of politics—is the series of documents that appears in 1827–30 under the editorship of the Comte de Saint-Victor,[38] setting forth the Jesuits' original answers to the original charges made against them in the seventeenth and eighteenth centuries.† Since the Liberals have organized their attack around the historical record of the Society, it is natural, inevitable, and typical of the Restoration that the Conservatives should refute these nineteenth-century attacks by reprinting the seventeenth- and eighteenth-century defenses. They must follow the Liberals back into history.

One can give only a brief idea of the range of these documents. The first series of pamphlets reprints the Jesuits' side of the controversy which led to their expulsion in 1764. There is a collection of favorable notices given the Jesuits by clergymen and Clement XIII, which is designed to meet the argument that the Jesuits were unpopular within the Church. A contemporary reply to the *Comptes rendus* is printed; it is necessary because "those today who declaim against the Jesuits do nothing else but stupidly or mechanically repeat the calumnies and abuses they get from the *Comptes rendus*."[39] One pamphlet is a defense against the specific charges presented

* See Chapter VII below for consideration of these Conservative defenders of the Restoration coalition.

† Saint-Victor was deeply involved in the defense of the religious Restoration. He had edited the *Défenseur religieux* until 1821 and had been connected in a publishing venture with Lamennais.

in 1762; another is a discussion of the events as reviewed in London four years after their exile.

In a preface, Saint-Victor notes that there is one lesson that this eighteenth-century controversy can teach the Conservative defender of the Jesuits; it is that in the eighteenth century, "the Jesuit apologias appeared late and perhaps too late."[40] The libelous attacks of Fleury and Chalotais had inflamed all France before the Jesuits could produce a reply. Further, since pro-Jesuit works were burned by order of the Parlement of Paris in 1762, the eighteenth-century defense of the Society is less accessible to Restoration France than the Liberal version. Saint-Victor set out to redress the balance; but for all his energy in assembling this Jesuit arsenal, he, like his predecessors, has arrived too late.

One pamphlet in the series, *Des Jésuites ligueurs et complices de Barrière et Jean Châtel,* offers us the rather confusing phenomenon of an apology for the Jesuits in 1827 consisting of a reprinting of a 1765 defense of Jesuit activities of the sixteenth century. Once again the Conservatives find the original defense the best way to combat the historical attack of the Liberals. Since the eighteenth-century court was trying the Jesuits of the seventeenth century, the Jesuits of 1762 naturally defended their historical conduct. The Conservative of the nineteenth century, interested in defending the Jesuits from essentially the same charges, can do no better than resurrect the defenses produced in the 1760's. As to the substance of the charge—the intimate attachment of the Jesuits to the League—the pamphlet (unlike the Liberal histories of the Restoration, a model polemic) flatly denies it. It refutes with equal efficacy the charge that Châtel was a Jesuit.

In this series, there is a pamphlet to meet virtually every charge of the Liberal historians, past and present. One hundred thirty-five pages are devoted to an elaboration of the doctrine of tyrannicide, the basis for the Liberal claim that Jesuits are regicides. To present the story graphically, two charts are included, one listing all the members of all orders who have approved of tyrannicide (there are more than sixty representatives of other orders and only sixteen Jesuits), the other listing merely "some" of the Jesuits who have flatly opposed this doctrine.[41] Another pamphlet refutes the wild fantasies surrounding the *Monita Secreta,* the secret instructions of the Jesuits; another is a full reprint of Archbishop Beaumont's pastoral Letter of 1763 in defense of the Jesuits.

Nor is the seventeenth century record neglected. A pamphlet, drawing heavily from the recently published *History of England* by the Catholic Lingard, explains the Gunpowder Plot. Saint-Victor also prints three original responses to the famous attack on Jesuit corruption in Pascal's *Les Provinciales,* which the Liberals had recalled to the attention of the Restoration.

In another attempt to answer the vilifications of Liberal historians, the authenticity of a supposed edict of Henry IV, banishing the Jesuits in 1595, is challenged. In two pamphlets, running to more than a hundred pages, the document is annihilated, and the efforts of the Liberals to exploit the hero king are headed off. The Conservatives want to have Henry IV on their side, and another essay is devoted to establishing that "it was not because he was afraid of the Jesuits that he recalled them."[42]

It is the imminent defeat of the Jesuits in 1828, and their decisive setback by the June ordinances, which finally provoke the fullest defenses. The message of these works is a warning to France that, in deposing the Jesuits for the second time, the Restoration is running the same risk as the eighteenth-century monarchy. It is one of the grim ironies of Restoration history that the fall of Charles X does come only two years and one month after the June decrees disestablishing the order.

In a series of articles in the *Conservateur de la Restauration,* Salaberry sought to turn the tide. Singling out the decisive charge, he insists: "It is not the Jesuits who kill kings, it is the Jacobins. . . . The tactic is always the same: regicides cry 'Regicide!' at others in order to conceal their own tracks." The Liberals have made the returning Jesuits a symbol for all that is wrong with Restoration France. For the Conservative, the attack upon the Jesuits is the most convenient way for the Liberals to express their true hatred for religion and monarchy: "It is the Catholic religion and legitimate monarchy which are persecuted in the Jesuit priests." In order to stress this point, Salaberry has only to hark back to the Revolution: "The tactics are the same as in '92; . . . the man of the Revolution must *écraser l'infâme* in order to attack next the anointed of the Lord; . . . he seeks to undermine the altar because the altar is in front of the throne."[43] Thus the attack upon the Jesuits in the Restoration is seen as parallel to the general attack upon religion in the Revolution—both preludes to the assault upon the throne.

In June of 1828, the Restoration campaign against the Jesuits meets with success; the Martignac administration closes the Jesuit seminaries and Jesuit "influence" is ended. Ironically, it is the defeat of the Jesuits that inspires their ablest defense, *Les Jésuites dévoilés à leurs amis et à leurs ennemis,* by Maritain de Neuwaches. The author hopes that his reappraisal of the Jesuits will help offset ten years of Liberal distortion. "Let us not reject the models of youth as its corrupters, banish the defenders of thrones as the enemies of the king, punish the benefactors and bulwarks of society as conspirators. . . . Finally, let us not brand as monsters men who are the ornament and glory of humanity."[44]

Maritain skips over the early centuries and quickly arrives at the eighteenth. Like other Conservatives, he attempts to read back into the eighteenth century the desired unity of throne and altar. This view supports his version of the Revolution, which he sees as a conspiracy among men who saw kings only as usurpers: "Two great obstacles stood in the way of the sacrilegious designs of these modern *philosophes*: Catholicism and monarchy." The men of the Revolution realized that this union rendered the two forces unassailable, so "they fawned on the great." They seized upon the issue of the Jesuits to split this mighty alliance. "Convinced that to break the religious bonds is to break the political bonds, that to overthrow religion is to overthrow the throne, . . . they chose religion as the principal object of their attack; and in order to avoid worrying the princes . . . they declared that they wished to separate the two causes." Thus, the present Liberal effort to split the coalition on the issue of the Jesuits is history repeating itself.

From the Jesuit point of view, the failure of the eighteenth-century monarchy was its failure to halt these seditious attacks, to realize that it was the monarchy itself which was being threatened. Remarkably enough, Maritain continues, the men of the Revolution did encounter strong and unexpected opposition. And from where?

They surveyed the ranks of the enemy, they looked for the men behind this sublime strength, this unalterable consistency, this invincible resistance. Alas, it was not difficult to recognize them; one has only to open one's eyes to perceive them. They are the same men who struck with dismay the spirits of Luther and Calvin, the same men who unmasked the hypocrisy of the savage Jansenist; these are the mortal enemies, the eternal scourge of the wicked—the Jesuits.

It was as a result of Jesuit opposition that the enemies of royalty "resolved above all to destroy this formidable phalanx. Despairing of destroying it themselves, they tried by calumny to render it suspect to its allies and to raise them against it. . . . The most antiquated accusations were resurrected; . . . all the great crimes, all the criminal attempts on kings, were grossly imputed to them." This description of the eighteenth-century campaign against the Jesuits mirrors nineteenth-century Liberal tactics; the dread result of these tactics is always visible to the Conservative reader. Successful in the eighteenth century, the Liberals have adopted the same formula in the Restoration.

In this discussion of the eighteenth century, one question embarrasses Maritain: How did the aristocratic parlement, the throne, and finally the pope himself, allow themselves to be persuaded by these arguments of the enemies of religion? We are asked to believe that even Pope Clement XIV succumbed to the pressure of the *philosophes*. It is one of the weaknesses of any Restoration defense of the Jesuit order that, no matter how delicately wrought it is, it must criticize the parlement and the king. At the very least, they failed to see their own interests; at worst, they are implicated in the conspiracy. The author handles this touchy problem brusquely. The parlements, "those great bodies, formerly the honor of France, paid no heed to their glorious tradition." Louis XV is treated even more harshly: "His corruption corrupted the nation's morals, his weakness undermined the monarchy, and while he slept the voluptuous and lethargic sleep of his old age, philosophy sapped religion and destroyed faith." This may be an honest verdict, but it is a killing honesty. The Liberal is in the far happier position of being able to agree with, even admire, an aristocratic parlement and a Bourbon king.

Maritain captures something of the early Restoration belief in the essential justice of the Jesuits' return in 1814, as well as the simple faith in the coalition: "Because religion had suffered more than monarchy, and because religion alone could support the newly created edifice, several measures were adopted which would restore the Jesuits to their former brilliance." The Jesuits are seen as merely one part of the general missionary task of the Restoration, "to uproot prejudices, to dissipate political suspicions, to disarm factions and reconcile them sincerely, in order to revive faith and morality."

There is something almost wistful about recalling, in 1829, the intentions of 1814. Indeed, caught in the career of the Jesuits is something of the history of the whole Restoration. Restored in 1814, they symbolize the return to stability. By 1825, they are under fire and the entire Restoration is called into question. They are defeated in 1828; this defeat marks the most successful penetration of the Restoration by the Liberals. And once again, as in the eighteenth century, their defeat heralds the larger disaster which is to engulf the regime of which they are so intimate a part.

To Maritain the pattern is all too clear. The tragedy for the Conservative is that the Restoration has neither understood nor appreciated the true history of the Jesuits: "It . . . is the history of Europe that the Society of Jesus saves nations from the shipwreck of ignorance, from heresy and anarchy, in order to establish forever the empire of believers." The Jesuit is the touchstone of loyalty to the Restoration: "History has spoken, we have heard its arguments, we know the facts, and through them we know the Jesuits and their enemies. Let us reflect and decide. What is a Jesuit? Who are the enemies of the Jesuits—who is a good citizen and who is a conspirator?"[45]

Maritain's eloquence comes too late; the June ordinances of 1828 have crowned the Liberal historians' efforts with success. At least one Conservative had seen, as early as 1825, what was behind this campaign against the Jesuits. In that year, J. F. Bellemare, a staunch defender of the Society, wrote an analysis of Liberal tactics called *Les Inquiétudes révolutionnaires.**

* Bellemare served as Commissioner General of Police under Napoleon; he was replaced by Carnot in 1814. He was extremely active in support of the Jesuits; in two years he wrote no fewer than six books in their defense: *Trois Procès en un an* (1827); *Le Conseiller des Jésuites* (1827); *Le Collège de mon fils* (1827); *La Fin des Jésuites et de bien d'autres* (1828); *Le Siècle de Fer des Jésuites* (1828); and *Les Jésuites en presence des Deux Chambres* (1828). Even in this short period, there were second editions of several of these works. Burnichon (*La Compagnie de Jésus*, I, 393, footnote) gives the numbers of copies sold.

He describes the Liberals as seeking constantly to cure the Restoration of diseases which do not exist. The first of these Liberal "worries" is the Jesuits. He sarcastically describes the motives that lie behind the Liberals' attack: "It is solely the love of royalty which inspires them; it is the perils of the realm that concern them; it is for the defense of royalty that they are armed; and if they display such bitterness in repelling the Jesuits, it is because two regicides have come from that school." Despite its sarcasm, this is an accurate summation of the Liberals' attempt to establish their own past and present loyalty to monarchy. To the Conservative Bellemare, there is only one answer to this impudence, and that is to remind the party of the Revolution that it, too, had regicides, and of more recent vintage:

Since it is as regicides that the Jesuits inspire in you such distrust and concern, kindly note that their crimes are a bit less personal and less verifiable than those of our good friends whose intentions are not suspect. . . . Take into consideration the date and the memories involved, and reflect that Jacques Clément and Ravaillac came earlier than Barère and David, and that the former are not as clearly Jesuits as the latter are regicides.

The Conservative is willing to play at comparative criminology with the Liberals on the question of regicides; he is ready to counter every reference to dubious Jesuits with real revolutionaries. Then Bellemare, with a quick twist, defends the present Jesuits from the charge of regicide with the aid of a favorite tactic of the Liberals—dissociation. Admitting that Jesuits may have been regicides, nevertheless "we recognize your principles of justice, and we know positively that they are opposed to the prosecution of children for their fathers' crimes."

Bellemare is at his most acute in seeing how the Jesuits function for the Liberals in the Restoration:

You have always needed a word of proscription with which to brand your enemies. Do you remember, among others, the words *aristocrat* and *monopolist* . . . ? Now it is the turn of *Jesuit*; it is this word that sums up all your sorrows, all your wounds, and all the calamities which can afflict the revolutionary world. You can find nothing unpleasant nowadays without assigning it this accursed name.[46]

This is indeed what the Jesuit came to be, the symbol of all that was antithetical to the New France.

For purposes of clarity, the Liberal attacks upon Ultramontanism and the Jesuits have been treated as two separate phenomena. Chronology also tends to justify this treatment, since the Gallican question dominated the early years of the Restoration, and the full-fledged attacks upon the Jesuits did not commence until after 1820. Actually, of course, the two were never entirely separate. Grégoire and Pradt take time out to snipe at the Jesuits in the midst of their general assaults upon Ultramontanism. The Ultramontanist Lamennais and even certain moderates who are anxious to preserve the coalition say an occasional kind word for the Jesuits. Bellemare lists both the concern over Gallican liberties and the fear of the Jesuits as examples of Liberal hypocrisy; it is clear to him that the Liberal assault is all of one piece. The link was as obvious in the Restoration as it appears today; the Jesuits were traditional opponents of Gallicanism and, more important, agents of Ultramontanism. One of the charges frequently directed against the Jesuits was, after all, their special oath of allegiance to the pope.

It is clear that by 1825 the two charges had merged and blurred in the mind and imagination of Liberal France, despite Conservative efforts to maintain the distinction between them. For the Liberal journalist or pamphleteer, Ultramontanist activity and Jesuit abuses were merely convenient reference points for attacking the same underlying evil. One of Béranger's verses displays the Liberal attitude, the easy linking of the two charges as part of one general indictment:

> Par Ravaillac et Jean Châtel
> Plaçons dans chaque prône
> Non point le trône sur l'autel
> Mais l'autel sur le trône.[47]

By 1825 the two attacks have, in fact, joined forces in what we now recognize as an attack upon the religious base of the Restoration. The first open challenge to this coalition can be seen in the trial of the *Constitutionnel* in 1825. Here, for the Liberals, all the threads of the preceding eight years—attacks on Ultramontanism, Jesuits, missions, and all the rest—are drawn together. Here the Restoration government seeks to strike down this threat by charging the *Constitutionnel* with crimes against religion.

CHAPTER VII

The Splitting of the Coalition

Throughout the year 1825, the Liberal campaign against the religious wing of the Restoration coalition mounted in intensity. Under the banner of Gallicanism, the Liberals assaulted Ultramontanists and Jesuits, seeking to sever the bonds between throne and altar. The government of Charles X decided that the challenge could no longer be ignored. After the Liberals' defeat in 1820, the government had cracked down on the Liberal journals, which were blamed for the assassination of the Duc de Berry. These journals, having found a fresh and popular line of attack, return with even greater vigor to batter at the coalition. The government finally decides to strike at the center of this Liberal agitation—the *Constitutionnel* and the *Courrier français.*

These are worthy foes of the coalition, particularly the *Constitutionnel,* the most popular of the Liberal dailies.* There are two separate trials; we shall concern ourselves only with the first, in which the *Constitutionnel* is charged with "outrages against the religion of the state."[1] The charge reflects the Villèle regime's awareness of the growing danger to the political-religious coalition. But it is the long-range awareness of what is at stake, expressed by both Conservative prosecution and Liberal defense, that is the most extraordinary aspect of this celebrated trial.

Bellart, who had once been named to defend Louis XVI and was attorney-general until his death in 1826, presented the case for the Crown. He begins by noting what was certainly obvious to any Conservative whose memory embraced the Revolution: that the Liberals had changed. With the usual Conservative penchant for seeing conspiracy, he conceives of this switch as conscious: "The enemies of all order, who sow trouble in order to acquire power, have had a change of plan."[2] This change, according to Bellart, was necessitated by the success of the Restoration monarchy: "Subdued by the wisdom and virtue of our kings, demagogy has lost all its guilty

* The *Constitutionnel* had 20,000 subscribers in 1825, having incorporated those of the *Minerve française,* which went out of existence in 1820. The editors of the *Constitutionnel* were Etienne, Jay, Tissot, and Thiers.

hopes; . . . it has renounced forever its senseless dreams of another dynasty." What precisely is the nature of this change?

> They no longer attack the monarchy, now that it is beloved of all; . . . but they have taken an equally unfortunate line, one that leads even further than the destruction of society itself. . . . It is religion which has today become the butt of their attacks. *Ecrasez l'infâme* is their secret rallying cry.

Bellart has perceived the principal drift of Restoration politics. The Liberals have long since abandoned any efforts to overthrow the monarchy; such sentiments remain only to a handful of Jacobins, isolated and outside of Restoration political life. By 1825, the Liberal attack is centered upon the threats emanating from the religious rather than the political Right.

Continuing his analysis, Bellart notes that these Liberals cannot attack religion openly, because "they know that would be revolt. Instead they use hypocrisy. . . . It is in the name of God that they blaspheme God." Bellart has nothing but contempt for these pseudo-Gallican Liberals: "There are those who touch theological matters only to sully them, who raise all these great questions only to inflame passions and create disorders, who feign such alarm at the ambitions of priests because they so earnestly seek their ruin, and who make such a great stir about assaults upon the liberties of the Gallican Church . . . because they wish to destroy both the Church and religion."

Next Bellart explains to the court why these Liberal journals have selected religion as their target. It is because religion is the cornerstone of society; if it falls, "the whole existing order will crumble, and every piece of debris in that universal ruin will be seized to serve as a pedestal for someone's ambition."

Bellart displays the faith of the Restoration Conservative in the efficacy of religion, as opposed to the Liberal fear of its encroachments. Here, he is less than fair to his opponents: the Liberals are trying to cut religion off from the sources of political power, but not necessarily to destroy religion or to injure the state. What Bellart fails to see and what most Royalist historians have since ignored, is that this fear of religion—though lacking an objective basis—was nevertheless real. Religious penetration of the state represented, for the men of the Revolution, all that they had fought against in the past, all that threatened them in the future. And when the Liberals turned to history to press their indictment, it was to gather ammunition to be sure, but it was also because history semed to reveal the menace of religious power even more clearly than the present.

Acquainted with this Liberal use of history, Bellart challenges its relevance to the present day: "No, it is not fanaticism that we should fear today, not the old phantom of the ambition of the clergy, evoked from the dust of tombs where its destroyed power reposes." For the prosecuting attorney, these Liberal fears are chimerical, because the spirit of the century is entirely opposed to any such resurrection of the power of the clergy. Thus, for the Conservative, the past has no relevance to the present—the danger emanates from an altogether different direction: from atheism and materialism, "the two great dissolvents of all social organization."

In this connection it is interesting to note that the *Constitutionnel* is being tried for some thirty-two separate violations—news items exposing alleged instances of clerical duplicity, Jesuit perfidy, and Ultramontanist fanaticism. This is the ground upon which the Conservative Restoration is best prepared to refute the Liberal charges. The Liberals are vulnerable at last, for they have shed the protective cloak of history; the *Constitutionnel* stands accused of attacking the religious order of the Restoration.

This is a problem for Dupin Aîné, the defense attorney, whom we have met previously (in Chapter III) as "avocat des maréchaux." By 1825, he is known as a defender of the Liberal press, and as an active anti-Jesuit. Dupin is not at all anxious to confine himself to a specific defense of the religious muckracking of his client. Instead, he turns to the larger implications of the controversy. First, he denies that the press has attacked religion by exposing "the abuses which dishonor it."[3] Indeed, for Dupin, the editors of the *Constitutionnel* are merely the most recent spokesmen in a long line of defenders of Gallican liberties. He blandly informs the court that "this cause is essentially *Gallican*,"[4] and somberly notes the recent widespread attacks on Gallicanism of which this prosecution is apparently a part. He then proceeds to convert the defense of the *Constitutionnel* into a prosecution of Ultramontanism. He seizes upon the incidents featured in the columns of the Liberal press—examples of clerical stupidity, venality, and fanaticism—and shapes them into a single thing, Ultramontanism. These minor abuses and irritants may in themselves seem insufficient to threaten society, but Dupin asks that they be examined in the light of history: "Remember these organizations, these diverse congregations, and then reread our history; think of how the League began . . . and ask yourself whether the present will not grow into the future, whether ultimately the state will not be menaced."[5] Thus, Jesuits and Ultramontanists are not to be judged by their present strength, but by what history has taught us they might become.

Still on the offensive, Dupin insists that it is not the *Constitutionnel* that is threatening society, but the forces it has exposed: "It is evident that they endanger the independence of the monarchy, since they proclaim the unlimited sovereignty of a foreign sovereign." Equally threatened are "civil liberties, which rest, as we have seen, upon the liberties of the Gallican Church and the Declaration of 1682."[6]

Ultramontanism is a charge that will convince the Liberals, who crowd the courtroom, but how effective is it as an appeal to the court? The royal court is presided over by Séguier, the descendant of a famous eighteenth-century magistrate, and this, perhaps, is all the inspiration that Dupin needs. He hits upon a tactic that is to play havoc with the Restoration coalition—the appeal to the class pride of the magistracy.* He draws an analogy between the eighteenth-century action of the parlements against the Jesuits and the present opportunity of this court; he offers the court the occasion to regain its eighteenth-century vigor and strike a blow for freedom: "When you have protected civil liberties by a decree that will go down in history with those of your predecessors, you will have earned the people's gratitude." He concludes with a bold plea to the magistrates to judge this case not in the light of the evidence alone, but in the light of tradition: "Examine your consciences, then; take counsel only of your doctrines, of your historical memories, . . . of your ideas on the future of France, of your love for the prince and the country, and finally, of your glory and your dignity."[7] Dupin's plea succeeded in fusing the Liberal attack; Gallican liberties are exalted, Ultramontanist pretensions scored, and the class pride of the magistrates flattered.

On December 3, 1825, the magistracy acceded to this powerful Liberal plea to reassert its venerable role as protector of the people, and reentered the arena to combat the pretensions of the clergy. In the words of the court:

> [We consider that] it is neither a lack of respect, nor an abuse of the freedom of the press, to dispute and contest the introduction and establishment of all associations not authorized by law; . . . and to point out the dangers and excesses of a doctrine which threatens, at the same time, the independence of the monarchy, the sovereignty of the king, and the civil liberties guaranteed by the constitutional Charter and by the Declaration of 1682, a declaration always recognized and proclaimed as a law of the state.[8]

Thus, for the first time, the courts enter this Restoration struggle over throne and altar. The decision was hailed by Liberal France; its dream had been partially realized—a new and powerful voice had been added; an ancient force in society, the aristocratic courts, had resumed its historic struggle with the clergy. Conservative France was stunned, but no one yet dreamed how significant this opposition was to become. Within three months this magistracy was to be involved in a celebrated trial in which its representatives were not only the judges but the prosecutors as well.

It began innocently enough. In January of 1826, an obscure bookseller decided to take advantage of the praise being heaped upon the courts as a result of the popular acquittal of the *Constitutionnel* and the *Courrier français*. To this end he reprinted a portrait of La Chalotais, a famous Breton magistrate, the author of the well-known *Comptes rendus*, and a key figure

* Bellart had also appealed to the magistracy; in concluding his opening accusation, he flattered the court by noting that thanks to the spirit of the magistracy, religion was not in danger.

in the eighteenth-century expulsion of the Jesuits. To have been a famous anti-Jesuit was sufficient reason to have one's portrait hawked on the streets of Paris in 1826. On January 27, the *Courrier français,* fresh from the legal vindication of its anticlerical campaign, casually and benignly commented on this portrait:

. . . it could be said that the noise of the chains now being rattled by Jesuitism has raised this illustrious attorney-general from the depths of his tomb. This face of a magisterial patriot attracts the passer-by's attention. What a lesson for those who, like La Chalotais, know how to stand fast before the disdain and disapproval of the powerful. . . . At his voice, the Jesuits were banished; a hydra, as it seemed, fled the soil of France.[9]

Thus far we have a rather commonplace Restoration example of the uses of history—a portrait is taken out of the historical attic, dusted off, and put to use as a reminder to Frenchmen that the Jesuits had been banished. What transformed this incident into a *cause célèbre* of the Restoration was a series of remarks in the Conservative clerically minded *Etoile.* In the issue of February 2, the *Etoile* notes the increasing tendency to revive the magistracy: "The people venerate the magistracy. Let us, then, say the enemies of religion, oppose the magistracy to the clergy; let us destroy this happy accord in which, with a single scandalous exception, the clergy and the courts have dwelt. They seize every opportunity to recall the ancient rivalry of the Jesuits and the parlements."

It is this "single scandalous exception" that concerns them:

To this end, they have just exhumed the supposed portrait of an obscure magistrate of the former parlement of Brittany, because he was courageous and powerful enough to sign the first indictment against the Jesuits; whereupon their journals instantly announced that there were throngs *chez* Soyer, 19 rue de Cadran, seeking to buy this fine portrait of the illustrious attorney-general La Chalotais. They have had the effrontery to single out for the nation's admiration a traitorous judge; a man who, contemptuous of duty and judicial impartiality and filled with the odious spirit of personal hatred, prosecuted a respectable body whose influence and learning amounted, in the eyes of a proud and ignorant magistracy, to the crime of *leze* [*sic*] *nation*; finally, a man who was soon afterward stripped of the honorable title his king had believed him worthy of, and dragged out his repentance in exile and ignominy.

Here, then, are the men who are held up to youth as noble apostles of the rights of the throne and of civil liberties.[10]

In these words are contained: (1) an attack upon the person of a French magistrate, including charges of disloyalty to monarchy as well as prejudice to religion; (2) an attack upon the trial that led to the expulsion of the Jesuits; (3) a general defense of the Jesuits; and (4) an attack upon those seeking to revive discredited historical figures as examples for present conduct.

It is no wonder that this paragraph had the force of a bombshell. In a single column, the *Etoile* achieved what all the Liberal historians had striven to produce—the reopening of the basic struggle between the eighteenth-century parlements and the Jesuits, as well as the still older, more general contest of aristocracy *vs.* clergy.

The reaction was immediate. The very next day, the *Constitutionnel* comes to the defense of La Chalotais in the name of the aristocratic magistracy, local pride, and national honor:

> A name venerated and esteemed throughout France becomes for *L'Etoile* the butt of the grossest calumnies.
>
> What will ancient Brittany say, where this name is revered almost as a titular divinity? Ghosts of Charette, Labourdonnaye, Kersalaun, La Fruglaye, forsake your tombs, you who share these noble sentiments and had the honor of sharing these disgraces and persecutions.[11]

For those Restoration readers who do not understand the references, the *Constitutionnel* helpfully provides a footnote identifying these men as Breton magistrates who were dismissed along with La Chalotais. The *Etoile*, in its attempt to discredit La Chalotais, had revived an old affair, one that had little to do with the controversy over the Jesuits: the struggle of the Breton parlement against the king. Coming after the successful prosecution of the Jesuits, this struggle had broken and disgraced La Chalotais and the other magistrates recalled by the *Constitutionnel.*

Significantly, the Liberal journal, before going on to the real issue, takes care to side with the aristocracy in this old struggle against monarchy. The importance of this shift cannot be overestimated. It is the measure of how completely the attack upon religion has supplanted the earlier attack upon aristocracy that the *Constitutionnel* can sing the praises of an independent Breton nobility. Moreover, it marks a fundamental rift in the coalition and a new realignment; prominent members of the aristocracy, Chateaubriand and Montlosier, are joining the camp of the Liberals on the issue of religious domination of the State.

Habitual readers of the *Constitutionnel* must have blinked at seeing a traditional aristocratic body warmly defended; at being asked, for example, to deplore the fact that "magistrates who, under the old monarchy, defended the rights of individual citizens, of the throne, and of the public are called traitors." But the *Constitutionnel* knows what it is doing. The eighteenth-century parlements, in their battle against the Jesuits, are models for the Restoration. That is why the *Etoile* has attacked La Chalotais and why the Liberals will defend him:

> Here is his crime in the eyes of *L'Etoile*. He attacked the Jesuits, the Jesuits who were suppressed by all the parlements of France by the edict of 1764; expelled by Spain, by Portugal, by Naples; abolished by the sovereign pontiff himself. For this, *L'Etoile* condemns him to exile and ignominy, and insults the entire magistracy. . . . Does *L'Etoile* know who these magistrates were? Has it

studied their procedures, their *doctrines* . . . Has it learned to recognize their . . . devotion to throne and country, their independence, their courage?

It would be abusing the patience of our readers to go into a long refutation of *L'Etoile*. Public indignation and contempt must suffice to render justice.[12]

Public indignation and contempt are, in fact, the order of the day. On February 8, the *Etoile* is forced to take note of the gathering storm. It answers the criticism by extending the attack on La Chalotais and introducing a fresh set of charges:

M. de La Chalotais was a friend of d'Alembert, the reputed editor of the *comptes rendus* of the atheist Diderot and Voltaire, two men who desired the destruction of the Jesuits in order to lead to the overthrow of religion. . . . Having become attorney-general of the Parlement of Brittany, he declared, despite the expressed command of the king, . . . that the king had been misled in religious matters; and he was one of those who contributed most to the fall of this celebrated Society, the first triumph of the enemies of monarchy and the social order. After the harm done to education by the suppression of the Jesuits, he produced a book on education at the same time as Diderot and Rousseau. *One finds*, said an apologist for M. de La Chalotais, *his plan very similar to Diderot's.*

In this way La Chalotais, the eighteenth-century aristocrat, is linked by the *Etoile* with the conspiracy of the *philosophes.* His attack upon the Jesuits is seen as part of the general Enlightenment effort to weaken the monarchy by removing the Jesuits. To cement this charge, the *Etoile* indulges in a bit of guilt by association and analogy—La Chalotais was a friend of the *philosophes,* and his eighteenth-century treatise on education, an edition of which had appeared in 1825, bears resemblance to the general educational theories of the Enlightenment.

This second attack in the *Etoile* went far beyond the first; to the charge of personal malice against the Jesuits is added conscious conspiracy against the State. And to strengthen this charge of treason, the *Etoile* goes into detail on La Chalotais's career, reviving forgotten chapters of eighteenth-century history:

In the affair of the Duc d'Aiguillon, M. de La Chalotais was one of those who were most noted for their opposition to the king's orders. Two infamous anonymous notes against the king were declared by experts to be written in his hand. He and his son were arrested and imprisoned in the chateau of Saint Mâlo. . . . M. de La Chalotais only left prison to be sent into exile . . . and it was only after ten years, and under Louis XVI, that he returned to Rennes.

History is an uncertain and treacherous weapon in the Restoration. In its effort to dispose of this early prosecutor of the Jesuits, the *Etoile* has unwittingly revived a deep and ancient bitterness in French life, the aristocratic revolutionary tradition which the Restoration coalition tries so hard to forget. According to the *Etoile,* the return of La Chalotais from exile presaged disaster: "Everyone knows that the parlements were recalled under that unfortunate prince [Louis XVI] and that they brought on all the innovations."

The reminder of the aristocratic revolution is a sensitive part of the indictment. The opposition press had been quick to recall that the son of this La Chalotais had been guillotined in 1794. For the *Etoile,* the death of the son is a judgment on the activities of the father:

> The son of M. de La Chalotais died under the revolutionary axe in 1794, a victim of the disciples of the *philosophes,* his father's friends, who will find defenders today only among those who never stop singing the praises of the Revolution of 1789.
>
> It is clear from all the facts we have just reported that M. de La Chalotais, whatever his intentions, was one of the men who contributed to the fall of the Bourbons. The admiration accorded him by the *Constitutionnel* and the *Courrier* is understandable, but it is not astonishing that we should have entirely different feelings toward him.[13]

The Liberal press reported the attack on La Chalotais as an insult to the aristocratic parliamentary tradition, but for the *Etoile,* Liberal admiration for La Chalotais can be explained simply as support of a fellow conspirator.

The controversy seemed to rest here for a moment, but in March it flares up again. The family of La Chalotais intervenes. In a letter published in the Liberal *Courrier français,* as well as in the *Journal des débats* and the Conservative *Quotidienne,* the family announces its intention to sue the *Etoile* for libel. The *Etoile* posts a reply to all the papers which printed the letter, noting, among other things, that the Liberal journals "only honor M. de La Chalotais for having served in the destruction of a body . . . approved by twenty popes, . . . and for having resisted royal authority."[14]

The trial is not scheduled to open until March 29, but interest does not flag in the interim. On March 22, the *Constitutionnel* publishes, on its front page, a warning of the Parlement of Paris of 1768 that the Jesuits expelled from France are slipping back. The following day, the *Etoile* sticks by its defense of the Jesuits: "It is terrible to be obliged every day to repel the attacks that Liberal fanatics and the ignorant direct against [the Jesuits]. . . . However, it is necessary to repel these attacks because history, especially ecclesiastical history, is not well known."[15]

Plainly disturbed at the turn of events, the *Etoile* tries to steer the discussion back to the basic question, the Liberal attack upon religion. The appearance of the powerful La Chalotais family and all that it represents convinces the editors that they must backtrack on the question of treason and emphasize instead the error of La Chalotais in attacking the Jesuits. They are defiant on the Jesuit question: "Nothing can prevent us from proclaiming aloud that La Chalotais vigorously served the enemies of religion by his charge against the Jesuits."[16] They are equally adamant on the general role of the parlements. "We still submit that M. de La Chalotais pushed the idea of the power of the parlements too far, and that he became the instrument of men who hoped to destroy royal power, with the aid of parliamentary maxims."

But they are least certain about the effort to discredit La Chalotais personally. They admit the possibility that the family may possess documents which will exonerate their ancestor: "*L'Etoile* only knows the accounts of the time, the public clamor, . . . a sort of notoriety often consistent with the truth but often contrary to it; often, at least, subject to great exaggeration." The editors are plainly uncomfortable at the turn of events and plead ignorance; God alone is the judge of men; the newspaper could be wrong; besides, it was only reporting the general consensus of eighteenth-century opinion on Chalotais. As a final concession to head off a trial, they agree to withdraw the charge of the anonymous letters, offering full rectification, "in order to avoid giving the Liberals the spectacle of a debate between Royalists, a debate which the Liberals themselves have provoked." The fear of the *Etoile*—the fear of the Conservative coalition—is clearly expressed: for the first time, an aristocratic family is suing a Royalist newspaper over the existence of a religious order. The *Etoile*, in a desperate bid to prevent this cleavage, accuses the Liberal newspapers, "who, far from seeking to excuse the conduct of M. de La Chalotais, propose that it serve as an example to magistrates present and future." But this plea to close ranks does not prevail; it is too late, the insult has been uttered. As the *Quotidienne* moaned: "Everyone has read the article in *L'Etoile*."[17]

The offended members of the family were grandchildren of the controversial La Chalotais—Mlle de la Chalotais and M. de la Fruglaye. The latter had been an émigré general and was, at the time, representing Brittany in the Chamber of Deputies. Both these plaintiffs had as their lawyer Berryer, already a distinguished Royalist spokesman. Two other descendants of La Chalotais, Kermarec and Montbourcher, were also suing; they were represented by Bernard, a Liberal lawyer from Rennes.[18]

The trial, which opened on March 29, had three sessions in all and was concluded on April 29. The atmosphere of the first session is caught in one pamphlet: "An extraordinary assemblage of spectators laid early siege to the doors of the police court. The Jesuits, who more than sixty years ago were condemned to eternal oblivion, were going to justify the assertion enunciated by the Parlement of Rouen in its decree of May 19, 1767: that *experience taught that the Society of Jesus had the gift of being reborn from its ashes*."[19] The affair was popularly conceived of as a trial of the Jesuits. But what gave the trial its special excitement was that the attack in the *Etoile* had brought into the arena no mere Liberal editor, no *philosophe*-turned-historian, but the surviving members of a distinguished family, themselves representing the French nobility and its supreme political expression, the parlement.

Berryer, an unimpeachable Royalist, immediately indicates the line he is to take, demanding "severe penalties for a journalist who, while affecting monarchical principles and sentiments, wounds consciences, stigmatizes the past, and insults names dear to the throne." For Berryer, the trial is an affair of honor, and he goes to great lengths to establish what is, in fact, the only legal issue at stake—the right of descendants to sue in defense of their family name.

Anticipating the *Etoile's* defense, Berryer raises the question of the rights of history, acknowledging that La Chalotais has been dead for many years. He professes all respect for the rights of history, but "the pen of the historian is not the knife of the *libelliste.*" He reads the offending paragraph and asks: "Is this the language of history, gentlemen? What is meant by historical facts, historical truths, historical judgments?"

Berryer sees that the basic charges against La Chalotais are two: his publication of the *Comptes rendus* and his activities against royal authority. To prove the *Etoile* libelous, it would appear necessary to return to the past and justify the ideas and actions of La Chalotais. Berryer seems on the brink of doing this, but he hesitates; he is too good a Royalist: "It would be wrong to summon up the passions of this battlefield where our fathers fought sixty years ago." Thus, on the issue of the Jesuits, Berryer is determined not to split the coalition, not to reopen a conflict that can only benefit the Liberals. Indeed, he attempts to heal the breach by picturing La Chalotais as having no basic animosity toward the Jesuits, and by arguing that the vigor of the eighteenth-century prosecution has been exaggerated. Berryer himself accepts the Conservative view of the necssity of the Jesuits, and tries—by the ingenious device of quoting favorable references to the Jesuits made by *philosophes*—to reduce the fundamental conflict to a simple case of mistaken identity.

If Berryer refuses to add fuel to the Jesuit controversy, he does take a strong stand on the second charge—La Chalotais's supposed treason to the monarchy. For if he is embarrassed by La Chalotais the anti-Jesuit, he is not ashamed of La Chalotais the representative of the tradition of independent parlements. He reminds the court: "Brittany had its parlement, Brittany had its estates. This fierce and generous province was jealous of its franchise, its customs, its privileges. At times its magistrates found themselves opposed to the royal will expressed in the name of the king; without ceasing to be faithful subjects, they knew how to reconcile liberty with obedience."

Thus, as a notable by-product of the religious controversy, the tradition of aristocratic independence is asserted. La Chalotais is seen as one of a long line of defenders of the ancient liberties. It is the charge that La Chalotais has been stripped of the title of magistrate that calls forth Berryer's bitterest words: "He was stripped, you said, of the honorable title of which his king believed him worthy. What ignorance and malice! Editor of *L'Etoile*, whom have you questioned about the rights and the dignity of a magistrate of France?"

In defense of La Chalotais's name, Berryer is driven to defend the aristocratic magistracy: "Consider what the magistracy was in the old days of the monarchy; look at Lavacquerie before Louis XI, the governor of Orthez writing to Charles IX; reread in the memoirs of Castelnau the touching and noble conversation between Francis I and M. de Mesmes." For Berryer it is not only La Chalotais who has been insulted, but the Breton nobility and the magistracy as a class. Having insisted upon their independence, he concludes by defending their loyalty in terms reminiscent of the Liberal Dupin's eulogy.

When Bernard takes up the defense of his clients, the atmosphere of the trial changes.* To Bernard, the Jesuits are the issue, and he reduces the whole affair to an epigram: "La Chalotais accused, the Jesuits accusers. That, gentlemen, is the spectacle offered you, and that is what astonishes me."[20]

But he gives his own version of this newest discovery of the Liberals, the parlements, which he regards as the only check to absolute power in their time, as indeed the eighteenth-century version of representative assemblies: "To the extent that one can make such comparisons, the parlements were the equivalent of the representative assembly, which today forms the essence of our government." Reading back into the eighteenth century his nineteenth-century Liberal prejudices, Bernard conceives of this ancient aristocratic body as the brake on all forms of absolute authority. Thus the collision between parlements and Jesuits—regretted by Berryer—is seen by Bernard as inevitable: "If the Jesuits had acted only in the realm of spiritual things, would the parlements have been alarmed?"

This version of the parlements as enemies of absolutism would seem to justify the *Etoile's* thinly veiled charge that the parlements had played into the hands of the Revolution by destroying the Jesuits. It is particularly important to refute this charge because it is the basis for the Jesuits' existence in the Restoration. In supporting the Jesuits, the Conservatives always asserted that the expulsion paved the way for the Revolution. Bernard denies any such connection: "What human mind could have predicted the course of this great and immense movement [the Revolution]? . . . In suppressing the Jesuits, the parlements had in mind the preservation of royal power . . . and to see the abolition of the Society as the move which thirty years later lost the throne of the unfortunate King Louis XVI, is to substitute the logic of passion for the logic of history." The Liberal indictment of the Jesuits

* Bernard had been appointed *conseiller* to the Court of Appeal at Rennes by Napoleon, a position which he lost under the Restoration. Like Dupin, he was a defender of General Travot.

is that they are jealous of royalty, a charge based upon the history of the order's dangerous and disloyal conduct toward kings. The eighteenth-century prosecutors must, therefore, be shown to have acted in the king's interests.

The parlements, according to Bernard, were both defenders of the people's interests and loyal supporters of the monarchy. These are not irreconcilable; indeed Bernard sees in them a foreshadowing of the constitutional monarchy of the Restoration. The parlements "gave men the first idea of this government under which we have the good fortune to live." And for Bernard it is not accidental that the *Etoile* has lashed out against La Chalotais, but rather part of a general campaign to destroy this ancient aristocracy, led by the Jesuits in alliance with the party of absolutism.

Having paid his respects to this ancient aristocracy—his real clients—Bernard proceeds to the matter that really interests him. The core of the *Etoile's* attack is La Chalotais's "persecution" of the Jesuits, and, as Bernard explains before carrying his audience back into the eighteenth century, "I must pursue the calumny."

Berryer had held that it was not necessary to discuss the *Comptes rendus*; Bernard, on the contrary, is most anxious to conduct his defense on the terrain of history, where, after all, the charges rest. Indeed, La Chalotais is such a windfall for the Liberals because the very nature of the charges compels an examination of the eighteenth-century quarrel. Bernard sees himself as defense counselor for that eighteenth-century verdict against the Jesuits: "I must justify that his prosecution . . . was just, that it was necessary, that it was the duty of a public official." Again he distinguishes his defense from Berryer's: "You have said that La Chalotais was neither a traitor nor a liar. . . . I will do more; I will prove it."

He grows indignant at the attempt to soft-pedal the Jesuit question:

> What! It has been printed and published that our ancestor prosecuted the Jesuits because he was "contemptuous of duty and judicial impartiality" . . . and you do not want me to speak of the Jesuits; and you bar me from proving that the *Comptes rendus* are neither the work of hatred nor the work of animosity, but a legal, serious, severe, impartial act of a magistrate faithful to all his duties!

The outcome of this eighteenth-century trial is relevant to the Restoration: "I hear the Jesuits spoken of everywhere. They are accused, they are defended, they are recalled, they are rejected; but ultimately, I do not see them in any sense legally reestablished in France. No . . . public act recognizes them, or even mentions their name." The importance of opening this case is that, as the Liberals have long insisted, the decision to expel the Jesuits has never been abrogated by the French government. The pope has reestablished the order, but officially the expulsion of 1764, stemming out of the prosecution by La Chalotais, has never been rescinded. Thus, to revive the trial that resulted in their expulsion is to recall to France that the Jesuits are still operating under this legal expulsion, that they have no legal existence in the Restoration.

From this point on, Bernard's plea is a familiar recital of the arguments of the Liberal historians. First the weight of history:

The Jesuits were condemned after long examination, and in a time when they could be more easily investigated than today; they were proscribed by the whole magistracy of Europe, by the entire Church rising against them, by kings who regarded them as enemies of their power, finally by the supreme head of Christianity. Do we wish to say today that so many voices were falsely raised against this Society? Do we wish, in order to absolve it, to condemn all those who declared themselves against it?

For those not impressed by the judgments of secular history, Bernard cites the opinion of Clement XIV.

Bernard succeeds in turning the La Chalotais case of 1826 into a retrial of 1762. The issue to be judged, then and now, is the Jesuits. If La Chalotais was right, the Jesuits were indeed a threat to France. One again sees the extraordinary relevance of the past to the present, in that an event sixty years past can be thought to bear so directly on the fortunes of the Restoration. And in retrying the eighteenth-century case, Bernard is compelled to use as evidence—as La Chalotais did—the accumulated evidence of the centuries. Fortunately for Bernard and the Liberals, the charges of La Chalotais against the Jesuits are essentially the charges of Restoration Liberalism.

Bernard insists that the Jesuit order should be judged not only by its crimes, but "by its spirit, its doctrine, its system of association, . . . by its potential influence on the State . . . , especially by its ability to endanger the safety of thrones and peoples." Clément and Châtel are of little importance compared with the Jesuits' basic fault—so pitilessly revealed by history—their threat to society. La Chalotais was justified because "the Society of Jesus was all-powerful, more powerful than kings, than peoples; for that reason alone, it should have been abolished." And Bernard becomes still more specific: The parlements attacked an order which "under the mask of religion . . . advanced openly to the domination of all temporal things, driving the State into the Church and the throne under the pulpit!"

More and more the prosecution of the *Etoile* takes on the character of a retrial, and just as La Chalotais provides Restoration Liberals with a precedent for getting rid of the Jesuits, La Chalotais himself is given the precedent of Louis XIV: "When Louis XIV made the clergy of France sign the Declaration of 1682, when he opposed this barrier to the pretensions of Ultramontanists . . . , was Louis XIV a 'proud and ignorant' monarch? Are all the kings who have defended their power against the enterprises of the court of Rome criminals?"

The links are forged: Louis XIV, La Chalotais, Restoration Liberals—

all have battled Ultramontanism. By establishing this tradition, that La Chalotais acted in the same interest as Louis XIV, Bernard has demonstrated the essential patriotism of this anti-Jesuit tradition. This is the key point of the debate. In defending the Revolution, and in attacking the Jesuits, the Liberals claim they are acting in the best interests of the monarchy.

Concluding his defense of La Chalotais, Bernard cries: "In attacking the Jesuits, he did more than make use of his right: he accomplished a duty. The existence of the Society was incompatible with the independence of the crown, with the safety of the State." As for the immediate issue of the litigation, Bernard reduces it to a simple choice: a choice "between the family of La Chalotais, which has been illustrious for six centuries, and the Jesuits, banished thirty-eight times from the states of Europe, and whose history is only a succession of *attentats.*" Herein is precisely the value of the La Chalotais trial for the Liberals: it forces a choice between two pasts upon a Restoration coalition which has sought to bury the past.

The La Chalotais affair presents one oddity, a reversal of the usual Restoration roles. This time it is not a Liberal journal that stands in the docket; it is a loyal, Conservative newspaper accused of libel. And though the Conservative is once again in the position of denying the validity of history, the *Etoile's* defense is predicated upon the inalienable right of the historian to judge the past. It is on this issue—the simple right of a newspaper to pass judgment on historical figures without incurring charges of libel—that Hennequin, the attorney for the *Etoile,* makes his strongest case.* Indeed it is this same, generally recognized principle which has allowed Liberals to operate under the relative immunity of history. Hennequin cleverly adopts a standard Liberal argument—the enormous changes wrought by the Revolution—to argue that, in a sense, the events of 1762 happened centuries ago; he refers to the "troubles of parlements in legendary times." To get the facts of the La Chalotais case, one must "sort out thousands of memories," and Hennequin is able to demonstrate convincingly that "M. de La Chalotais belongs to history."[21] Ironically, it is this argument—the immunity of the past—that is critical in the decision. The *Etoile* is chastised for having unjustly accused La Chalotais, but the rights of history are upheld and the complaint is dismissed.

An interesting sidelight on the trial is Bernard's effective refutation of the charge of La Chalotais's hatred and bias against the Jesuits by reading long quotations from La Chalotais himself. Bernard asks: How could the editors of the *Etoile* have been so mistaken? Clearly, the *Etoile* has chosen the worst possible ground upon which to refute the attackers of Jesuitism. La Chalotais is revealed as a careful gatherer of facts, and an intelligent,

* Hennequin was Dupin's Conservative counterpart. He had defended Fiévée in his difficulty in 1818 (see Chapter IV above), and appeared in all the great trials in defense of throne and altar.

subtle, and essentially fair-minded critic. The Liberals, who have accepted the eighteenth-century verdict unquestioningly, are now delighted to discover how damaging a case La Chalotais did build. Bernard himself unwittingly offers a clue when he wonders "how to explain such a slander at the very time when the most alarming rumors about the reestablishment of the order are heard every day."[22] It is possible that, in a period of embittered attack upon the Jesuits and of Liberal espousal of the eighteenth century, the *Etoile* simply read back the virulence of contemporary critics without checking. Whatever the explanation, its assault on Louis René de Caradeuc de La Chalotais was an unfortunate mistake, for not only did it antagonize the aristocracy, but it provided the Liberals with a fresh and powerful voice in their campaign to oust the Jesuits.

With the battle raging in the press and in the court, the Liberals were quick to exploit the "obscure" eighteenth-century magistrate. *La Petite Bibliographie,* selling for only fifty sous a volume, announces La Chalotais's *Résumé des doctrines des Jésuites* as the second volume in its series, which is also to include a translation of the Jesuit institutes and a life of Saint Ignatius. In the course of the year 1826, three editions of La Chalotais's famous *Comptes rendus* were reprinted, as well as two of his Résumés, and three editions of the memoirs. All these reprintings illustrate the political uses of history in the Restoration; the original indictments of the Jesuits, the accounts of the struggle, scarcely need any retouching before being thrown into the Restoration campaign.

Nevertheless, the publishers of these volumes leave no doubt about their intentions. The publisher of the *Résumé des constitutions des Jésuites* proudly announces that he is reprinting "in convenient and portable form, this résumé of the Institutes of the Jesuits which was presented in 1762. It is the work of Caradeuc de La Chalotais, a Breton magistrate of laudable virtue." The work itself is a long extract from the institutes, so arranged as to indict the Jesuits for their shiftiness, their secrecy, their independence of all authority. The publisher concludes: "Add to these the testimony of all the histories, the constant and uniform complaints from one continent to the other, and know that you will seek in vain to reform a body which counts as one of its prerogatives that of being unreformable. . . . Everything there smacks of abuse; everything calls for dissolution."[23]

Gilbert de Voisins, an enemy of the Jesuits whom we have already encountered, exploits the trial in a typical Liberal manner. He rushes the memoirs of La Chalotais into print even before the trial is over. "The plea . . . of the descendants of M. de La Chalotais reawakens public interest in this illustrious magistrate and offers a natural occasion to reprint his memoir to the king." He gives the background of this eighteenth-century trial: "A financial scandal on the part of the Jesuits furnished the occasion to examine their institutes, their secret ambitions, their plans for universal domination, their perverse doctrines, and their monstrous teachings on homicide and regicide."[24]

Whatever the outcome of the trial, Gilbert de Voisins feels that the La Chalotais family has done its duty; it has fought well for the rights of Brittany, and he hopes it will not abandon these rights "when they have become the heritage of all Frenchmen, . . . that it will employ this noble energy in the defense of the Charter."[25] The Liberals hope that this conflict will lead to a realignment; that the aristocrats—on the issue of the Jesuits—will heed their traditions and unite with the Liberals.

During the trial, the debate continues to rage in the press. The *Etoile* pursues its defense of the Jesuits: "It is clear today that the same ideas which caused the Jesuits to be expelled are those which caused the Revolution. . . . Everything comes down to this: You defend the ideas which made the Revolution; we defend those which could have prevented it and which alone can prevent its return."[26] The *Etoile,* disturbed by the La Chalotais case, is trying to reassert the traditional alignment; those *against* the Revolution should be *for* the Jesuits. That is the logic of the Restoration, and that is why the La Chalotais case is such a threat.

Despite these pleas, it is noteworthy that the *Etoile* is attacked on all sides for its Ultramontanism, and for refusing to subscribe to the principles of 1682.[27] Its editors reply: "We believe ourselves far happier to be Christians than Frenchmen."[28] On April 23, the *Etoile* reprints (in the seventeenth-century spelling) Henry IV's order of 1603, reestablishing the Jesuits. And though the court's decision has already been rendered, on May 1 another article appears, proving that Jacques Clément, the assassin of Henry III, was not a Jesuit but a Dominican; that Jean Châtel was only educated by the Jesuits, as was Voltaire; that Ravaillac was refused admission to the Society and told to go home. So much for the charge of regicide, shouted "by those who assassinated . . . [three kings] and the Duc de Berry."[29]

Perhaps the most piercing analysis of Restoration politics to emerge from the La Chalotais affair is the *Etoile's* discussion of a question that perplexed many Conservatives—the origin of all this talk about the Jesuits. The *Etoile* gives a brief synopsis of French history since the Revolution. At first the cry was "aristocrats to the lamppost." The return of the Bourbons posed a problem for the Liberals: "They found it difficult to reproach the Royalists with loving the king, so they hit upon the idea of reproaching them with loving him too much, and an assassin of Louis XVI invented for them the sobriquet Ultras. . . . The disciples of Robespierre and Marat became the constitutionalists *par excellence*; they alone loved the Charter."[30] This is, in fact, an accurate description of the early Liberal emphasis upon the aristocrats as their enemy.

In attempting to explain when and how the Jesuits supplanted the aristocrats as the Liberal scapegoat—a legitimate historical question—the *Etoile* can offer only invective. The Liberals simply grew tired of the old slogans, the newspaper explains; they needed new ones, but

> the most industrious minds could not find an idea. . . . Suddenly someone or other pronounced the word Jesuit, and flagging spirits revived. "Jesuit," repeated all the echoes . . . , "we are saved." Since this happy moment, indeed, the children of Ignatius are everywhere . . . ; they command our armies and our fleets, administer our departments; they have allowed the king only his throne, and God knows if some day . . . Already our old *conventionnels* and their pupils tremble for the brother of Louis XVI.[31]

While the La Chalotais trial was cutting across all natural alliances, confusing and dividing the coalition, an even larger clash was brewing. This was the Montlosier case; a product of the religious agitation of the Restoration, it marks the culmination of the Liberal effort to split the coalition by driving the aristocracy into combat with the clergy.

The name of La Chalotais burst upon the Restoration in 1826; a name out of the past, it might have remained there but for the accidental confluence of an enterprising Liberal book dealer and an intemperate Conservative editor. But Montlosier was a name well known to the Restoration, and there is something almost inevitable in his step-by-step career that led to the explosion of 1826.

Montlosier had been a Liberal aristocrat in 1789 and had emigrated in 1791.[32] Ironically, his revolutionary fame rested upon a passionate defense of the French clergy. In exile he belonged to the Liberal Royalist group of Lally-Tollendal and Mallet du Pan, and quarreled with the more extreme of his fellow émigrés. He returned in 1801 and served Napoleon, under whom he began his four-volume *De la Monarchie française,* a historical defense of aristocracy. At the outset of the Restoration, Montlosier placed himself in opposition to the Ultras and to the attempt to form French society upon the union of Church and Throne. As early as 1815, he recognized the curious role he was to play: "I approve of the nobility, and I am forced to criticize the conduct of the nobles. I approve of liberty, and I am forced to speak against the doctrines dearest to the friends of liberty. I approve of religion, and I am obliged to write against the pretensions of priests."[33]

This statement gives us the clue to Montlosier's special strength in the Restoration. As historian and champion of the role of the French aristocracy, he was often referred to as a nineteenth-century incarnation of Boulainvilliers, unimpeachable credentials for the Restoration aristocracy.[34] As Royalist, he is equally sound; he stood between the Liberals who wanted to continue the Revolution and the Ultras who called for a blind return to the past. Guizot's *Archives* rejected Montlosier's peculiar brand of compromise ("an effort to employ the men of the Revolution to unmake the Revolution"), but noted the difficulty of handling him. "His ideas are aristocratic; his sentiments liberal and generous."[35]

As for his religious attitude, Montlosier was that special amalgam to be found in French history, the religious anticlerical. With curious logic, he charges the clergy with the crime of being hated throughout French history, observing with relish that "je rénie Dieu" was on the lips of his Frankish ancestors and common in the army at the time of Henry IV. According to Montlosier, this hatred of priests—not to be confused with hatred of religion—was responsible for everything from the earliest heresies to the French Revolution.

As early as 1815, Montlosier had already singled out as his special enemy the newly returned Jesuits. With a candor that is seldom to be matched in the Liberal campaign, Montlosier reveals that he is hostile to the Jesuits because they represent the extension of all the unfortunate tendencies within the clergy as a whole, notably the desire to invade the temporal order. They have suffered accordingly: "A great deal has been said about the cause of their fall, but the true cause has not been understood; Calvinism, Jansenism, the philosophic spirit, impiety itself—all these never had the hatred of religion for their true object, only the hatred of priests."[36]

In the first years of the Restoration, Montlosier undertook an active career as a publicist in defense of his program of a Liberal royalism, a revived aristocracy, and the elimination of the priests from the political life of the Restoration. In 1818, the spread of missions worries him, and on the question of education, he takes a view exactly opposite to Lamennais—priests should remain in the Church.

In explaining the mounting pressure of the Liberal attack in 1825 and 1826, we must take note of the Conservative provocation. The Liberals, to be sure, hoped to split the coalition by raising the specter of religious domination—*parti prêtre,* papal pretensions, Jesuits—but their chances were not particularly bright until after the death of Louis XVIII in 1824, when the Conservatives, under the direction of Charles X, did much to give the specter substance.* Charles X embodied the Restoration dream of the perfect union of throne and altar. More devout than either of his brothers, he was firmly convinced that the security of the Restoration lay in the traditional safeguards of religion. The coronation of 1825 seemed to mark the full return of the clergy;[37] even more ominous was the Jubilee of 1826, on which occasion Charles was found marching without distinguishing costume in a crowd of priests. And these fears of the power of a resurgent clergy received their biggest boost in the Law of Sacrilege and Love of 1825. Never did a piece of legislation more clearly indicate its sponsorship; that a relatively

* This is the traditional explanation offered by the Liberal Republican historians to explain the religious agitation of the Restoration. Vaulabelle, Charléty, Weill, and others state that Ultramontanism and the Jesuits represented a real threat. The treatment of Lamennais and the defeat of the Jesuits in 1828 would seem to me to indicate otherwise.

small band of religious Ultras had the Villèle ministry sufficiently under its control to pass laws punishing religious desecration by death was proof of the reality of the danger.

Whatever the causes, the time was clearly ripe for a major attack. The acquittal of the *Constitutionnel* and the *Courrier* in December 1825 had whetted the appetite of Liberal France. On February 25, in the midst of the La Chalotais controversy, Montlosier delivered his bombshell: *Mémoire à consulter sur un système religieux et politique tendant à renverser la religion, la société et le trône.* Only Lamennais's publications rivaled the success of this extraordinary volume.[38] It quickly ran through eight editions, in three months it sold more than 10,000 copies, an abridgment went for five sous, and by June 16 it was on the Index. Examining the work, modern critics have professed surprise at this sensational reaction. But to understand it, one has only to examine the contents, keeping in mind the peculiar position of the author and the state of France in 1826. What Montlosier did in a single volume was to sum up a whole decade of attack on religion, and to do so, as his title suggests, in the name of religion and royalty.[39]

Further, he had succeeded in absorbing, simplifying, and classifying the attacks under four headings. The enemies of France were, according to Montlosier: the Jesuits, Ultramontanism, the *parti prêtre,* and the Congregation.* The first two, as we have seen, were major targets of Liberal attack, and the *parti prêtre* had become a cliché of the Liberal press. The charge against the Congregation, an active lay group of religious enthusiasts about whom the Liberals worried a great deal during the Restoration, was Montlosier's own contribution. Actually, however, despite this careful breakdown, these forces represented the same thing. As a biographer of Montlosier observes: "At this time, the three expressions, *Ultramontanist, clerical, Jesuit,* were already synonymous; they designated the same party."[40]

The work is actually a little masterpiece of political propaganda, a clear distillation of all the Liberal histories, written with unquestionable sincerity and designed to appeal to every group in Restoration France. In a letter written to Chateaubriand a few months before publication, Montlosier states his intention clearly: "It remains for us to preserve the King and the State from ecclesiastical, self-styled religious preponderance. . . . Doctrines covered with the blood of Louis XVI and Charles I have consented to leave their place to doctrines stained with the blood of Henry IV and Henry III."[41] Here is Montlosier's great achievement: Convinced himself that the real threat

* Burnichon, naturally, feels that the Jesuits were the major target; Grandmaison tends to emphasize his subject, the Congregation, as the real focus of Montlosier's attack. In Montlosier's own mind, the words *parti prêtre* seemed to be the all-inclusive term, although in the Restoration reception of his work, critics tended to concentrate on the Jesuits. For the role of the Congregation in the Restoration, see Bertier de Sauvigny, *Ferdinand de Bertier et l'énigme de la Congrégation.*

to Restoration monarchy emanated from the religious power and not from the Revolution, he succeeded in convincing France.

At the very beginning of his work, Montlosier is careful to identify himself: "For forty years, I have fought against . . . opinions steeped in the blood of Louis XVI and Charles I." It is this clear antirevolutionary record that allows Montlosier to advise the king and the aristocracy of the dangers of religious penetration: "Always faithful to the true and legitimate sovereignty, I fight that of the priests."[42] Having established his own voice as from within the coalition, Montlosier proceeds to indict the forces which are threatening the Restoration. His second chapter is devoted to the Congregation, his third to the Jesuits—the familiar Liberal story, the usual documents brought forward, including an early decision of the Sorbonne.

Throughout the book, Montlosier directs his argument to people who would be immune to the editorializing of the *Constitutionnel.* This is the advantage of his position—as both an anti-Jesuit and an antirevolutionary, he can draw a series of damaging parallels. What if the Jacobins have plotted against monarchy? The Jesuits' history is a procession of such plots. There is only one difference: the Revolution has paid for its crimes against royalty; the Jesuits have not. As for the expulsion of the Jesuits in 1762, Montlosier rejects the Conservative thesis that this was a prelude to the Revolution; instead, the Jesuits themselves are blamed for having trained a whole generation of *philosophes.** Finally, Montlosier is angry at the Liberals for having so confused the issue that a good Royalist cannot attack the dangerous Jesuits without being accused of striking at religion.

The Conservative replies attest to the impact of Montlosier's work. Saint-Chamans's *Du Croque-mitaine de M. le comte de Montlosier, de M. de Pradt, et de bien d'autres* reflects one nervous reaction of the Royalist Restoration.[43] The title indicates that Montlosier is fighting windmills and suggests that, despite his protestations, he has joined Pradt and the Liberal pack in sniping at religion. Saint-Chamans professes surprise at the conclusions of Montlosier's work; he had always thought that the enemies were Liberalism and irreligion, but now he discovers that the real enemy is an excess of religion and piety. He answers Montlosier's attack on the clergy by noting that the clergy has been a part of French society for thirteen hundred years. The specific charges against the Jesuits are disposed of: they are not Ultramontanists because they supported the Declaration of 1682; they cannot be ambitious because there are no Jesuit cardinals or bishops. The Jesuits are accused of being regicides, yet their enemies are the regicides; the Jesuits want to overthrow the king, yet everywhere they are summoned and protected by kings.[44]

* Montlosier even reads something sinister into the fact that the Jesuits and *philosophes* appeared together in the eighteenth century and returned together in the Restoration.

Saint-Chamans is most revealing in his analysis of the spirit of Montlosier's work. As a man of the Conservative Restoration, he is bewildered by what appears to him the revival of the spirit of the eighteenth-century aristocracy. Doesn't Montlosier realize, he asks, that enormous changes have taken place, that religion is in fashion again? The French, he reminds Montlosier, have had a chance to reflect on the true meaning of the eighteenth century, when people found themselves delivered up to impiety and natural law. Saint-Chamans claims that it is only reasonable that religion should have become a dividing line in the Restoration, separating those who saw firsthand the evil effects of irreligion, and the "democrats, revolutionaries, Bonapartists, and Liberals."[45] In the Restoration, the attack upon religion is the mark of the Liberal opposition; and for Montlosier to cross the line, to renew the aristocratic attack upon priests reminiscent of the eighteenth century, is to throw the whole Restoration into question. Saint-Chamans dutifully explains to Montlosier that the problem of the Restoration is precisely how to prevent the age from growing irreligious, and that those truly concerned with the stability of the Restoration should support the Jesuits in their efforts to reestablish faith.

For Saint-Chamans, Montlosier is an unfortunate example of the effect "of the ideas of the Revolution upon persons who have always been most opposed to it"; by attacking the Jesuits, Montlosier is playing into the hands of the Revolution he despises. This is a telling argument and a shrewd piece of analysis. Montlosier does represent a crack in the dike, a defection in the coalition; overnight he has become the hero of Liberal France.* Saint-Chamans's reply is, in effect, an attempt to heal this breach, to persuade Montlosier to come back into the fold. He calls upon Montlosier to recognize this simple axiom of the Conservative Restoration: that "monarchy and religion have felt the need to be closely united for their mutual defense; . . . to weaken the rightful influence of the clergy is to weaken monarchical doctrines and their defenders." Saint-Chamans is intelligent enough to realize that the Restoration coalition has been split before, that the fear of the Ultras allowed the Liberals to triumph in 1819. He concludes by asking Montlosier not to allow the Liberals to succeed this time; to realize that the Jesuits are no danger, that the Congregation is only the party of the Restoration, that Ultramontanism is merely a smoke screen, that a party of the clergy should not be alarming. Above all, Montlosier is asked to remember that the clergy, far from being a threat to monarchy, carries a "standard . . . inseparably united to the white flag of our Bourbons."

Another Conservative reply to Montlosier was Bonald's *Réflexions.* It was inevitable that Bonald should reply, since he was singled out as a member

* See, for example, the reception given Montlosier in the *Constitutionnel,* March 4 and March 7, 1826. To improve relations, Montlosier has even apologized to the *Constitutionnel* for having previously called it revolutionary!

of the Congregation and had always been a staunch defender of the Jesuits in the Chamber. Montlosier had raised the basic question of a conspiracy directed against throne and society by four religious armies. To Bonald this is nonsense: The real threat is the anti-Christian conspiracy of the Liberals. And it is typical of this Liberal conspiracy to accuse someone else: "It was thus at the beginning of the Revolution; the Jacobin party accused the Austrian cabinet, Pitt, and Coburg of meddling with France, and the nobles of pillaging their own property and burning their own châteaux. Likewise, note the eager alacrity with which the Liberal party has welcomed, reprinted, and blown up the sally of M. de Montlosier."[46] Bonald's reply to Montlosier is symbolic of the Jesuit debate in the Restoration: a struggle waged over historical figures, dead controversies, and far-off lands. Elsewhere Bonald quotes d'Alembert on the virtues of the Jesuits in seventeenth-century Paraguay.

Bonald hits upon a new way of defending Ultramontanism without openly attacking Gallicanism. Instead of denouncing Bossuet, Bonald patronizes him. What Bossuet lacked—what all France of 1682 lacked—was experience, the experience of the French Revolution, "the irreligious Revolution." "If M. Bossuet had been able to foresee this Revolution—for which the profound revolutionary Mirabeau gave the rationale in these few words, 'It is necessary to decatholicize France in order to demonarchize her, and to demonarchize her in order to decatholicize her'—he would have taken a more cautious and less peremptory tack." For Bonald, as for so many of the religious Ultras, the French Revolution had been a solemn judgment on the Gallican liberties of 1682, and offered a clear guide to present conduct: "The French Revolution . . . by overthrowing society . . . laid bare the abysses beneath it. It brought into existence a new way of considering politics in religion and religion in politics, their affinities, and the analogies in structure which inevitably result from these affinities."

The decision to mix politics and religion, then, is something born out of the disasters of the Revolution, disasters brought on by the absence of any strong religious feeling at the base of the eighteenth-century monarchy. The Restoration has profited from this experience, but Montlosier has not, and this is what separates him from the coalition.

Bonald tries to dispel Montlosier's fear, shared by the Liberals, that the temporal power is in danger of being submerged by the "spiritual." He notes that even Lamennais admits that popes cannot depose kings any more, and that "nothing is more solidly established, more certain, more necessary, than the full and complete independence of the temporal power of kings from all spiritual power." If this fear of the subservience of the temporal is unreal, where does it come from? Bonald offers this analysis of the agitation over Ultramontanism: "The leaders of the two societies, political and religious . . . , must always remember that the men of the Revolution are thirsting for a schism between France and the court of Rome, as the final step in our imitation of the Revolution of England, in which we have already gone so far." Here the purpose of the anti-Ultramontanist campaign is seen as a break with Rome. This, for Bonald, is the logical result of Gallicanism, as well as an objective of the Revolution. And again Montlosier finds himself allied with the Revolution.

Finally, Bonald must confront the phenomenon of Montlosier himself, the anticlerical aristocrat: "Certainly not all the adversaries of the Jesuits and the missions are enemies of religion and the throne, but all the enemies of religion and the throne are the natural enemies of Jesuits and missionaries." Montlosier must choose; if he adopts the Liberals' enemies as his enemies, then he has in fact become a Liberal.

Bonald wonders aloud at the fate of these Royalists who mix with the Liberals on common ground: "Can one share thus with one's enemies the same views, the same hates, the same fears . . . ? Is it wise to be guided by the sentiments and counsel of an enemy?" This suggests to Bonald a depressing historical analogy, another group of Royalists who imagined that they could support the cause of their enemies and remain immune from the consequences: "And when the parlements allied for a time with philosophy, in order to overthrow one of the most solid supports of religion, the parlements were sacrificed several years later on the scaffold which this same philosophy had raised; are they not a terrible example of the danger of these imprudent alliances?" Here the eighteenth-century La Chalotais can be used as a historical precedent for Montlosier's joining the Liberal chorus against the Jesuits. The parallel is exact. It was fear and distaste of the Jesuits that drove the eighteenth-century magistrates into an alliance with the *philosophes* to destroy the Jesuits. It is the same repugnance for the same order which has driven Montlosier into the camp of the enemy. On April 8, recognizing that Montlosier had placed the coalition in jeopardy, Saint-Chamans raised a Royalist distress signal in the Chamber of Deputies: "The evil has come from the divisions between Royalists. This evil is further enlarged by the influence that the Liberal party exercises . . . on a certain number of Royalists misled by false theories. In order to frighten the Royalists, old memories are invoked; they are told about the supremacy of the pope over the temporal power of kings; they are threatened with the Jesuits." To Saint-Chamans it is amazing that some Royalists let themselves be so deceived and exploited: "It is in the nineteenth century, in the midst of irreligion and incredulity, that the excesses of religious zeal are decried. . . . The remnants of the Jesuits are still pursued after more than sixty years, by the remnants of the Jansenists, to the cries of our self-styled *philosophes*."[47]

By May 15, the magistrate Agier had spoken for those Royalists who were genuinely disturbed by the revelations of Montlosier and La Chalotais:

"France can hardly master her emotion at the threat of spiritual power invading the temporal."[48]

By May 25, the issue is squarely joined in the Chamber. The question under discussion is the religious budget. Blangy rises to urge strong financial support for the clergy because of the severe attack to which it has been subjected by a wave of antireligious writings: "These writings have produced a frenzy which cannot be explained by the horrible lies they contain; this sickness which they spread, this division among Royalists who formerly marched together—where does it come from, if not from these writings born of passion and hate?"[49]

Here Blangy shifts from the usual Restoration attack upon "dangerous books" to a more immediate concern: that these works are not merely appealing to impressionable minds but literally dividing the Restoration coalition. This is the newest danger, for impiety is not menacing if confined to its traditional audience: "If public opinion is false and perverted, to what can we attribute its perversion? To our internal divisions, fed by these lying writings which exaggerate the evil." To halt this movement Blangy calls for unity.

He is refuted by Agier, who admits that deep divisions have been opened in the ranks of the Royalists, but insists that these divisions are not the result of books. There is a deeper issue, of which the books are only a troubled reflection: "It is not bad books which are the cause of our divisions; it is Ultramontanist ideas."[50]

This disagreement sets the stage for Frayssinous's delivery of one of the great speeches of a Restoration Chamber in which oratorical greatness is coin of the realm. Ostensibly present to defend his budget, Frayssinous attempts, without mentioning Montlosier, to meet and resolve the charges, and to quiet the disturbance they have created. He reiterates the firm stand on Gallicanism that he had taken in 1817: "Our doctrines are those of Bossuet and Fleury."[51] As always he is the master of compromise. Some Gallicans, he finds, have gone too far—practically into heresy. On the other hand, there is too much Lamennais-inspired Ultramontanism in the seminaries. He reduces the Liberal fear of Ultramontanism to a question of educational administration: some way must be found to "convince the young . . . that Gallican liberties are not incompatible with the Catholic faith, that Gallican maxims . . . have never been condemned."

As for the specific charges raised by Montlosier, Frayssinous acknowledges the existence of the Congregation only to dismiss its importance: "I have never felt the yoke of this mysterious empire." But the Jesuits cannot be dismissed in so cavalier a fashion. Indeed, Frayssinous produces a full and documented refutation of claims of undue Jesuit influence in the educational institutions of the Restoration. If the attacks upon the Jesuits had been based upon their Restoration activity, Frayssinous would have silenced the Liberal campaign right there, but the Jesuits are under attack not for what they are doing, but for what they have done. He is aware of this—"The past is being ransacked for scandalous anecdotes."

Frayssinous's reply, instead of soothing France, unleashes a fresh wave of discussion. The Liberals, led by Casimir-Périer, later to be the first prime minister of the July Monarchy, continue the pressure, forcing Frayssinous to defend the Jesuits where they are most vulnerable—their history. Lainé carries the Liberal history into the Chamber: "Edicts have abolished the Society; it has been denounced by all the laws of Catholic Europe, even by by the laws of countries where the ideas of the *philosophes* never penetrated. . . . Justice has made itself heard above all the Society's oracles. . . . Surely all these kings, these peoples, the pope himself, cannot be dismissed as abettors of godlessness."[52]

Fraysinnous, badgered, is driven back to history. On July 4, the Liberals force him into a discussion of the secret nature of the Jesuit institutes: "Everyone knows that, from their origin, the Jesuits were the butt of attacks from other religious orders and from the University, and were exposed to the . . . surveillance of the parlements."[53] If it is true that the Jesuits were condemned by unanimous opinion, "the various causes must be weighed to separate the true from the false, to see what part was played by party spirit, by ambition, by false zeal, by the prejudices of philosophy, by time and circumstance."

Frayssinous attempts to answer as many individual distortions as possible, but basically his plea is that of a reasonable man for perspective on the history of the Jesuits: "Religious bodies have played . . . a part in the events which have filled French annals. If they have made mistakes, let us agree that . . . [others] have not been entirely without reproach." It is an indication of the passions aroused, the prevalence of party spirit, that Frayssinous's dispassionate analysis is taken by the Liberal press as a virtual admission of the power of the Jesuits. Actually, the opposite is true; when Frayssinous was not being driven into history, he was convincing in his demonstration that the Restoration was able to control its Jesuits.

On July 6, the Chamber closes and the next move is up to Montlosier. Not yet satisfied that the Jesuits and the Congregation have been sufficiently exposed, he is determined to see his crusade through to the finish. He thereupon addresses to the royal court his second work, *Dénonciation aux cours royales*. Essentially, the new book repeats the charges of the earlier one: "History teaches us, in point of doctrine, that popes have claimed the right to dethrone and depose kings; in point of fact, they have actually dethroned and deposed them." Montlosier concludes with his address to the court, noting that he has consulted with some eighty lawyers and has been duly advised that "it is not only my legal right, but . . . my rigorous duty to uncover the said offenses and denounce them to the authorities as attacks upon religion, and upon the safety of the king and the State."[54] By this stroke, Montlosier converted the political issue of the Jesuits into a legal question. If his charges can be upheld, the Restoration must do something about this religious penetration. But even more important than the possibility of a favorable decision is Montlosier's opportunity to throw the Restoration spotlight once again upon the courts, the descendants of the old magistracy, who must now decide—as did their eighteenth-century counterparts—on the legality of the Jesuits.

Fifty judges sit in deliberation on this momentous case. Meanwhile the Liberals are active. Dupin organizes the Liberal barristers, who present a defense of Montlosier's charges as incontestably legal.[55] The press tries the case in its columns; bishops thunder from pulpits. Finally, on August 18, a decision is reached. The court has clearly conceived of itself as judging nothing less than the admissibility of the Jesuits' presence in France; its conclusion is that French legislation is "opposed to the establishment of the Society called Jesuit." This legislation, it continues, "is based on the recognition that the principles professed by the said Society are incompatible with the independence of any government."[56]

Having echoed in essence the opinions of 1762, the court goes on to disqualify itself from judgment; it abdicates to the government the right to decide whether such institutions are a menace. "The court declares itself incompetent." Nevertheless, the opinion expressed by the court was, like the acquittal of the *Constitutionnel*, an enormous triumph for the Liberals. The court is not yet ready to smash the Restoration coalition on the issue of the Jesuits, but it is clearly in sympathy with Montlosier's views. By declaring itself incompetent, it passes the accusation on to the Chamber of Peers, which is to be the stage for a full-dress debate that commands the attention of all France.

Montlosier petitions the Chamber of Peers for action on his *Dénonciation*, "to recognize the immediate danger presented by the flagrant offenses of the numerous Jesuit and Congregation establishments in France, and to advise the promptest measures to dissolve them."[57] On January 18, Montlosier's petition is reported out by Baron Portalis, son of the Empire diplomat, who is to play a key role in the ousting of the Jesuits in 1828. The outcome of the debate is no more decisive than the verdict of the royal court, yet it is crucial for an understanding of what was happening to the Restoration coalition. The aristocrats of the upper Chamber are bitterly divided by the charges of a fellow aristocrat, Montlosier. And the division cuts across and goes far deeper than the distinction between the old and the new aristocracy, which can account for most of the earlier disagreements in the upper Chamber. This controversy is nothing less than the split between the political and religious forces of the coalition.

For Portalis, the issues raised by Montlosier are simple enough. The Jesuits were destroyed by an act of royal will in 1764, a judgment confirmed by Louis XVI in 1777: "Here then are the Jesuits, and that should end the matter."

But that does not end the matter for the Cardinal Duc de La Fare, who reminds the hushed Chamber of an experience so many of its members had gone through: "Hurled out of France by the revolutionary turmoil, . . . I came to accept the prevailing opinions on the Society of Jesus. Everywhere I noted strong regret at its suppression, a profound indignation against the calumnies which blackened it, a general veneration for such of its members as the times had spared."

The Liberals of the Restoration had rested their case against the Jesuits on the eighteenth-century decision of court and king. But for Conservatives like Cardinal de La Fare, the memory of the Revolution has priority over the history of the eighteenth century. It was the Revolution that taught Conservative France the worth of the absent Jesuits. Given the frightful experiences of the Revolution, religious France can now truly reevaluate this action of the eighteenth-century parlement: "This formidable coalition against the Jesuits was composed of sectarians of all opinions, of all those skilled in philosophy, of all the enemies of religion, the Church, and royalty. From one end of Europe to the other arose the cry: 'Let us unite against this Society which resists us.' " Actions are to be judged by their results, and "Who in France profited from the destruction of the Jesuits? Unquestionably those who, for many years, secretly plotted the ruin of altar and throne."

This was the intention of the anti-Jesuits, then as now. "It is well known that their plan is to extinguish the Catholic faith. . . . The name of Jesuit is for them a curse which applies equally to all ecclesiastics, all Catholics, all men of good will." Equating the Jesuits with religion, and religion with society, the religious Conservative naturally finds that any attack upon the Jesuits is an attack upon society and religion.

Cardinal de La Fare concludes bitterly that these men, whose only wish is to execute the laws of the eighteenth century against the Jesuits, have themselves destroyed the most sacred laws of monarchy. Here again is the Conservative insistence that opposition to the Jesuits is the mark of the revolutionary. But La Fare is no sooner seated than a man speaks who is the living proof that hatred for the Jesuits is not the exclusive possession of Liberal France. It is the Duc de Choiseul, the namesake of an outspoken eighteenth-century enemy of the Jesuits.

In rising to defend Montlosier, Choiseul proudly proclaims his lineage:

> More than anyone else, gentlemen, I stand for the values handed down to us by our fathers. A member of the ancient peerage, brought up to respect this ancient magistracy that has been the glory of France, . . . I rejoice in never having

deviated from that respect. . . . My opinion is further strengthened by the principles and examples of the pious and venerable bishops in my family . . . [whose] religious and political sentiments always ranged them against this dangerous Society.

Choiseul has thus made a family matter of his anti-Jesuitism. The Montlosier and La Chalotais affairs are behind his speech, with their forceful reminder to the French aristocracy of its traditional opposition to the Jesuits; it is impossible to imagine Choiseul making this speech in the first part of the Restoration. In a burst of family pride, he quotes the famous Choiseul on the dangers of the Jesuits, and then concludes:

Supported by such memorable examples and by such notable authorities, enlightened by the great and grievous lessons that history has taught us, . . . struck by the terrible accusations handed down to us from the century of the League, accusations from the very mouth of Henry IV, . . . after the knowledge that we have acquired of this long chain of intrigues from the reign of Henry IV to the reign of Louis XV, . . . convinced and fearful of the dangers which threaten the throne and society, I support . . . the petition of M. de Montlosier.

The efficacy of history is remarkably demonstrated in the debate over the Jesuits. Choiseul is not primarily concerned with the present menace of the order; he is led to support Montlosier because history has already spoken, because of Henry IV and the late Duc de Choiseul rather than Montrouge and Saint-Acheul.

The Duc de Fitz-James, a zealous Ultra in the Chamber as in the press, seizes upon this curious reliance upon history and the apparent unwillingness of the anti-Jesuits to deal with the present: "Do the seminaries publicly preach anti-Gallican doctrines? Are the young people who leave the seminaries imbued with principles contrary to our existing laws? Has it been discovered that education in these seminaries is immoral, anticonstitutional, or anti-Gallican? Rage against them if this is so; close their colleges; I will be the first to call the just severity of the laws upon their heads."

But this is not so, as would be clear to everyone if everyone had not turned historian: "If people are content to repeat accusations leveled against the Jesuits one or two centuries ago, Pascal's pleasantries or the arguments of Port Royal; . . . if people persist in seeing in a handful of college rectors either the same fanatics as in the days of the League, or the same theologians as in the days of Sanchez and Molinas"—if, ultimately the anti-Jesuits are merely playing historical games—Fitz-James wonders if the whole enterprise is not suspect:

I wonder if the word Jesuit is not a word artfully chosen to hide other designs, a false attack in order to mask the real attack; a word which, touching old worn-out questions, awakening old prejudices, rekindling the hatreds which once seemed smothered in the common misfortune, is more suitable than any other to alienate from this coalition those who feel they have been forced into it.

As for himself, Fitz-James tells us he cannot feel the historic pull of anti-Jesuitism: "It is useless to cry *au Jésuite* at me. . . . I have taken my stand. I will always fear a Jesuit less than a Jacobin." But to those who *are* captivated by the turbulent historical past of the Jesuits, Fitz-James addresses this plea:

If you had to pronounce on the fate of these men, you would examine what they are, not what they were; what they do, not what they did. What is important to us is not the fact that the Jesuits of old, poisoned by the passions of the League, concurred and even participated in some of the outrages in which all men and all parties of this sad epoch of our history had their share; or that theology textbooks which are no longer read imputed to them erroneous or perverse doctrines that have time and again been disavowed by their successors.

Fitz-James is willing to concede history to the Liberals—yes, the Jesuits did wrong—but he challenges the whole enterprise of the Liberal history: What is the relevance of this admittedly vulnerable past to the peaceful present, to the students and teachers of Montrouge?

Despite his brilliant attack upon the tactic of judging the Jesuits through their history, Fitz-James himself succumbs and is driven to examine the eighteenth-century question. For the Liberals, the eighteenth-century decision is clear cut—the expulsion of a demonstrably treasonous society. Fitz-James is not so certain: "What happened in France in 1764 is at best unclear." La Chalotais was sensible, but all the other factors seem to suggest that a "very complicated intrigue dominated this great affair, and that the Jesuits were condemned without having been judged." After a brief foray into this despised history, Fitz-James draws the appropriate lesson, that the past is so complicated it can never be really understood: "Between the past and ourselves are abysses: it would be folly to think of crossing them. A single step backward can destroy us." This is Fitz-James's expression of the Conservative fear of history—to putter around the past and dig up family skeletons can lead only to disaster.

Lainé led off for the pro-Montlosier forces the next day (January 19). He seems to accept Fitz-James's strictures, and disclaims any intention of using history: "Let others forage in the public archives, . . . sharpen up the old weapons of the *procureurs-généraux*, and invoke history. May it please God that I never draw upon these dangerous arsenals! There are already all too many new causes of discord without exhuming old ones."[58] Lainé nonetheless proceeds to demonstrate a flair for universal history. Conceiving of the Jesuits' experience as one long trial, he echoes the verdict of history:

I see on one side the Jesuits, . . . forming . . . a state within a state. On the other, I see six Catholic kings with their courts, their councils, their ministers; a venerable body of officials—all interested in upholding religion. . . . The case was judged by each state . . . ; finally, after many years of troubled meditations, the sovereign pontiff confirmed the decrees of the monarchs by his bull. Is it blasphemy to range oneself on the side of kings and a sovereign pontiff?

The Restoration is not yet an age of public opinion, but it does display an enormous respect for historical opinion. Lainé does not have to judge the Jesuits of the Restoration; they have already been judged.

Thus far in the debate, the Conservatives have followed the Restoration pattern and conceded that history is a Liberal science. For Cardinal de La Fare, the Revolution has wiped out the previous history of the Jesuits; for Fitz-James, the history of the order is irrelevant to its standing in the Restoration. But at last there comes forward a defender of the Jesuits on historical grounds, in the person of Vicomte Louis de Bonald. Says Bonald, "The idea of making any apology here for the Society of Jesus is far from my thoughts . . . ; its apology is in its history." And it is this apology that Bonald utters, a moving word picture of the contributions of the Jesuits to Western civilization. The Jesuits are the natural opponents of Protestantism, and all their strong characteristics—their obedience, flexibility, desire to expand—are the natural responses to their historic mission: "They invade society to regulate it, and the world to convert it; but these ambitions are one."

Bonald makes no apologies for the Jesuits in history. Most Conservatives find the eighteenth-century expulsion by monarchy and papacy at least an embarrassment, but Bonald can explain it to his own satisfaction. The Jesuits fought the Reformation, and the Reformation won a temporary victory "under the name of philosophy." The Jesuits were forced to succumb, and the "same hatred which crushed them pursues them today." Bonald is typical of the Ultra Conservatives who refuse to give ground: the Jesuits have been right historically; they are right in the Restoration.

In defense of his friend Montlosier, Barante surveys the Conservative arguments, and observes the inconsistencies of their defense of the Jesuits: Bonald using history, Fitz-James asking that history be ignored. Of the two arguments, Barante elects to answer the latter. Bonald's historical hymn can be countered by any Liberal history; Fitz-James's demand that the Jesuit record since 1814 be confronted is more challenging. Barante is disarming in reply: "Let us frankly agree that the new Jesuits give no indication that they practice or preach regicide. Let us laugh at the affected terrors, at the tender concern which has been lavished on sovereigns. Let us say that the Jesuits will not kill kings, because there is no need to kill kings."

This is the voice of a Liberal aristocrat who has not been seduced by the vulgarities of the Liberal history, and who has seemingly recognized the illogicality of flaying the Jesuits with their antecedents. But, Barante continues, one quality of the Jesuits cannot be gainsaid, "the essence of their order, the cause of their renown: the insatiable need to dominate." Though the Jesuits are wearing a new suit of clothes, they are still Jesuits subscribing to unalterable principles. It is ironic how unhistorical the school of Liberal history can be in regarding the Jesuits as an immutable essence rather than as an institution susceptible to historical change. Barante concludes by refusing the Jesuit-or-Jacobin Hobson's choice: "Are we already at the point at which we can no longer reply, neither one nor the other? That would be deplorable; for, by accepting the Jesuits, we would not be sure of avoiding the Jacobins, and the real way to be safe from either of them is not to bear ill will against the other."

Throughout the Restoration, the Liberals have insisted that there is a third way, a position between Jacobin and Ultra from which both may be attacked. Again in the Jesuit debate, the Liberal aristocrats seek to recommend this position, to create a body of opinion, of men like Montlosier himself, somewhere between the politico-religious coalition and Liberal France.

And there were those present at the debate who saw the Restoration coalition dissolving before their eyes. The Marquis de Villefranche rose to remind the aristocrats who were attacking the Jesuits of some very recent history. The word Jesuit is "the new byword that the enemies of the government are exploiting; it replaces the old word *aristocracy*." Villefranche, like his fellow Ultras, deplores the historical approach and assails the Liberals for "digging up the old quarrels of the parlements against the Jesuits, quarrels which had not been spoken for sixty years."

By 1827 the affair has progressed through the press, two debates in the Chambers, a trial before a royal court, and another work by Montlosier. When in that year Antoine Madrolle, a literary protégé of Bonald's sets down his full refutation of Montlosier, the implications of Montlosier's attack are clear. The whole Conservative case is contained in the title of Madrolle's book: "Defense of the Social Order, attacked at its foundations in the name of the Liberalism of the nineteenth century by M. Montlosier, in which it is demonstrated to the King, the Chambers, and the Courts that the works of this writer epitomize the errors of philosophy that led to the Revolution." It is the "social order" that Montlosier has attacked, that is, the order of the Restoration coalition; this refutation is addressed to "the King, the Chambers, and the Courts," the three sensitive areas to which Montlosier has carried his fight. And finally the title charges Montlosier with repeating the errors that led to the French Revolution—that is, with attacking "in the name of Liberalism."

Madrolle accurately registers the Conservative fears regarding Montlosier's impact upon the coalition. He documents his charge that Montlosier "has hurled the apple of discord at the heart of monarchy" by citing the Conservative press on Montlosier's effort to stir up the courts. The *Quotidienne* has deplored the possibility of any breach between the magistracy and the monarchy: "Magistracy and monarch have been allied too long for their interests not to be common, their dangers similar, their enemies the same." The *Journal de Paris,* attempting to head off Montlosier's new alliance between the Liberals and the magistracy, has reminded Liberal France that the same parlements which struck down the Jesuits had also decreed the destruction of many books that are now dear to Liberal hearts.[59]

Madrolle pays Montlosier the compliment of a point-by-point rebuttal; no argument is too small, too absurd, to go unanswered. Montlosier is now much too serious to be dismissed as a crank, much too influential to be ignored.

Montlosier had found the simultaneous reappearance of *philosophes* and Jesuits suspicious; Madrolle finds nothing unnatural in it. Yes, the Jesuits were condemned by the eighteenth century, but that is proof of their innocence; yes, they were condemned by a pope, but they were also restored by a pope. Whereas Saint-Chamans has tried to bring Montlosier back into the fold, Madrolle prepares a Conservative counterattack. He remarks that although Montlosier has "set himself up as the apologist of the people and of liberty," his historical works, some as recent as 1821 and 1822, teem with aristocratic bias and attacks on the middle class.[60] Clearly, then, Montlosier's attack on religion comes from a direction altogether different from the Liberals', and is based on aristocratic assumptions that no Liberal can share.

Madrolle finds an unwilling ally in the Liberal *Globe,* which considers Montlosier highly suspect. The *Globe* has not forgotten Montlosier's previous associations, nor has it entirely abandoned its antiaristocratic campaign of the early Restoration. It has characterized Montlosier as

> the advocate of the nobility, the defender of the system of castes and corporations. . . . Montlosier seeks to restore the old society, to which he is deeply attached, by blending in with it certain elements of the Revolution. If he pursues the priest with such rigor, it is because he sees in him a rebellious cleric in the dungeon. . . . If tomorrow he should triumph over the priest, he would want to go back to fortified castles, low and high justice, seigneurial prerogatives. Is that what we ask of society . . . ?[61]

Next Madrolle switches ground; Montlosier is seen no longer as the spokesman for a resurgent aristocracy, but as a man who has always been willing to compromise with the Revolution. Here it is not his service to Napoleon or his pronouncements on the Revolution that are the most damning; rather it is his disloyal attitude toward the Bourbons, as expressed in his *De la Monarchie française,* and particularly his deprecating treatment of Louis XIV.[62]

Once again we observe how, in the Restoration, a man can be undermined by showing an improper attitude toward the facts of French history. Montlosier stands accused of having adopted the pure aristocratic line on the French monarchy, and Madrolle makes the connection between this view and Montlosier's *Mémoire à consulter*. In this book, he "seems to carry to the point of irreverence, to the point of outrage, and even to the crime of *lèse-majesté*, the expression of illegitimacy." Thus Madrolle provides Montlosier with a consistent position—whether supporting aristocracy or attacking religion, Montlosier is antimonarchical: "Such are the antimonarchical opinions of M. de Montlosier. And it should not be imagined that his perpetual apologies for the nobility are a contradiction; they are rather a consequence."

Madrolle even offers an explanation for why this aristocracy, once the natural support of monarchy, is troublesome in the Restoration; it has lost its function in society. Typified by such mavericks as Montlosier, it is for Madrolle the weak link in the coalition. It is indifferent to the king and attacks the clergy; it would cheerfully sacrifice them to advance its own interests. Here Madrolle underscores the real divisions of the coalition. He regards the antics of Montlosier and his class as the desperate efforts of a group seeking status where it formerly held power.

This irresponsible activity would be bad enough, but the aristocracy has made it worse by adopting the platform of the king's Liberal enemies. Madrolle defines their platform as "to make religious power terrifying to political power"—an excellent condensation of the whole Liberal religious campaign. Madrolle indicates that he would have no fear of this party, except that "they appear to have M. de Montlosier." Montlosier has to be answered, for he represents an important convert to the opposition.

Madrolle rips into the supposed danger from the religious Right as factually absurd. The contrast between Madrolle's description of the state of the French clergy and the powerful armies described by Montlosier is direct. The clergy has "some members in the upper Chamber . . . and not one in the lower, or in the councils of the king; only a single member in the ministry [Frayssinous], where the Church has always been well represented, under the most absolute reigns as under the weakest; . . . such a clergy is presented as *in possession of France*." This reply of Madrolle's helps us to understand the feeling on support of Lamennais. To the true supporter of the clergy, Montlosier's charges are absolutely preposterous; the truth is that the clergy has made a series of degrading compromises with the Revolution and has little real power in the Restoration.

The crucial fact for Madrolle is that "Montlosier is a thousand times more frightened of even the most legitimate action of the universal church than of the conspiracies of all the *philosophes* and Jacobins combined." This consideration is vital, for Montlosier's strength lies in his claim to represent the Royalist cause; if Madrolle can equate Montlosier with Restoration Liberalism, can prove that he had sold out, then his ability to divide the coalition is curtailed. Madrolle offers two proofs of Montlosier's Liberalism. First, he places Montlosier in the tradition of the eighteenth century and the Revolution by reminding his readers that it has always been the task of "philosophy, the great master of the theory of revolutions, to separate the king and the clergy," and that charging priests with conspiracy is an old revolutionary stratagem, one which had been used as a justification for Robespierre's government. Second, Montlosier has adopted the latest line of Restoration Liberalism, the effort to "sap royalty in its Catholic foundations while seeming to flatter and sustain it." Montlosier is quoted as having said, "Everywhere, and especially in France where royalty is so strong, it is necessary to have the king on one's side when one wishes to strike at royalty."[64]

Madrolle has even more direct evidence than doctrinal similiarities, namely the Liberal reception of Montlosier's work. Here Madrolle is on unassailable ground: whatever Montlosier's intentions, he is clearly welcomed by the Liberals. As early as April 1826, a Liberal lawyer in Toulouse has cited Montlosier to prove that a clerical conspiracy exists, and by 1827 he has become the "rallying point . . . of all the Liberals in France." But even Madrolle cannot quite understand the warmth of his reception: "His arrival in Paris was solicited and announced by the newspapers immediately after the news of the court."

At this point, the argument takes an unexpected turn. After more than 350 pages of denunciation and refutation, Madrolle—as if suddenly aware of the urgency of the situation—offers a final appeal to Montlosier to rejoin the Restoration coalition: "You belong to a great class of society. You have served in high office; . . . you have enjoyed great renown; and today more than ever, you exercise a rather great influence on public opinion." And then, almost apologetically, Madrolle explains: "It was urgent to demonstrate to society the venom with which your writings are imbued, and to fortify the people and the young against your seductive doctrines." Madrolle discloses much by this final desperate bid for reconciliation. In some way, Montlosier does still represent the aristocracy. A breach has been opened; it must be closed.

The Chamber of Peers passes the petition on to the ministry and this officially ends the Montlosier affair. But anti-Jesuit sentiment continues to smolder; the divisions do not mend. Within the year, the Villèle regime falls, and within eighteen months the Jesuits are expelled again. It is a mark of the success of the campaign that more and more Frenchmen have come to believe that religious power is incompatible with the power of the State. So widespread is the fear of clerical domination that Dupin has the temerity to address Villèle in 1827: "Remember well, Monseigneur, that the men of old-fashioned ideas support you only to exploit you and later set you aside. You are not an archbishop, and therefore you can only be a temporary leader in their eyes; Your Excellency must know this."[65]

By the end of the year 1827, the *Gazette universelle de Lyon,* though hostile to Montlosier, sadly concedes the success of his attack; his triumph has been "complete and undisputed."[66] The influence of the Montlosier affair on public opinion is recorded by Barante in 1828: "I see men who eighteen months ago would have burned the *philosophes* invoking Voltaire with all their hearts against the clergy."[67]

The June decrees of 1828 are the biggest political victory for the Liberals since the dispersion of the Chambre Introuvable in 1816. But even more important than this triumph was its by-product, the break-up of the politico-religious coalition.* In the process of attacking the Jesuits, the Liberals not only had eliminated an important source of Conservative strength, but had divided the Royalists.† Monarchists were convinced of the dangers of Ultramontanism; aristocrats feared the returned Jesuits—and both groups fought those who were trying to hold the Restoration coalition together.

Long after the July revolution, the Ultra Frénilly and the Liberal Guizot, thinking back upon the failures of the Restoration, reflected on the man and the event. For Guizot,

> No one was less an eighteenth-century *philosophe* or a nineteenth-century Liberal than Montlosier; he had passionately defended the Church and fought the Revolution in the Constituent Assembly. He was a sincere Royalist, Catholic, aristocrat. Not without reason, he was called the champion of feudalism. But the modern bourgeoisie did not accept ecclesiastical domination any more than did the feudal nobility. M. de Montlosier rejected it in the name of the New as well as the Old France.[68]

It is a great stroke of Liberal good fortune that the Liberal objectives in the Restoration and the sentiments of the aristocracy coincide on the issue of religious domination.

Frénilly describes the Jesuit question as "an apple of discord cast into our ranks; it caused division even among the best Royalists."[69] "Even among the best Royalists"—there is no clearer indication of Montlosier's deadly role.

Thus far we have traced a pattern of Liberal success. The trial of the *Constitutionnel*, the La Chalotais battle, the Montlosier affair—everything seemed to lend substance to the fear of Ultramontanist pretension and Jesuit domination; everything served to split off the aristocracy from the Resto-

* To Ultras like Salaberry, 1828 seemed like 1793 . . . or 1830.

† "It can be seen from this exposition that my ideas on Christianity differ from those of M. le Comte de Maistre and those of Abbé Lamennais. The former wishes to reduce the people to a common servitude, dominated by a theocracy; the latter seems to me to summon the people to a general independence under the same theocratic domination." Chateaubriand, *Etudes historiques*, in *Œuvres*, IV, 118.

ration coalition.* The Restoration might have survived this loss had the forces of political and religious Conservatism closed ranks against this alliance of Liberals and aristocrats. But this was not to be, for in their attack upon the coalition, the Liberals had revived, along with memories of papal supremacy and Jesuit perfidy, something positive—Gallicanism. And it was this third force, Gallicanism, which was to complete the dissolution of the coalition by dividing the French clergy at the very time it was under severest attack.

The year 1826 is a fateful year for the French clergy; not only is it attacked by the La Chalotais family and by Montlosier, but it continues to be rent by the internal disagreement which has been seething since Lamennais's "Essay on Indifference" in 1817. The condemnation of Lamennais in the affair of the *Drapeau blanc* in 1823 had been an official check to Ultramontanism, but like the political Ultras, Lamennais was not one to stay chastened. In 1824, he created *Le Mémorial catholique* as the house organ of Ultramontanism, awaiting only fresh Gallican provocations to call him back into action.

A strong Gallican stand was the inevitable response of the government of Charles X to the pressure from the Liberal Gallicans. Frayssinous, the king's minister of ecclesiastical affairs, in order to steal this Gallican thunder from the Left, proposes on January 16, 1826, the establishment of an ecclesiastical school for advanced studies. Frayssinous explains the purpose of this university: "The king . . . has formed the plan of reviving higher ecclesiastical studies in the ancient Sorbonne, whence have come so many doctors and illustrious pontiffs. . . . Supported by his influence, the clergy of France will show itself more ready than ever to render unto Caesar what is Caesar's and unto God what is God's."[70]

This proposal is, for Lamennais, the clarion call to arms. An attempt to revive the old Sorbonne, the center of Gallican heresies, is nothing less than an official effort to Gallicanize the entire French clergy. Lamennais enters the lists with the second part of *De la Religion considerée dans ses rapports avec l'ordre politique et civil.* Thus, at the very moment that the Liberal campaign against Ultramontanism has reached its greatest intensity, a work of pure Ultramontanism is published.

As in 1823, the government decides to move against Lamennais and formally charges him with provoking disobedience to the laws of the state. At this juncture, the French Church itself again decides to register its loyalty

* It is noteworthy that two of the best historians of the Restoration, L'Epinois and Thureau-Dangin, are Royalists writing in the early 1870's. Their insight into the Restoration as a tragedy, their awareness that the monarchy was doomed by the rift in the aristocracy, clearly comes from their contemporary situation, in which a new rift among Royalists—the dispute between the counts—is so prominent a factor.

to the government and its opposition to Lamennais. Ten days before the date set for the trial, fourteen bishops of France issue their famous *Exposé des sentiments des évêques*. The bishops are shocked at Lamennais's anti-Gallicanism. "Maxims accepted in the Church of France are boldly denounced as an assault upon the divine constitution of the Catholic Church, as the sullied work of schism and heresy, as a profession of political atheism."[71] And like the descendants of La Chalotais, the Gallican bishops resent any insult to their predecessors: "We reject the epithets that have been leveled at the maxims and memories of our predecessors in the episcopacy; and we remain inviolably attached to the doctrine that has been handed down to us on the rights of sovereigns and on their full and absolute independence from all ecclesiastical power in the temporal order." Thus, the bishops close ranks with Frayssinous on the issue of pure Gallicanism. To reaffirm the loyalty of the Gallican clergy to the principle of the independence of the sovereign is the most effective answer to the Liberal cry of Ultramontanism. The bishops' statement is impressive evidence that the throne is not threatened by the altar. Indeed, the bishops profess astonishment at Lamennais's effort to revive Ultramontanist doctrines discredited by history. Ultramontanism is defined as "an opinion born out of Europe's former state of anarchy and confusion, constantly rejected by the clergy of France, and fallen into an almost universal neglect." The bishops' accusation is just. Ultramontanism has risen from the ashes to embarrass the Restoration.

Lamennais presents himself for examination on the very day the La Chalotais decision is rendered. Stung by the La Chalotais case, the government is not happy at the prospect of this new engagement. The *Quotidienne* notes that no one except a Liberal can rejoice to see a priest in the docket. Bellart, the public prosecutor who saw the Liberal motives so clearly in the *Constitutionnel* affair, is called in for his advice. His memorandum reflects the Royalist dilemma: "I cannot, Monseigneur, be other than unhappy at the necessity of this prosecution. It is unfortunate for religion in these indifferent times . . . that this conflict should come before the courts."

Yet Bellart recommends prosecution because "tolerance would be worse than repression." Lamennais has committed the unpardonable sin: "He has created a sect within the religious party and introduced new doctrines in the State. And even more unforgivably, from Bellart's viewpoint, Lamennais has played into the hands of the Liberals, has furnished the enemies of religion with their strongest arguments: "On all sides the enemies of the Catholic religion represent it as incompatible with the existence of a politically independent order. By this kind of attack they do great harm, and they will end up by alienating a great number of people." If we are going to suppress Liberals for arguing that the Catholic religion is incompatible with the State, Bellart argues, surely we must suppress "a priest who has said the same thing, and who says more than they have dared to say." Lamennais is the only writer who has openly supported papal supremacy, and by so doing, "he has given an irresistible force to those warnings with which unbelievers have continued to regale the public." Lamennais has told his audience that it is not just the clergy, but religion itself, that is "incompatible with the independence of the civil power." By trying Lamennais, the government hopes to convince France that it is the enemy of Ultramontanism, that it is capable of upholding the Gallican liberties of 1682.

Lamennais is defended by his close friend Berryer, himself the author of a series of anti-Gallican articles for the *Quotidienne* in December 1825. Berryer was especially bitter about the Liberal "street-corner Gallicans": these Liberals, these modern Gallicans, these utterly improbable protectors of the liberties of the Church—wouldn't they be surprised if the royal authorities took their rhetoric seriously?[74] But Berryer the lawyer was even more interested in proving that Gallican liberties were not laws but debatable opinions, and this is the approach he takes in defending Lamennais. The trial consequently resolves itself into a single question: Is the Declaration of 1682, or is it not, the law of the land? Just as the La Chalotais case was essentially the retrial of the 1762 prosecution of the Jesuits, it is not Lamennais who is on trial here, but the Four Articles of 1682. And Berryer, before the court, proceeds to arraign these Articles as guilty: as unjustified by any previous legislation, as the mistaken product of circumstance, and as ultimately repudiated by Louis XIV. Lamennais is defended for having reminded France of these "salutary lessons of the past."[75] Berryer's voice is that of a Conservative genuinely bewildered by this revival of Gallicanism in the face of "all the great and terrible lessons of history." Lamennais concludes with a word in his own defense: those who recognize the Four Articles as the law of the land "recognize a law incompatible with my religion."

The details of this trial are less important than the outcome. With Lamennais's conviction, Gallican liberties are no longer a prize to be fought over by Liberal and Royal Gallicans; they are the law. The decision sends a shock through Conservative France, for as long as Gallicanism was a matter of opinion, the coalition could contain theological differences. But the Liberals have won their battle—Gallicanism is official, and there is no room in the coalition for supporters of the papacy. Commenting on the decision, the *Quotidienne* despairs: "The consequences of this judgment are so vast that it will be impossible for us to make them comprehensible in a single article." The fact that Lamennais has been convicted for violating the principles of 1682 "gives a theological character to the trial, and consequently something extraordinary and new even to the eyes of the Gallicans—we are speaking of Catholic Gallicans."[77] From the vantage point of the *Quotidienne,* the conviction of Lamennais is a victory not for the Catholic Gallicans, but for the Liberal Gallicans. In the eyes of Lamennais himself, the decision had done nothing less than establish a national Church, analogous to the Church of England.[78]

It is difficult to calculate the exact influence of Lamennais's attack on the Restoration monarchy.[79] His was so overwhelming a voice that he tended to have fanatical disciples rather than articulate supporters.* There are evidences that he represents a deep undercurrent in the religious sentiment of the Restoration. In 1825, a *curé* of Orleans is imprisoned for three years for telling his parishioners, "My dear brothers, Charles X is not a Christian, since he upholds the Charter, which is an act against religion; we must not pray for him any more than for Louis XVIII, who was the originator of this Charter. Both of them are damned. Those who concur, please rise."[80] The charge of a royal court is that two or three hundred rose in assent—this is the logic of Lamennais's stand carried into action.†

The extreme sensitivity of the government to the possible damage he can do is perhaps the best index of his influence. Frayssinous, in the same address in which he defends the Church from the charges of Montlosier and the Liberals, attacks Lamennais for attempting to "revive a completely superseded opinion."[81] Further, through his connections, Frayssinous throws into the struggle some of the great names of Conservative France: Clausel de Coussergues, his brother Clausel de Montals, Baron Frénilly, and Abbé Boyer.[82]

The Restoration coalition must deal with the enemy in its midst. Madrolle, in his volume directed against Montlosier, concludes by attacking Lamennais for "destroying with one hand what we are building with the other, misusing words and misinterpreting history, alone or almost alone against the entire Church of France. . . . This system of his is rejected by the Jesuits, rejected by Bonald, rejected by the great majority of Catholic writers . . . ; it is even rejected by Liberal writers and journalists."[83] But this effort to dismiss Lamennais only reveals the Royalist irritability at an attack upon the coalition from an unexpected quarter. Lamennais belongs in a book on Montlosier, for just as Montlosier represents a rift in the aristocracy, Lamennais represents a division within the clergy. Both have revived disturbing historical issues that the Restoration would rather forget.

* He adopts a position so extreme that he alienates the other famous Ultramontanists, including Maistre; "he loses himself in the excesses of an Ultramontanism unknown to Rome." (Thureau-Dangin, *Royalistes et républicains*, p. 257.) But it was this very intransigence, the fact that he quarreled with every other famous Ultramontanist, that he insulted every famous leader of the Conservative Restoration (Corbière, Lainé, Frayssinous, Archbishop Quélen), that made him so fertile a source of dissension.

† Another example of how Mennaisianism cuts across the Restoration coalition is found in the discussion that dominates the last year of the Restoration—the possibility of revolution. As we have seen, the Conservative coalition insists that it is in imminent danger. But J. B. Férat, a disciple of Lamennais, writes an essay entitled *Une Révolution, est-elle encore possible?* (1829), in which he argues that it is impossible since democracy has in fact won the day!

The events of the Restoration drove Lamennais further and further from the coalition. His own trial and conviction had indicated that the Restoration was determinedly, officially Gallican. By 1829, Lamennais is prepared to make the final break. The Montlosier affair, the Martignac regime, the June ordinances against the Jesuits, have convinced him that there is no security possible for the French clergy within the framework of the Restoration.

The Restoration is generally a period of great turnabouts: young Royalists like Lamartine and Hugo emerge as Republicans; three vigorous Liberals—Guizot, Thiers, and Casimir-Périer—are later to become Conservative premiers of France. But none of these shifts is as remarkable or dramatic as that of Lamennais. In 1829, this man who found Maistre and Bonald too Gallican, who found the Villèle regime too Liberal, considers the possibility of the French clergy's uniting with the Liberal opposition! For Lamennais, this is nothing more than the rigid application of his own Ultramontanist logic. He decides that Gallicanism is the only true enemy, and weighs Liberalism as the alternative to the Gallican position. Gallicanism he views as simply an adjunct to despotism, an attempt to make the king "an object of real idolatry."[84] Then he launches a vituperative attack upon the monarchy, which he sees as the historic tormentor of Catholics. He specifically takes issue with Royalists who call for censorship to halt the flow of Liberal propaganda: "In the present state of Europe, with governments having no doctrines or only false ones, the oppression of censorship would weigh almost exclusively on the Catholics . . . as it did during the Revolution and long before, beginning with Louis XIV under the Gallican despotism and the degenerate monarchy." Having linked Gallicanism to monarchical despotism, Lamennais quite naturally seeks an alliance with the enemy of despotism, liberty.

Once he has suggested this startling alliance, it quickly captivates him, and he proceeds with his customary brilliance to justify it historically and philosophically: "Is it not indeed under the empire of Catholic Christianity that all European liberties have been conceived and developed, in Spain, Italy, France, and England?" The idea of the historical congruence of Catholic Christianity and liberty appeals to him more and more; he sees the League—"this great Catholic confederation"—as an example of this union, the Vendée rising against the despotism of the Revolution as another. A contemporary event affords him the opportunity to speculate further. A national Liberal Catholic movement exists in Belgium, and Lamennais considers: "Thus, even in our own day, we see the Low Countries, arms in hand, regain their religious and political liberties in a noble upsurge of patriotism and faith." Patriotic *and* religious *and* political liberty—this combination of words had never occurred to Lamennais before, and in this observation on the Belgian situation is the foreshadowing of his own drift to the Left.

At this point he seems about to cross the line, but he is not quite ready. He must first examine Liberalism to ascertain that it is a possible partner; he decides that Liberalism is misdirected Christianity.

The balance of *Des Progrès de la Révolution* is devoted to an attack upon the Restoration monarchy and its supporters. Lamennais flatly says that the Church is, at the present time, the enemy of the State. "She [the Church] has constantly more to fear than to hope from princes." He sees a pattern of antireligious activity from the establishment of the "democratic republic" in 1814 to the ordinances against the Jesuits, "an inquisition for which Henry VIII at his worst did not supply a model."

This discussion of the Jesuits reminds Lamennais that the Liberals' stand on this issue was far from satisfactory. He professes to find their attitude inconsistent: Don't they realize, he asks, that by supporting Gallicanism they are supporting the despotism of Louis XIV? He is sorry to see them duped by the Royalist Gallicans: "Most of those who are called Liberals . . . do not even suspect that they are cooperating in this wretched development." He realizes that they are not true Gallicans, that their Gallicanism is merely a device for proving their loyalty: "The Liberals . . . affect an ardent zeal for the rights of royalty, making themselves Gallicans and parliamentarians." Lamennais's real venom is reserved for the sincere Gallicans, who are, of course, Royalists. He even credits the Liberal Gallicans with not intending to destroy the Church: "They think they can go just so far, weakening the Church but not destroying it. Vain thought!" Given this Gallican party—one part Liberal, one part Royalist—what can the Church do? "The Church must perpetually battle against this twofold assault."

Lamennais concludes his work with a chapter on the duties of the French clergy in the existing state of affairs. Here he is addressing his own loyal following as well as that part of France which is unhappy with the Galliacan party of the Restoration. He at last raises the question implicit throughout the book—can we ally with the Liberals? He rejects the alliance, but in the very same sentence he also rejects any agreement with the Restoration monarchy: "The clergy cannot ally itself with Liberalism, . . . nor can it ally itself with the political power which seeks to destroy and abolish it, in order to establish an absolute despotism on its ruins."

Neutrality in the struggle that looms ahead is the only other possibility, and this is the course Lamennais urges upon the Church. It should "fortify itself in the middle of the battle of peoples and kings, without taking any direct part. The conquerors, whoever they may be, will one day fall at its feet." This is the death knell of the Restoration; in this final struggle which Lamennais so clearly foresees, he advises the French clergy—that integral part of the coalition—to remain outside. There is no ambiguity about this advice; Lamennais emphasizes his recommendation: "We cannot repeat too often, the most pressing duty of the clergy in the present circumstances is to isolate itself completely from an atheistic political society. . . . Disengage yourself from all parties."

Lamennais's *Des Progrès de la Révolution* appeared in January 1829. The religious interests turned upon him savagely, everyone from *L'Ami de la religion* to the papal nuncio. A friend, Benoît d'Azy, writing to Lamennais, records the excitement: "This is a time of strife for your friends. The salons ring with discussions of your book. . . . A long work in reply to yours is being prepared at the seminary of Saint Sulpice, in the spirit that you have already seen in the *Gazette de France* articles. Unbelievable vehemence is going into it."[85]

In the fatal concluding year of the Restoration (1829–30), Lamennais himself keeps the controversy alive, answering the attacks of Gallican churchmen and Conservative spokesmen who struggled to soften his charges and weaken his influence. He engages in full-scale controversies with Flottes, who speaks for the Gallican Church, and Frénilly who speaks in behalf of the monarchy of Charles X.[86]

But again, as in 1826, the Church officially moves against Lamennais. In February 1829, the Archbishop of Paris issues a pastoral letter chastening "the fondness for -isms, that sad and dangerous temptation of the finest talents, . . . [which] threatens us with an internal war." Lamennais is specifically attacked for having abused "one of our greatest kings and one of the most intelligent of our pontiffs."[87] In addition, he is charged with having insulted the Church of France by suggesting that the clergy almost unanimously reject the Articles of 1682. And the Archbishop summarizes, in a single sentence, Lamennais's fatal error. He is one of those bold writers who "render religion suspect to the powers established by God himself, who bear out all the warnings of heresy against Gallicanism, and who call down the mistrust and hatred of peoples upon the Church."[88] This is the threefold danger of Mennaisian Ultramontanism in the Restoration: that he has made Royalists suspicious of religion; that he has supported the Liberal claim of a threat to Gallicanism; that he has aroused fresh fears in the minds of Liberal France.

In a series of letters to the archbishop of Paris, Lamennais replied to this latest effort of the Gallican Restoration to muzzle him. He makes no effort to deny that he is a thorn in the flesh of the Restoration; indeed he reiterates his attack on Gallicanism. Yes, he admits, he has attacked Louis XIV, "but what is this strange respect which, after 150 years, would impose a silence upon history?"[89] In a letter to the editor of the *Quotidienne*, he clarifies his views: "In truth, I believe . . . that in saying that Louis XIV substituted despotism for the ancient constitutional monarchy I was in agreement with the judgment of history and with Fénelon."[90] As for the Gallicanism so dear to the heart of Louis XIV, it is simply the Protestantism of Catholicism; for

Lamennais looks upon Gallicanism and Catholicism as a contradiction in terms.

Despite attacks on the Gallican clergy and intrigue in Rome,[91] Lamennais continued his fifteen-year struggle against the Gallican Restoration. If anything, the assaults of the official Restoration drove him further and further into a rapprochement with the Liberals. By March 1830, he devotes an article in the *Revue catholique* to the work of a Belgian Liberal Catholic whose position anticipates Lamennais's during the July Monarchy. L. F. Robiano de Borsbeek had in fact laid the foundations for the Liberal-Catholic alliance when he wrote:

Catholics do not know how to be free alone; liberty for all has become the necesary condition of their liberty. . . . The Liberals ask for the same liberties as ours. Their aversion to despotism and their just horror of the yoke it seeks to impose are always laudable, and in that we [Catholics] will aid those of stout heart. In resisting with us, they [Liberals] obey an inner sentiment common to all men, and without knowing it, the ancient impulse of Christianity. Thus we believe that their distance from Christianity is not too great to close. . . . The Liberals have thrown away a great part of their anti-Catholic prejudices, and they are close to us.[92]

After quoting at such great length, Lamennais comments: "What dignity, and at the same time what wisdom, in this language."[93] In Robiano's argument we find the rationale that will drive Lamennais completely outside the coalition and, later, from Ultramontanism to Social Christianity.

It is now possible to see that Lamennais's Ultramontanism and his fierce anti-Gallicanism are stages in a personal development that is to make him one of the nineteenth-century apostles of Liberal and Social Catholicism, and ultimately carry him out of the Church. When, in October 1830, Lamennais founds his new journal *L'Avenir,* he selects as his motto "Catholicism and Liberty." The campaign he then launches is the complete repudiation of everything he stood for in the Restoration. Modern scholars friendly to this later and admittedly more sympathetic Lamennais have tended to ignore his Restoration "phase," to regard the Restoration as an experimental laboratory where Lamennais worked out his religious ideas. Lamennais may have "outgrown" the Restoration, but not before he had played his part, had helped divide the coalition, and had helped deliver the death stroke to the Restoration, that last effort of Conservative France to direct the destinies of the nation.

CHAPTER VIII

Conclusion

> A new generation has risen; it delves into the monuments of our history and fashions itself anew in the image of these monuments.
>
> Benjamin Constant

With regard to the Liberal historians, this work has fallen into a natural division between political historians, concerned principally with defending the French Revolution, and religious historians, interested in reviving Gallicanism and exposing Jesuits. At this point some comparisons are in order.

The need to whitewash the French Revolution was a continuing problem for the Liberal historians. The Revolution was lurking beneath every political issue; again and again it had to be explained and defended, right up to the very day the revolution of 1830 successfully enshrined it. On the other hand, the histories analyzing Gallicanism or Jesuitism were generated for immediate occasions to illuminate specific controversies. The Gallican histories were a response to the debate over the Concordat; the attacks upon the Jesuits picked up where they left off and reached their greatest intensity in the Montlosier affair.

This circumstantial difference can account for the varying character of the works. The Liberals' version of French history represents a considerable achievement. Created out of the most intense partisanship, it nevertheless succeeded in illuminating the Revolution. In defending themselves, they laid the groundwork for a general defense of the Revolution which is to dominate historical debate and serve French Liberalism throughout the nineteenth century.

Further, faced with the Conservatives' version of the French past, the Liberals were compelled to reëxamine all of French history, to ransack the past for instances of Liberal virtue or Conservative skulduggery. This may be the key to the greatness of the Liberal historians of the Revolution. The political history of France was a vast lacuna, a challenge big enough for the energies of men like Guizot, Thierry, Barante, Trognon. In this enterprise of unlocking musty chambers clogged with official apologia, their Liberal bias was their strength. Finally, it is interesting to note that, in the best of them, there was a reaction to the abuses suffered by history in the service of politics. Thierry, writing in 1827, chides the eager polemicist of 1820. Guizot's 1829 lectures are richer, fuller, and sprinkled with warnings about a narrow political commitment to history. Trognon, that fierce resuscitator of medieval communes, by 1829 is praising a historian for "not having dreamed of placing history in the service of political theories."[1] Evidence of this late Restoration drift—a natural reaction to the over-politicization of history—is to be found in Guizot's *Revue française*, where the Restoration tendency is attacked as "transforming history into a veritable novel, a monarchical novel in one century, republican in the other."[2]

This reaction in the direction of a more balanced, scientific history raises the Liberal historians in the judgment of the modern scholar. But it must not be forgotten that the historical virtues of Thierry, Mme de Staël, Guizot, Mignet—and they possess virtues, from great intelligence to great readability—are the result of their Liberal commitment.

When we turn to the Liberal historians of religion, their very undertaking dooms them to mediocrity. Since their purpose is not to convince but to divide, they are content merely to dredge up the religious record. There is no need for original work, for fresh versions of the Jesuits or the Concordat of 1516. These Liberals do not have to quarrel with the previous views of the religious history of France—there exists sufficient dissension within that history; there is no necessity to uncover a Liberal side. Thus, their function is merely to present these facts, to collect the damaging and divisive sources, to display them appropriately, and to watch them work. Indeed, it is the special strength of this Liberal operation that it needs little Liberal doctoring—eighteenth-century aristocratic critics of the Jesuits are far more effective than nineteenth-century unbelievers.

Thus, in rejecting the Conservative version of the political past, the Liberals have become historians; in gladly accepting the Conservative version of the religious past, the Liberals have become judicious compilers of old calumnies.

As for the Conservatives, we have seen them become divided in the process of replying to the Liberal historians. The attack on the Old Regime called forth defenders of the special interests of monarchy, aristocracy, and clergy. The revival of Gallicanism called Gallicans and Ultramontanists to arms. In both cases, 1830 was the measure of the Liberal success. In that year, the Liberals succeeded in convincing France of the necessity of insurrection in order to preserve a Charter which embodied the French Revolution. By 1830, the Liberals have been equally successful in this second campaign:

the Jesuits are eliminated; Lamennais has broken with the Gallican Church and the French monarchy.

Perhaps the real symbol of the triumph of the Liberal version of history in selling the Revolution and splitting the coalition is the figure of Chateaubriand. Chateaubriand, the voice of the Restoration in 1814, the fierce Ultra of 1820, the Royalist leader of 1823, writes on the French Revolution in 1830: "It is clear that massacre, injustice, looting, are not, as has been believed, peculiar to our revolutionary times. The terrorists of St. Bartholomew and the League were aristocratic nobles, kings, princes, *gentilshommes* . . ."[3]

Shades of the Liberal history!

Notes

NOTES TO CHAPTER I

1. *Revue encyclopédique* (1827), XXXII, 679.
2. Joseph Fiévée, *Histoire de la session de 1817* (1818), p. 149.
3. Louis de Bonald, *Pensées sur divers sujets* (1817), II, 53.
4. A. G. P. de Barante, *Mélanges historiques et littéraires*, 3d ed. (1835), II, 43.
5. Quoted in E. Hatin, *Histoire politique et littéraire de la presse en France* (1859–61), VIII, 226.

NOTES TO CHAPTER II

1. See François Guizot, *Mémoires pour servir à l'histoire de mon temps*, 3d ed. (1861), I, 157, 193, for summations of this situation.
2. On the attitude of the Empire toward history, see Dacier's remarks on Napoleon in Louis Halphen, *L'Histoire en France depuis cent ans* (1914), p. 4. There was some historical writing contemporary with the event. See Aulard, *Premiers Historiens de la Révolution française, Etudes et leçons sur la Révolution française* (1910), VI, 32–134.
3. A. Jubé de la Perrelle, *Quelques Mots sur la proclamation de M. le comte de Chateaubriand* (1818), p. 5.
4. Guillaume N. Lallement, ed., *Choix de rapports, opinions et discours prononcés à la tribune nationale* (1818–23), I, viii.
5. Mme. de Staël, *Considérations sur les principaux événemens de la Révolution françoise*, 2d ed. (1818). The page numbers cited in the present book are those of the first English translation, *Considerations on the Principal Events of the French Revolution* (London, 1818); here Vol. I., p. 2.
6. Benjamin Constant, *De la Doctrine politique qui peut réunir les partis en France*, 2d ed. (1817), p. 10.
7. M. N. Rioust, *Carnot* (1817), p. ix.
8. Guizot, *Discours prononcé pour l'ouverture du Cours d'histoire moderne* (December 7, 1820), p. 10.
9. Staël, *Considerations*, I, 16–17. Cf. Guizot, *Des Moyens de gouvernement et d'opposition dans l'état actuel de France* (1821), p. 188. "Scrupulous champions of law show us one empire, one society formed under its auspices alone, tell us of a single victory exempt from pillage and blood."
10. Staël, *Considerations*, I, 17.
11. Guizot, *Discours prononcé*, pp. 9, 12. This entire address is a landmark in the changing conceptions of history.
12. "The Revolution of 1789 had then no other object than to give a regular form to the limitations which have existed all along in France." Staël, *Considerations*, I, 146.
13. A. Carrion-Nisas, *De la Liberté et des factions, ou coup d'oeil sur l'état de la liberté publique aux divers époques de notre histoire et sur son état présent* (1819), p. 5.
14. *Ibid.*, p. 6.
15. *Ibid.*, p. 8.
16. *Ibid.*, p. 28.
17. *Ibid.*, p. 37.
18. *Ibid.*, p. 76. Carrion-Nisas cites two specific examples of this ancient liberty, one a statement of the Estates of 1438, and the other a demurrer by a deputy from Burgundy objecting to a treaty made by Francis I with Spain.
19. *Ibid.*, p. 90.
20. Augustin Thierry, *Lettres sur l'histoire de France*, new edition (1859), Preface

to 1827 edition, p. 3. See also Fritz Stern (ed.), *The Varieties of History* (New York, 1956), pp. 66–70. See also *The Historical Essays Published Under the Title of "Dix Ans d'Etudes Historiques" and Narratives of the Merovingian Era* (Philaphelphia: Carey & Hart, 1845), p. 9. For a summation of the case for Thierry as a racial historian and under the influence of poetry, see Emery Neff, *The Poetry of History* (New York, 1947).

21. Thierry, *Dix ans d'Études Historiques* (bound with *Lettres sur l'Histoire de France*), Preface to 1834 edition, p. 300.

22. *Ibid.*, p. 301. The 1818 article is quoted.

23. *Ibid.*, pp. 301–2.

24. Thierry, *Lettres*, p. 20. It is "absurd to base a history of France upon the Franks alone."

25. Thierry, *Dix ans*, p. 501.

26. *Ibid.*, pp. 502, 503.

27. See articles V, IX, and XIV, *ibid.*, Part II.

28. Thierry, *Lettres*, pp. 3–4.

29. *Ibid.*, p. 4, my italics; pp. 12, 13–14, 10.

30. *Ibid.*, p. 12.

31. For a discussion of the impact of the book, see Charles H. Pouthas, *Guizot pendant la Restauration* (1923), pp. 272–75.

32. Guizot, *Du Gouvernement de la France depuis la Restauration et du ministère actuel*, 2d ed. (1820), pp. 1, 2.

33. *Ibid.*, pp. 2–3.

34. Guizot, *History of the Origin of Representative Government*, English translation (London, 1852), Opening of Course in Modern History on December 7, 1820, p. 6. Pouthas, *Guizot pendant la Restauration*, p. 312, gives a brilliant summary of Guizot's history: "To place all history in the service of representative government . . . , to discover *des titres séculaires de la noblesse* for constitutional monarchy, and to successfully oppose them to the theories of divine right and aristocracy."

35. Guizot, *Representative Government*, p. 5.

36. *Ibid.*, p. 12.

37. Guizot, *History of Civilisation in Europe*, translated by William Hazlitt (London, 1873).

38. Auguste Trognon, *Etudes sur l'histoire de France* (1836), p. 400.

39. Trognon, *Etudes*, p. 123.

40. *Ibid.*, pp. 131, 133–34.

41. Félicité de Lamennais, *De la Religion considérée dans ses rapports avec l'ordre politique et civil* (1825), in *Œuvres complètes*, V, 128. "The French Revolution was a rigidly precise application of the final consequences of Protestantism."

42. Staël, *Considerations*, I, 24.

43. Trognon, *Sur les Guerres de religion du seizième siècle en France, in Etudes*, p. 282.

44. Léon Thiessé, *Résumé de l'histoire de la Révolution française* (1828), p. 7.

45. Guizot, *Mémoires*, I, 318.

46. Carrion-Nisas, *De la Liberté*, p. 103. Note Saint Giraud's remark in Stendhal's *Le Rouge et le noir*: "The history of England serves as a mirror to show me our future." *The Red and the Black*, English translation (New York, 1926), II, 10.

47. Abbé de Montgaillard, *Histoire de France*, 2d ed. (1827), IX, 231.

48. See Introduction to P. V. de Besnavel, *Mémoires du Baron de Besnavel* (1821), in *Collection des mémoires relatifs à la révolution française*, III, xxvi. "But the Baron de Besnavel was mistaken in imputing this great insurrection to the work of the *philosophes*." Cf. Thiessé, *Résumé de la Révolution*, p. 11; "Voltaire, Rousseau, and the other writers were the organs, not the authors of it."

49. Victor Cousin, *Cours de l'histoire de la philosophie* (1829), Lecture I, pp. 35–36.

50. *Ibid.*, pp. 8, 9, 34, 36.

51. Staël, *Considerations*, I, 88.

52. "Politique spéciale," in *Archives philosophiques, politiques et littéraires* (1827), I, 139; C. L. Le Sur, *La France et les Français en 1817*, 2d ed. (1818), p. 5. Le Sur managed to hold on to his job as inspector of the Paris lottery until 1825. He was also editor of the *Annvaire historique universel.*

53. Thiessé, *Résumé de la Révolution*, p. 10.

54. Montgaillard, *Histoire de France*, IX, 217.

55. Alexis de Tocqueville, *Democracy in America*, translated by Henry Reeve (New York, 1945), II, 87–88.

56. André Dupin, *Mémoires* (1855), I, 194. Cf. Félix Bodin, *Résumé de l'histoire de France*, 3d ed. (1823), p. 172. "The Revolution was already made when Louis XVI mounted the throne."

57. Charles de Rémusat, "Sur la situation du gouvernement" (1818), in *Critiques et études, ou Passé et présent*, new ed. (1857), p. 72.

58. Guizot, *Des Moyens*, p. 119.

59. Montgaillard, *Histoire de France*, IX, 280.

60. Staël, *Considerations*, I, 182–83.

61. *Ibid.*, p. 188.

62. Le Sur, *La France et les Français*, p. 5; C. H. Richard, *Aperçu de la Révolution française et des véritables intérêts de la royauté dans l'état actuel des choses* (1820), p. 30. Cf. Thiessé, *Résumé de la Révolution*, p. 11.

63. Thiessé, *Résumé de la Révolution*, p. 6.

64. Jacques Antoine Dulaure, *Causes secrètes des excès de la Révolution* (1815), p. 4.

65. Dulaure, *Equisses historiques des principaux événemens de la Révolution* (1823), I, 31.

66. Lazare Carnot, *Mémoire addressé au roi en juillet 1814* (Brussels, 1814), pp. 14–16.

67. *Ibid.*, pp. 17–18.

68. Jubé de la Perrelle, *Lettre à M. le Vicomte de Chateaubriand . . .* (1816), p. 19.

69. Staël, *Considerations*, I, 46–47.

70. *Ibid.*, p. 434.

71. Guizot's article, originally in *Archives*, reprinted in *Moniteur*, August 21, 1818.

72. Thiessé, *Résumé de la Révolution*, pp. 218–19.

73. Benjamin Constant, *Des Effets du régime qu'on nomme révolutionnaire relativement au salut et à la liberté de la France* (1797), reprinted in *Mélanges politiques et historiques relatifs aux evénemens contemporains* (1829), p. 348.

74. *Ibid.*, p. 348 n.

75. See also Constant, *De la Doctrine*, p. 10.

76. "Politique spéciale," in *Archives* (1818), III, 50.

77. Guizot, *Du Gouvernement représentatif et de l'état actuel de la France* (1816), p. 2. See also Rémusat, "La Révolution française" (1818), in Rémusat, *Critiques*, p. 99.

78. Guizot, *Du Gouvernement de la France*, Preface to 3d ed., p. xviii.

79. Guizot, *Des Moyens*, pp. 26–27.

80. Carrion-Nisas, *La France au dix-neuvième siècle* (1821), pp. 53–54. See also Rémusat, "La Révolution française," in Rémusat, *Critiques*, p. 108.

81. Carrion-Nisas, *La France au dix-neuvième siècle*, p. 139.

82. Bodin, *Résumé de l'histoire de France*, p. 184.

83. *Ibid.*, p. 198.

84. *Ibid.*, p. 199. Also see Thiessé, *Résumé de la Révolution*, pp. 92, 112, 171.

85. M. S. Foy, *Discours du Général Foy* (1826), II, 29.

86. Staël, *Considerations*, I, 275, 284–85.

87. Jacques de Norvins, *Tableau de la Révolution française* (1819), Preface. See also Carrion-Nisas, *La France au dix-neuvième siècle*, p. 87.

88. C. E. de Ferrières, *Mémoires du marquis de Ferrières*, 2d ed. (1822), in *Collection des mémoires*, V, vii.

89. Montgaillard, *Histoire de France*, I, 3, 5.

90. Bodin, *Résumé de l'histoire de France*, p. 190.

91. Thiessé, *Résumé de la Révolution*, p. 190.

92. François Mignet, *History of the French Revolution*, English translation (London, 1846), p. 1.

93. Benjamin Laroche, *Considérations sur l'ouvrage de M. Guizot* (1820), p. 33.

94. Richard, *Aperçu*, p. 34 n.

95. *Mémoires sur les journées de septembre 1792* (1823), in *Collection des mémoires*, XLIV, xiv.

96. *Ibid.*, pp. xiv–xv.

97. Montgaillard, *Histoire de France*, IX, 218–19, 224, 222.

98. *Ibid.*, p. 223. For another example of comparative criminology, cf. J. D. Lanjuinais, *Constitutions de la nation française* (1819), II, 34–35. "Must one speak of the frightful League, of the ridiculous though bloody Fronde, of the wars of La Rochelle, of the *dragonnades* of Louis XIV and the war of the Cevennes; of the tortures ordered by Richelieu's commissioners; of the *visirats* of Mazarin, Dubois, Fleury and the hundred thousand exiles and arbitrary imprisonments which these favorites ordered?"

99. Montgaillard, *Histoire de France*, IX, 229.

100. Thiessé, *Résumé de la Révolution*, p. 6.

101. Rémusat, "La Révolution française" in Rémusat, *Critiques*, p. 99.

102. Cousin, *Cours*, p. 33.

103. *Ibid.*, p. 34.

104. *Ibid.*

105. Guizot, *Du Gouvernement représentatif*, p. 1. Sully's remark was often quoted: "It is the refusal of justice that wrecks states."

106. Guizot, *Du Gouvernement de la France*, Preface to 3d ed., pp. xxvi–xxvii.

107. *Ibid.*, p. xxviii.

108. Guizot, *Des Moyens*, p. 187. Cf. Richard, "The French Revolution was legitimate." *Aperçu*, p. 21.

109. Camille Jordan, *La Session de 1817, aux habitans de Bain et du Rhône* (1817), p. 24.

110. Thiessé, *Résumé de la Révolution*, p. 5.

111. *Ibid.*, p. 219.

NOTES TO CHAPTER III

1. J. S. Bailly, *Mémoires de Bailly* (1821–22), in *Collection des mémoires*, VIII, i.

2. J. B. Louvet de Couvray, *Mémoires de Louvet de Couvray*, in *Collection des mémoires*, XLIII, iv.

3. *Ibid.*, p. iii.

4. P. T. Durand de Maillane, *Histoire de la Convention nationale* (1825), in *Collection des mémoires*, XXVII, ii.

5. In the upper Chamber, Lanjuinais fights to preserve the Revolution, to prevent the return of property to the clergy, to prevent the suppression of married priests, to broaden the general amnesty. See details in biographical sketch by Victor Lanjuinais in J. D. Lanjuinais, *Œuvres complètes* (1832), Vol. I. See also Montgaillard, *Histoire de France*, IX, 16.

6. Lanjuinais, *Œuvres*, I, 316.

7. For other examples of this phenomenon, see Rioust, *Carnot*, p. ix, and the defense of Danou by the *Courrier français*, February 6, 1829.

8. *Refutation de l'opinion de M. le comte de Lanjuinais*, quoted in Lanjuinais, *Œuvres*, I, 333.

9. *Ibid.*, p. 343. Lanjuinais did not confine himself to self-defense. In 1815, he helped defend Ney. In 1817, he fought for pensions for Monge, Grégoire, and twenty-nine other peers who sat during the Hundred Days. In 1819, he defended his brother, who was deposed as canon of Rennes.

10. P. T. Tissot, *Précis ou histoire abrégé des guerres de la Révolution française* (1821), p. ii.

11. F. A. Doppet, *Mémoires politiques et militaires du Général Doppet* (1824), Vol. XL; L. M. Turreau de Linières, *Mémoires pour servir à l'histoire de la guerre de la Vendée* (1824), Vol. XXXV; C. F. D. Dumouriez, *La Vie et les mémoires du Général Dumouriez* (1822–23), Vols. XVI–XIX; J. J. M. Savary, *Guerres des Vendéens et des Chouans contre la République française* (1824–27), Vols. XXVIII–XXXIII. All in *Collection des mémoires* series.

12. Dumouriez, *La Vie*, p. iii.

13. Foy, *Discours*, I, 258–59.

14. Dupin, *Mémoires*, I, 64, 127, 124–26, 112–14, 66–72. For the Royalist efforts to punish the Napoleonic army, see Edmund Bonnal des Ganges, *Les Royalistes contre l'armée (1815–1820)* (1906).

15. *Ibid.*, pp. 133–35, 114–16, 142–48.

16. Writing to Dupin in 1834, Marshal MacDonald calls him this. *Ibid.*, p. 81.

17. *Ibid.*, p. 79.

18. *Archives parlementaires*, 2d ser., January 15, 1818.

19. *Ibid.*, January 16, 1818.

20. *Ibid.*, January 25, 1818.

21. *Ibid.*, January 24, 1818.

22. *Ibid.*, January 17, 1818.

23. On the authorship of this speech, see Pouthas, *Guizot pendant la Restauration*, p. 184.

24. *Archives parlementaires*, January 26, 1818.

25. Pouthas has gathered together these reactions, *Guizot pendant la Restauration*, p. 185.

26. *Ibid.*, p. 184.

27. See *Remède unique aux maux de l'église et de l'état*, par un curé de campagne, 3d ed. (1817), which expresses dissatisfaction with the penitence of January 1816, and urges a greater expiation.

28. Achille de Vaulabelle, *Histoire des deux restaurations* (1874), IV, 29.

29. *Archives parlementaires*. The debate begins December 2, 1819.

30. *Ibid.*, December 6, 1819.

31. *Ibid.*, April 20, 1819.

32. *Ibid.*, December 6, 1819. Quotations in the next four paragraphs are all from the same source.

33. Carnot, *Mémoires addressés au roi*, p. 11.

34. *Ibid.*, p. 23.

35. *Ibid.*, pp. 23–24, 26.

36. *Ibid.*, p. 27.

37. *Ibid.*, p. 30.

38. Carnot, *Exposé de la conduite politique de M. le Lieutenant Général depuis le 1 juillet 1814* (1815).

39. F. R. de Chateaubriand, *Réflexions politiques* (1814). See also F. M. Guillot, *Le Jacobinisme réfuté, ou Observations critiques sur le mémoire de M. Carnot addressé au roi en 1814* (1815).

40. See *Moniteur*, March 31, 1817, for details of the case.

41. *Ibid.*

42. Rioust, *Carnot*, p. ix.

43. Rioust, *Procès du Sr. M.-N. Rioust pour son ouvrage ayant pour titre Carnot* (1817), p. 32.

44. *Ibid.*, p. 33.

45. *Ibid.*, p. 50.

46. This charge is based upon the words in the text, "The revolution of the eighteenth century was the crisis by which philosophy wished to separate itself . . . from the errors, false maxims, the arbitrary procedures of governments, of religious absurdities." *Ibid.*, p. 34. (Rioust, in the *Procès*, frequently quotes from his *Carnot* to refute the charges.)

47. Rioust, *Procès*, p. 35. Quotations in the next four paragraphs are from the same source, pp. 38–44.

48. *Moniteur*, March 31, 1817.

49. Rioust, *Procès*, p. 162. The decision is given in full on pp. 161–63.

50. Tissot, *Mémoires historiques et militaires sur Carnot* (1824), in *Collection des mémoires*, LI, 1.

51. *Ibid.*, p. xi.

52. Constant, *De la Doctrine*, p. 10; the footnote contains a special plea for army.

53. "Politique spéciale—choix des hommes," in *Archives* (1817), II, 65. Cf. Guizot, *Des Moyens*, pp. 256–57: "A minister devoted to the Bourbons ought to know that the very men of the revolution, those who took part in its actions and grew old under its banners, are no longer intractable."

54. Jean Baptiste Billecocq, *De l'Influence de la guerre d'Espagne sur l'affermissement de la dynastie légitime et de la monarchie constitutionnelle en France* (1823), p. 7. For the best recent treatment of the whole Spanish question see Bertier de Sauvigny, *La Restauration*, pp. 240–69.

55. *Archives parlementaires*, February 8, 1823.

56. *Ibid.*, February 24, 1823. Subsequent quotations are from this same speech of Royer-Collard.

57. *Ibid.*, February 25, 1823.

58. *Ibid.*, February 24, 1823. Subsequent quotations are from Labourdonnaye's same speech.

59. *Ibid.*, February 25, 1823. Subsequent quotations are from this speech by Chateaubriand.

60. Guizot, *Du Gouvernement représentatif*, p. 5.

61. "Politique Spéciale," in *Archives* (1817), I, 138.

62. *Ibid.*, p. 141.

63. Guizot is replying to a pamphlet of Chateaubriand, *Remarques sur les affaires du moment* (1818). Guizot's answer appears in *Archives*, and is reprinted in *Moniteur*, August 21, 1818.

64. *Ibid.*

65. *Ibid.* Guizot quotes this from a speech of Royer-Collard (*Archives parlementaires*, January 27, 1817)—an example of Doctrinaire teamwork.

66. *Archives parlementaires*, May 1, 1820.

67. Guizot in *Moniteur*, August 21, 1818.

68. Royer-Collard in *Archives parlementaires*, January 27, 1817.

69. Guizot, *Du Gouvernement de la France*, p. 3.

70. For a full treatment of this complex development, see Paul Thureau-Dangin, *Royalistes et républicains* (1874).

71. Guizot, *Des Moyens*, p. 142. Subsequent quotations, *ibid.*, pp. 156–57, 186–87, 205–17 *passim.*

72. Carrion-Nisas, *La France au dix-neuvième siècle*, chap. iv.

73. Cousin, *Cours*, pp. 36–38.

74. For a full statement of the Conservative position, see Chapter IV below.

75. *National*, January 15, 1830.

76. *Ibid.*, January 17, 1830.

77. *Ibid.*, January 22 and 23, 1830.

78. *Ibid.*, January 29, 1830. Subsequent quotations from same issue.

79. *Journal des débats*, January 21, 1830.

80. *Ibid.*, February 1830.

81. *Ibid.*

82. Charles Cottu, *De la Nécessité d'une dictature* (1830).

83. *Globe*, March 7, 1830.

84. *Ibid.*

85. The following quotations are all from Agier's speech, *Archives parlementaires*, March 15, 1830.

NOTES TO CHAPTER IV

1. Joseph de Maistre, *Considérations sur la France* (1796) in *Œuvres complètes . . .*, new edition (Lyon, 1884–86), I, 15. See also p. 12, speaking of the regicide, "Never has so great a crime belonged to so great a number of guilty persons."

2. *Ibid.*, I, 22.

3. *Ibid.*, pp. 4–5, 7, 9.

4. See, for example, Chateaubriand's work of 1796 on revolution (*Essai sur les Révolutions*), which he tries hard to suppress in the Restoration. For a discussion of the Conservative historians in exile, see Paul Beik, *French Revolution Seen from the Right, Social Theories in Motion*, pp. 63–90.

5. Chateaubriand in the *Conservateur* (1818), I, 475–76.

6. *Les Principes de la Révolution française* (Chalons-sur-Saône, 1820), p. 1.

7. *Les Fastes de l'anarchie, ou Précis chronologique des événemens mémorables de la Révolution française* (1820), p. iii.

8. *Ibid.*, pp. 1–5. Jouffroy's attack is an attempt to split the Empire and the Revolution apart, to argue that the Revolution should not get the credit for the work of Bonaparte: "We do not deny the good that was produced in the course of the Revolution, but we deny that the Revolution produced this good."

9. [A. Madrolle], *De la Révolution dans ses rapports avec ses victimes et particulièrement avec les émigrés* (1824), p. iii.

10. *Ibid.*, pp. iii, footnote, and ix.

11. *Du Seul Moyen de sortir de la crise actuelle* (1829), p. 71.

12. Louis de Bonald, *Observations sur l'ouvrage de Madame la baronne de Staël* (1818), in *Œuvres*, V, 400–401.

13. Maistre, *Œuvres complètes*, VIII, 487.

14. P.L.B., *De la Restauration considerée comme le terme et non le triomphe de la Révolution et de l'abus des doctrines politiques; en réponse à l'ouvrage de M. F. Guizot . . .* (1820), p. 9.

15. *Ibid.*, pp. 13, 14.

16. *Ibid.*, pp. 19, 20.

17. J. C. Clausel de Coussergues, *Du Sacre des rois de France et des rapports de cette auguste cérémonie avec la constitution de l'état aux différens âges de la monarchie* (1825), pp. vii–viii. The works quoted by Clausel are Barante, *Histoire des ducs de Bourgogne*, and Ségur, *Histoire de la campagne de Russie*.

18. See Gilbert Stenger, *The Return of the Bourbons* (New York, 1909), pp. 97–98.

19. Baron Henrion, *Vie de M. Frayssinous* (1844), I, 84, 125.

20. Hyacinthe Louis de Quélen, *Oraison funèbre . . . [du] duc de Berry* (1820), pp. 10, 11–12, 13–14.

21. *Mémoires de la vie et de la mort du duc de Berry* (1820), p. 9.

22. Joseph Fiévée, *Correspondance politique et administrative* (1815–19), III, No. 11, p. 15.

23. *Ibid.*, III, No. 13, p. 14.

24. *Discours du Général Foy*, I, 4.

25. Claude H. Clausel de Montals, *Réponse aux Quatre Concordats de M. de Pradt* (1819), p. 81.

26. Henrion, *Vie de Frayssinous*, I, 281.

27. *Ibid.*, II, 381–82. For other defenses of Louis XIV, see J. L. H. F. Roche, *Essai analytique sur l'histoire universelle* (1823), II, 90–110 (this work is recommended by Frayssinous for teaching history in the schools), and F. T. Delbare, *Le Siècle de Louis XIV* (1823).

28. For examples of the Liberal attack on Louis XIV, see Mme de Staël, *Considérations*; L. de Sainte-Aulaire, *Histoire de la Fronde* (1827); P. E. Lemontey, *Essai sur l'établissement monarchique de Louis XIV et sur les altérations qu'il eprouva pendant la vie de ce prince* (1818). For the aristocratic attack, see Chateaubriand, *Analyse raisonnée de l'histoire de France, in Œuvres complètes*, IV, 435–36; and Jouffroy, *Les Fastes de l'anarchie*, p. 39. For the attack from the theological Right, see Lamen-

nais, *Des Progrès de la Révolution et de la guerre contre l'Eglise* (1829); and Maistre, *De l'Eglise gallicane* (1818).

29. *Du Sacre*, p. vii.

30. See Chapter II for a discussion of Carnot's *Mémoire au Roi.*

31. *Réflexions politiques*, in *Œuvres complètes*, XXIV, 126.

32. F. M. Guillot, *Le Jacobinisme réfuté, ou Observations critiques sur le mémoire de M. Carnot adressé au Roi en 1814* (1815), pp. 27, 39.

33. Saint-Marcelin, "Sur l'Armée," in *Conservateur* (1818), I, 519–20. Saint-Marcelin was a natural son of Fontaine. He had soldiered for Napoleon all during the Empire, but in 1814 he had switched. He was a protégé of Chateaubriand's and was killed in a duel at the age of twenty-eight. See also J. Delandine de Saint Esprit, *Le Panache de Henry IV, ou Phalanges royales en 1815* (1817), a defense of the Royalist armies in the campaigns of 1814 and the Hundred Days.

34. *Les Principes*, pp. 48–51.

35. For summation of the trial (July 31, 1820), see Dupin, *Mémoires*, I, 196–98.

36. [Madrolle], *De la Révolution*, p. 51. See also in this "campaign literature," Nicolas Bergasse, *Essai sur la Propriété* (1821).

37. Félix Conny de la Fay, *Observations sur les confiscations révolutionnaires, et le projet de loi d'indemnité* (1825), p. 6. See also Saint-Roman, *Opinion de M. le comte de Saint Roman sur le projet d'une loi tendant à indemniser les anciens propriétaires des biens-fonds confisqués . . . , Session de 1825, séance du 11 avril* (1825), pp. 32–34, for refutation of revolutionary calumnies.

38. A. Antoine de Saint-Gervais, *Histoire des émigrés français* (1828), p. xxxix.

39. Delille, quoted in Conny de la Fay, *Observations*, p. 46.

40. J.A.P., *De la Monarchie avec les philosophes, les révolutionnaires et les Jacobins* (Lyon, 1817), pp. 7–8.

41. Marquis d'Herbouville, "Sur les Mots *France Nouvelle, Nation Nouvelle, Intérêts Révolutionnaires*," in *Conservateur* (1818), I, 356. See also Riambourg, *Les Principes*, p. 2.

42. *Du Sacre*, p. 201.

43. *Quelques Considérations sur la marche du parti libéral dans les premiers mois de 1822* (1822), p. 23.

44. Maistre, *De l'Eglise gallicane dans son rapport avec le Saint Siège* (1818), in *Œuvres complètes*, III, 6. See also Bonald, *Observations*, V, 396.

45. [Madrolle], *De la Révolution*, p. 2.

46. Bonald, *Œuvres*, V, 402. Subsequent quotations, pp. 404–14.

47. *De la Monarchie selon la Charte* (1816), chap. 60.

48. "Réflexions sur un article du *Moniteur*, du 21 août," in *Conservateur* (1818), I, 63.

49. *Quelques Considérations*, p. 115.

50. *Les Principes*, p. 13.

51. Dampierre, *Historique de la Révolution tiré des Saintes Ecritures* (Dijon, 1824), p. 7.

52. E.g., [Madrolle], *De la Révolution*, p. 2.

53. Cottu (*De la Nécessité d'une dictature*, p. 26) approvingly quotes Napoleon on Necker: "It is he who overthrew the monarchy and led Louis XVI to the scaffold. Robespierre himself, Marat, Danton, did less evil to France than M. Necker. It was he who made the Revolution."

54. For classic statement of this view, see Abbé Augustin Barruel, *Mémoires pour servir à l'histoire du Jacobinisme* (Hamburg, 1797).

55. Herbouville, "Sur les mots . . . ," in *Conservateur*, I, 355–56.

56. See Charles Lacretelle, *Histoire del Assemblée Constituante* (1821), Vol. I.

57. Pierre Chaillot, *Histoire des révolutions de France* (1817), I, 6.

58. J.A.P., *De la Monarchie*, pp. 5–6, 11.

59. *Les Fastes*, p. 12.

60. *Tableau des trois époques, ou les Philosophes avant, pendant, et après la Révolution* (1829), p. 377.

61. Abbé de Pradt, *Les Quatre Concordats* (1818), I, 387, 391.
62. *Ibid.*, p. 407.
63. *Réponse aux Quatre Concardats,* p. 9.
64. *Ibid.*, p. 111.
65. *Ibid.*, p. 114.
66. Pierre de la Gorce, *La Restauration* (1926–28), II, 58. Gorce's judgment on the importance of the reprinting of Voltaire's works: "The opposition has raised the ghosts of two great men against the Bourbons: first Bonaparte, then Voltaire. Formerly, under Louis XVIII, the formidable ghost was, above all, Bonaparte: now [under Charles X], more than Bonaparte, it is Voltaire." *Ibid.*, II, 7.
67. Clausel de Montals, *Questions importantes sur les nouvelles éditions des œuvres complètes de Voltaire et de J.-J. Rousseau* (1817), pp. 15, 16; subsequent quotations, pp. 21–26, 44–45.
68. Edouard Lepan, *Vie politique, littéraire, morale de Voltaire, où on réfute Condorcet et ses autres historiens,* 2d ed. (1819), pp. xi, xiii. The first edition appeared in 1817. There were five editions in all, as well as commentaries and a collected Voltaire.
69. E. A. Boulogne, *Instruction pastorale de Monseigneur l'évêque de Troyes sur l'impression de mauvais livres et notamment sur les nouvelles œuvres complètes de Voltaire et de Rousseau* (1821), pp. 1, 3–4.
70. *Ibid.*, p. 19.
71. *Ibid.*, p. 30.
72. Clausel de Coussergues, *Du Sacre,* p. 438. See also Abbé Boyer's attack on Abbé de Pradt's glorification of Rousseau.
73. Riambourg, *Les Principes,* p. 31. See also *Remède unique aux maux de l'Eglise et de l'Etat,* p. 12.
74. See Chateaubriand on why the magazine was founded, in *Conservateur,* I, 5–45.
75. Vicomte de La Rochefoucauld, "Réflexions sur le système que suit le ministère," in *Conservateur,* I, 323.
76. "Inventaire de ce que la Révolution française a coûté en hommes et en argent distribué à ses principaux agens, au-delà des dépenses ordinaires de l'Etat," in *Conservateur,* I, 378.
77. *De la Nécessité pour les rois des souvenirs de la Révolution* (1819), pp. 4, 9.
78. See also [Madrolle], *De la Révolution,* p. ix, and T. F. Jolly, *Mémorial sur la Révolution française* (1824), p. 505.
79. *Le Jacobinisme réfuté,* pp. 17–19.
80. Abbé Pierre Denis Boyer, *De la Liberté des cultes selon la Charte avec quelques réflexions sur le doctrine de M. de Pradt* (1819), p. 77.
81. "M. Feuille-Morte, ou Revue critique de quelques opinions," in *Conservateur,* I, 530–32. This is quite a complicated story, a reply to Tissot writing in the *Mercure* of November 29, 1817.
82. These are actual quotations from Thiessé, *Lettres normandes,* a work suppressed in the Restoration. I have taken the liberty of titling the speakers.
83. For the best statement on this group and the politics of the Restoration, see Thureau-Dangin, *Royalistes et républicains.* See also the works of Bertier de Sauvigny; and Nora Hudson, *Ultra Royalism and the French Restoration* (Cambridge, England, 1936).
84. *Observations,* p. 3.
85. *Opinion,* p. 4.
86. Quoted in Eugène de Guichen, *La France morale et religieuse à la fin de la Restauration* (1911–12), I, 8.
87. See, for example, A. Chuquet, ed., *Recollections of Baron de Frénilly,* translated by F. Lees (London, 1909). For the thoughts of a typical Ultra, see for example, p. 248.
88. F. Montlosier, *De la Monarchie française depuis le retour de la maison de Bourbon jusqu'au premier avril 1815* (1815), p. xv.
89. A. Madrolle, *Défense de l'ordre social attaqué . . .* (1827), p. 181.

90. *Quelques Considérations sur les tyrannies diverses qui ont précedé la Restauration, sur le gouvernement royal et la dernière tyrannie impériale* (1815), p. 102.

91. Henrion, *Vie de Frayssinous*, II, 486. Henrion resurrects this statement in treating a work which appeared much later in the Restoration. This accounts for its curious position in the text.

92. *Ibid.*, I, 88. Voltaire is the "man who raised the standard of incredulity in the heart of France." *Ibid.*, I, 89.

93. *Ibid.*, I, 95; subsequent quotations from II, 483–84.

94. *Du Seul Moyen*, p. 153.

95. *De la Nécessité d'une dictature*, p. 146.

96. Riambourg, *Les Principes*, p. 31.

97. *Histoire de l'Assemblée Constituante*, I, 1.

98. *Plaidoyer de M. de Marchangy . . . prononcé le 29 août 1822, devant la cour d'assises de la Seine, dans la conspiration de la Rochelle* (1822), p. 27.

99. *Histoire des révolutions*, I, 138.

100. *Les Principes*, pp. 47–48, 42, 93, 36.

101. "Sur le dernier ouvrage de Madame de Staël," in *Conservateur* (1818), I, 208. Subsequent quotations, pp. 208–10.

102. *Des Résultats nécessaires de la situation actuelle de la Couronne et de la Chambre des Députés* (1829), p. 29.

103. "Sur le dernier ouvrage," in *Conservateur*, I, 205.

104. *Archives parlementaires*, May 30, 1820.

105. See, for example, a series of articles published in 1821 by *La France chrétienne*, entitled "Plan des Libéraux pour recommencer la Révolution" (March 31 and April 18, 1821).

106. V. Lombard de Langres, *Des Jacobins depuis 1789 jusqu'à ce jour, ou Etat de l'Europe en janvier 1822*, 2d ed. (1822), p. 5. The first edition appeared in 1820. Lombard had been active in the Revolution, as president of the revolutionary tribunal of Villeneuve-sur-Yonne and as ambassador to Holland. But 1799 had marked the end of his career. And in the Restoration he adopts a classic conservative position.

107. *Quelques Considérations*, p. 92.

108. Marchangy, *Plaidoyer*, pp. 6–7.

109. *Preuves frappantes de l'imminence d'une seconde révolution* (1827), p. 15.

110. *Tableau des trois époques*, pp. 388, 409, 415.

111. *Journal du nord*, January 18 and 19, 1830.

112. "Coup d'œil sur la situation du ministère de la France en 1818, 1819, et 1820," in *Conservateur*, I, 447–49.

113. T. de Boisbertrand, "Sur les opinions révolutionnaires," in *Conservateur*, I, 498–500.

114. "Plan des Libéraux," p. 3.

115. *Plaidoyer*, pp. 236–37.

116. Madrolle, *Défense de l'ordre social*, p. 198.

117. *Ibid.*, pp. 71, 198. See Maistre, *Œuvres complètes*, VIII, 487; Joseph Bernardi, *Lettre à M. le comte de Lanjuinais . . .* (1818), p. 6. See also Chapter V.

118. Clausel de Coussergues, *Du Sacre*, p. 308.

119. Conny de la Fay, *Les Révolutionnaires de 1792 et les Révolutionnaires de 1820* (1820).

120. Herbouville, "Sur l'inégalité des conditions," in *Conservateur*, I, 538–39.

121. Cottu, *Du Seul Moyen*, p. 101.

122. *Réflexions politiques*, in *Œuvres complètes*, XXIV, 184.

123. *Ibid.*, pp. 213, 221. A general spokesman for Royalism until 1816, Chateaubriand becomes a violent Ultra during the years 1816–20; he is back in the government between 1820 and 1824; he breaks with Villèle and moves further and further into the Liberal opposition. With the Martignac regime he returns to the government; he is made ambassador to Rome; he opposes Polignac. For the details of these shifts and vagaries of Chateaubriand's political career, see Emmanuel Beau de Loménie, *La Carrière politique de Chateaubriand de 1814 à 1830* (1929), 2 vols.

124. *Considérations*, I, 143.

125. Charles Constance Agoult, *Lettres à un jacobin, ou Réflexions politiques sur la constitution d'Angleterre et la Charte royale considérée dans ses rapports avec l'ancienne constitution de la monarchie française* (1815), p. 95. Subsequent quotations, pp. 110, 124, 148–53.

126. *Les Constitutions révolutionnaires en opposition avec la volonté générale de la nation* (1815), pp. 26–27.

127. C. P. Ducanel, *La Constitution non écrite du royaume de France et les épreuves qu'elle n'a jamais cessé, un seul instant, d'être en vigeur depuis Clovis jusqu'à ce jour* (1814). Ducanel had been an enthusiastic Jacobin in the first years of the Revolution, but he broke and, in 1795, was already numbered among the supporters of Constitutional monarchy. He was one of the founders of the *Bibliothèque Royaliste* in 1819 and, two years later, wrote a history of the Revolution.

128. Delbare, *Les Constitutions*, pp. 35, 39.

129. Henrion de Pansey, *Des Pairs de France et de l'ancienne constitution française* (1816), p. 91. Henrion was regarded by his contemporaries as a "pure" legal talent, above politics. In 1828 he was appointed president of the Cour de Cassation.

130. *Œuvres*, V, 418.

131. *Des Pairs*, pp. 177–78.

132. *Du Sacre*, pp. 457–62.

133. "Réflexions sur un article du *Moniteur*, du 21 août," in *Conservateur*, I, 66–69.

134. P.L.B., *De la Restauration*, p. 33. Subsequent quotations, pp. 87, 111, 67.

135. Foy, *Discours*, I, 182.

136. *Ibid.*, II, 105.

137. Maistre, *Correspondance*, in *Œuvres complètes*, XIV, 339.

138. Clausel de Coussergues, *Quelques Considérations*, p. 27. This work differs in viewpoint because Clausel is battling the Liberals in 1822, whereas in 1825 (see above) he is celebrating the coronation of Charles X.

139. *Ibid.*, pp. 116–17.

140. *De la Nécessité d'une dictature*, pp. 103–4.

141. *Archives parlementaires*, March 15, 1830. The following quotations are from the same speech.

NOTES TO CHAPTER V

1. Jubé de la Perrelle, *Lettre à M. le vicomte de Chateaubriand* (1816), pp. 29, 34–35.

2. *Pensées sur des divers sujets* (1817), II, pp. 17–18.

3. Quoted in *Archives* (1817), I, 110.

4. *Ibid.*, pp. 111–12.

5. *De la Liberté des cultes et du concordat* (1818), p. 36. Subsequent quotations, pp. 37–69.

6. D. Baillot, *Dialogue entre François I, Louis XI, Charles VII, et Louis XII sur le nouveau concordat* (1818).

7. Note, for example, the reprintings of *Concordat entre Léon X, Souverain Pontife, et François I, roi de France, en latin et en français* (1818); and Abbé Fleury, *La Congrégation religieuse* (1826), a speech reprinted to illuminate the discussion of religious congregations. The Liberal periodical *Bibliothèque historique* (1818), I, 32, publishes an article on concordats, in which extracts from the opinions of Vély, Mézeray, and Voltaire are included.

8. Baillot, *Dialogue*, p. 3. Subsequent quotations, pp. 29–36.

9. *Les Quatre Concordats* (1818), I, 220.

10. *Ibid.*, p. 280.

11. *Ibid.*, p. 295.

12. *Ibid.*, p. 354.

13. *Ibid.*, II, pp. 25–26.

14. "Such was the fate of the clergy through the mistake of emigration; it had nothing in common with a measure whose purpose was the taking of arms." *Ibid.*, p. 59.

15. *Ibid.*, p. 407.

16. *Ibid.*, III, 39, 43. This is an obvious reference to Lamennais's *Essai sur l'indifférence* and the spread of Ultramontanist ideas.

17. *Ibid.*, pp. 85, 91, 143. Subsequent quotations, pp. 197–217.

18. *Appréciation du projet de loi relatif aux trois concordats* (1817), pp. 28–29.

19. Abbé H. B. Grégoire, *Essai historique sur les libertés de l'eglise gallicane* (1820), p. 206.

20. *Ibid.*, p. 255.

21. *Ibid.*, p. 212.

22. Abbé D. L. Frayssinous, *Les Vrais Principes de l'eglise gallicane* (1818), p. 207. This is a matter of intense debate. See Abbé Dillon, *Réponse . . . à la réplique de M. l'abbé Clausel* (1818), pp. 74–75.

23. Frayssinous, *Les Vrais Principes*, pp. 205–6.

24. Note the replies like that of L. Silvy, *Difficulté capitale proposée à M. l'abbé Frayssinous* (1818).

25. *Des Livres et des pamphlets sur le Concordat*, printed in *Le Publiciste* (1818), p. 3. Subsequent quotations, pp. 3–13.

26. The author attempts to discredit Ultramontanists by noting that they have joined forces with those hostile to religion in order to defeat the concordat.

27. *De la Monarchie selon la Charte*, p. 230.

28. *De la Religion prouvée par la Révolution*, 2d ed. (1817), p. 3.

29. Clausel de Montals, *Réponse aux Quatre Concordats*, p. 81. This is quoted by Clausel from Saint-Chamans.

30. Antoine Kentzinger, *Les Préceptes, ou la Religion sous les rapports politiques* (1820), pp. 13–14.

31. These discussions are doubly interesting because, after 1820, there is proposed legislation on all these matters.

32. *Les Préceptes*, pp. 8–9, 12.

33. *Ibid.*, pp. 33, 34.

34. *De la Monarchie selon la Charte*, p. 72.

35. *Quelques Considérations*, p. 94. "Establishing" is of course used in the sense "granting civil status to."

36. *Du Sacre*, pp. 310, 328. On the fascination of Conservative France with the League, see Louis Vitet's play, *La Ligue* (1824), and the discussion in Lamennais, *Des Progrès de la Révolution*, in *Œuvres*, VI, 53 ff.

37. *Tableau des Trois Epoques*, pp. 314–15, 413.

38. Maistre, *De l'Eglise gallicane* (1818), II, 91.

39. *Ibid.*, p. 106. For an example of what Maistre is referring to, see Abbé Grégoire, *Essai historique*, p. 211. "In the shadows of the Middle Ages, the *chapitres* of the cathedrals usurped the right to name bishops from the clergy and the people; . . . the popes in their turn usurped . . ."

40. *Ibid.*, pp. 246, 247.

41. *Ibid.*, p. 120.

42. *Ibid.*, p. 272.

43. *Ibid.*, p. 281.

44. Maistre, *Œuvres*, VIII, 489.

45. See C. Maréchale, *Lamennais, la dispute de l'Essai de l'indifférence* (1925).

46. See, for example, his attack on Biblical societies in the *Conservateur*, III, 49, 291; for his articles on education, *ibid.*, I, 145, 297, 585.

47. Lamennais, *Observations sur la promesse d'enseigner les quatre articles de la Déclaration de 1682* (1818).

48. For an account of the affair of 1823, see F. Duine, *Lamennais, sa vie, ses idées, ses ouvrages* (1922), pp. 94–97.

49. Lamennais, *De la Religion considerée dans ses rapports avec l'ordre politique et civil* (1825–26), in *Œuvres*, V, 112, 117.

50. *Ibid.*, pp. 128, 140. Lamennais takes the latter quotation from the *Etoile*. Subsequent quotations, *De la Religion*, pp. 159–67.

51. *Ibid.*, p. 185.

52. *Ibid.*, p. 165. Lamennais broadens this into a general attack upon Liberal historians like Thierry, who have discovered a Liberal past.

53. "It comes to this, that Philip, Ferdinand, Henry, oppressed their people." *Ibid.*, p. 194.

54. *Ibid.*, pp. 195–96.

55. *Ibid.*, p. 222.

56. Fiévée, *Correspondance politique et administrative*, III, No. 10, p. 3.

57. *Ibid.*, p. 5. For Fiévée, to argue as the Liberals do is "to know little about the conflict of interests by which Europe was torn; it is to forget that the first attempts of the Protestants in France had taken place under the reign of his prince, and that worry over the political consequences . . . more than love of conquest, made him decide to seek in the court of Rome a direction of which he felt the need." *Ibid.*, pp. 5–6.

58. Fiévée, *Histoire de la session de 1817* (1818), pp. 143, 149–50.

59. *De la Situation du clergé, de la magistrature, et du ministère* (1826), pp. 3–4.

60. *Ibid.*, p. 18. Guizot expresses the same idea: "Is the power of the Church so great and its existence so deeply, so universally, bound to the whole of society that the government is uneasy about resisting its pretensions? Does the king need the clergy's consent to raise taxes, to render justice, for citizens to be born, marry, and die legally; in a word, for the political order to run smoothly, for the interests of civic life to be orderly and satisfied?" Guizot, *Des Moyens*, p. 199.

61. Cottu, *De la Situation*, pp. 18, 20.

62. *Ibid.*, p. 29.

63. *Ibid.*, p. 121.

64. *Lettre à M. le comte de Lanjuinais* (1818), pp. 6, 8.

65. *Ibid.*, p. 8. Bernardi had himself been a general before the Revolution. Deprived of his command and arrested, he fled in 1793.

66. *Ibid.*, p. 10. Subsequent quotations, pp. 17–23.

NOTES TO CHAPTER VI

1. For example, Fiévée joins Chateaubriand and attacks Frayssinous and Lamennais in the *Journal des Débats*.

2. Note the attention given to religious issues in Guizot, *Des Moyens de gouvernement et d'opposition dans l'état actuel des choses* (1821); Ganilh, *De la Contre-révolution en France* (1823); Domeny de Rienzi, *Adresse au gouvernement et au peuple français* (1820).

3. Joseph Burnichon, *La Compagnie de Jésus en France, histoire d'un siècle 1814–1914* (1914–22), I, 538–39. The petition is included as a *pièce justificative*.

4. Maistre, *Œuvres*, XIV, 357.

5. See Tarabaud, *Du Pape et des Jésuites* (1814); Silvy, *Les Jésuites tels qu'ils ont été* (1815).

6. Abbé Grégoire writing on this subject in the *Minerve* and Cauchois-Lemnire in *Le Nain jaune* are two examples of this early preoccupation with the Jesuit question.

7. See, for example, Abbé de Pradt, *Les Quatre Concordats*.

8. *La Compagnie de Jésus*, I, 550.

9. *Histoire abrégée des Jésuites* (1820), title page. Goubeau had served the Revolution and the Empire in France and Piedmont. For a brief period in the Restoration he had suffered the loss of his position in the courts, but he was "restored" in 1819.

10. *Ibid.*

11. *Ibid.*, I, ii.

12. *Ibid.*, p. iii. The reference to the exploits of the League is probably provoked by Bonald and the *Conservateur.*

13. *Ibid.*, p. iv.

14. *Ibid.*, p. v.

15. *Ibid.*, pp. i, xiii.

16. *Ibid.*, p. xii.

17. *Ibid.*, p. 491.

18. Goubeau's accuracy may be called into question: at one point he refers to Lamennais as a Jesuit. *Ibid.*, II, 369. Subsequent quotations, pp. 337, 349–54.

19. *Ibid.*, p. 400.

20. *Ibid.*, p. 450.

21. Gilbert de Voisins, *Procédure contre l'institut et les constitutions des Jésuites suivie au Parlement de Paris* (1823), p. xii. Subsequent quotations, pp. xii–xvi.

22. *La Galère jésuitique* (1826), pp. 9–10. For the eighteenth-century description, see pages 25–26. Today the painting hangs in the history museum of the National Archives.

23. *Ibid.*, pp. 24–25.

24. *Ibid.*, p. 31. Subsequent quotations, pp. 11–12, 1–6.

25. This advertising notice is pasted in the front of the book, opposite the title page.

26. See Pierre Nicolas Collin d'Ambly, *Les Jésuites condamnés d'après leurs maximes et leurs actions* (1825).

27. Burnichon, *La Compagnie de Jésus*, I, 323–24.

28. *Histoire des confesseurs des empereurs, des rois, et d'autres princes* (1824), p. 303.

29. *Ibid.*, p. 11. Another example of the conscious use of history is Picard and L. N. Achaintre, *Les Jésuites peints par Henri IV et jugés par Montesquieu, Voltaire, Raynal, Buffon* (1825).

30. *Du Jésuitisme ancien et modern* (1826), p. 262.

31. *Ibid.*, p. 327.

32. Laumier, a prolific writer, was curator of the library at Dôle. His *Histoire de la Révolution d'Espagne* was published in 1820.

33. Charles Laumier, *Résumé de l'histoire des Jésuites* (1826), p. 483.

34. *Ibid.*, p. 494. Subsequent quotations, pp. 518–26.

35. *Ibid.*, pp. 494–500. He adds an analysis of the weakness of the Jesuit regulations. Subsequent quotations, pp. 551–58.

36. Abbé, J. F. Georgel, *Mémoires pour servir à l'histoire de la fin du dix-huitième siècle*, 2d ed. (1820).

37. J. P. P. Montfleury, *Le Mensonge détruit par la vérité, ou Réfutation des erreurs politiques et religieuses contenues dans l'ouvrage intitulé Le Jésuitisme de M. de Pradt* (1826), p. 151.

38. J. de Saint-Victor, ed., *Documents historiques, critiques, apologétiques concernant la Compagnie de Jésus* (3 vols.; 1827–30).

39. *Le Rédacteur véridique* (1827), p. 8 (in Saint-Victor, ed., *Documents*, Vol. I).

40. *Précis pour servir de réponse aux accusations faites contre les Jésuites* (1827), p. 1 (in *Documents*, Vol. I).

41. *De la Doctrine du Tyrannicide* (1828), pp. 83–86 (in *Documents*, Vol. III).

42. *Du Rappel des Jésuites* (1827), p. 6 (in *Documents*, Vol. II).

43. Salaberry, *Aux Hommes de Bien* in *Conservateur de la Restauration* (1828), pp. 6–9 of ninth letter. For Salaberry's disgust at the events of 1828, see *Souvenirs politiques sur la Restauration* (1900), II, 211–14.

44. C. Maritain de Neuwaches, *Les Jésuites dévoilés à leurs amis et à leurs ennemis* (Lyon, 1829), p. 1. Subsequent quotations, pp. 65–80.

45. *Ibid.*, pp. 114, 117.

46. J. F. Bellemare, *Les Inquiétudes révolutionnaires, ou les Maladies que nous n'avons point, suivies de celles que nous avons* (1825), pp. 4–6.

47. P. J. Béranger, *Procès fait aux chansons de P. J. de Béranger* (1821), p. 96.

NOTES TO CHAPTER VII

1. Quoted in Dupin, *Mémoires*, I, 210.
2. Bellart, *Réquisitoire de M. le procureur général près de la cour royale de Paris contre le Constitutionnel* (1825), p. 1. Subsequent quotations, pp. 1–8.
3. Quoted in *Moniteur*, November 27, 1825.
4. Quoted in E. Hatin, *Histoire politique et littéraire de la presse en France* (1859–61), VIII, 403.
5. Dupin, *Plaidoyer pour le Constitutionnel, accusé de tendance* (1825), p. 455.
6. *Ibid.*, p. 456.
7. Hatin, *Histoire . . . de la presse*, VIII, 403.
8. *Moniteur*, December 4, 1825.
9. *Courrier français*, January 27, 1826.
10. *Etoile*, February 2, 1826. The editor of the *Etoile* was M. Aubry.
11. *Constitutionnel*, February 3, 1826.
12. *Ibid.*
13. *Etoile*, February 8, 1826.
14. *Ibid.*, March 18, 1826.
15. *Ibid.*, March 23, 1826.
16. *Ibid.*, March 24, 1826. Subsequent quotations from the same issue.
17. *Quotidienne*, March 30, 1826.
18. For details of the trial, consult *L'Annuaire historique* (1825). Kermarec was *avocat général* of the court at Rennes. Montbourcher was—like La Fruglaye—a member of the Chamber of Deputies from Brittany.
19. Berryer, *Cause célèbre; Plainte en diffamation des petits-fils de La Chalotais contre l'éditeur de L'Etoile, Plaidoirie* (1826), p. 1. Subsequent quotations, pp. 7, 14–22.
20. Bernard, *Cause célèbre; Plaidoirie, Plainte en diffamation des petits-fils de La Chalotais contre l'éditeur de L'Etoile* (1826), p. 3. Subsequent quotations, pp. 15–28, 45–46.
21. Hennequin, *Cause célèbre; Plaidoirie, Plainte en diffamation des petits-fils de La Chalotais contre l'éditeur de L'Etoile* (1826), p. 67.
22. Bernard, *Cause célèbre*, p. 33.
23. La Chalotais, *Résumé des Constitutions des Jésuites* (1826), publisher's note.
24. Gilbert de Voisins' Introduction to La Chalotais, *Mémoires* (1826), pp. v, vii.
25. *Ibid.*, pp. xxxiv–xxxv.
26. *Etoile*, April 2, 1826.
27. See *Drapeau blanc*, March 21, 1826, and *Quotidienne*, April 10, 1826, for examples of the hostility of the Conservative press to the *Etoile*'s stand on La Chalotais.
28. *Etoile*, April 3, 1826.
29. *Ibid.*, May 1, 1826.
30. *Ibid.*, April 16, 1826.
31. *Ibid.*
32. For a discussion of Montlosier's pre-Restoration career, see Joseph Brugerette, *Le Comte de Montlosier et son temps* (1931).
33. Montlosier, *De la Monarchie française* (1815), p. xvii.
34. The *Etoile* (March 10, 1826) puts it neatly: speaking of Boulainvilliers, "Cet homme on le retrouve tout entier dans M. le Comte de Montlosier." For a typical statement of Montlosier's aristocratic sentiments, see *De la Monarchie française*, p. 90.
35. *Archives*, III, 391, 398.
36. *De la Monarchie française*, p. 145.
37. Apparently it even worried some Royalists. See Barante, *Souvenirs*, III, 245.
38. For the details, see Guichen, *La France morale et religieuse à la fin de la restauration* (1912), pp. 164–66.
39. In the words of Barante, the work was "in complete harmony with the public temper." *Souvenirs*, III, 322.
40. E. Michaud, *Le Jésuitisme politique et le comte de Montlosier en 1826* (Berne, 1889), p. 9.

41. Chateaubriand, *Memoirs* (London, 1842), IV, 124.

42. Montlosier, *Mémoire à consulter sur un système religieux et politique tendant à renverser la religion, la société et le trône* (1826), pp. 5, 14.

43. Saint-Chamans was *maître des requêtes* in 1820, and a deputy from 1824 to 1827.

44. Saint-Chamans, *Du Croque-mitaine du comte de Montlosier, de M. de Pradt, et de bien d'autres* (1826), pp. 38–39.

45. *Ibid.*, pp. 113–14. Subsequent quotations, pp. 120, 129, 134.

46. Bonald, *Réflexions sur le Mémoire à consulter de M. le comte de Montlosier* (1826), p. 16. Subsequent quotations, pp. 29–31, 38, 62.

47. *Archives parlementaires*, April 8, 1826.

48. *Ibid.*, May 15, 1826.

49. *Ibid.*, May 25, 1826. Subsequent quotations from this same speech.

50. *Ibid.*, May 25, 1826.

51. *Ibid.*, May 26, 1826. Subsequent quotations are from Frayssinous's speech.

52. *Ibid.*, July 4, 1826.

53. *Ibid.* Subsequent quotations are from this same speech.

54. *Dénonciattion aux cours royales* (1826), pp. 256, 277.

55. For Dupin's activities in relation to the Jesuits, see the interesting account in Burnichon, *La Compagnie de Jésus*, I, 331 ff.

56. The court decision is quoted in Vaulabelle, *Histoire des deux Restaurations*, new edition (1874), IX, 68–69.

57. As read by Portalis before the Chamber of Peers. *Archives parlementaires*, January 18, 1827. Subsequent quotations from this same issue.

58. *Ibid.*, January 19, 1827. Subsequent quotations from this same issue.

59. *Défense de l'ordre social*, pp. 10–15.

60. *Ibid.*, p. 165.

61. *Globe*, as quoted *ibid.*, p. 173. Note that *Le Producteur*, Saint-Simon's periodical, also remains outside the chorus of Liberal praise. In this journal, Montlosier is referred to as belonging to the "temporal section of the retrogressive party." *Le Producteur*, II, 623.

62. *Défense de l'ordre social*, p. 186. Subsequent quotations, pp. 186–98, 224.

63. *Ibid.*, p. 286. Madrolle even compares him to Benjamin Constant, *De la Doctrine politique qui peut réunir les partis en France.*

64. *Défense de l'ordre social*, p. 280. This quotation is taken from an earlier work; Montlosier is referring to the Liberal policy in 1816–20. Subsequent quotations, pp. 347, 354.

65. Villèle, *Mémoires et correspondance du comte de Villèle* (1891–92), V, 256.

66. *Gazette universelle de Lyon*, December 9, 1827. Quoted in Guichen, *La France morale et religieuse*, p. 217.

67. Barante, *Souvenirs*, III, 345.

68. Guizot, *Mémoires*, I, 282–83.

69. A. Chuquet, ed., *Recollections of Baron de Frénilly*, trans. by F. Lees (London, 1909), pp. 351–52.

70. Henrion, *Vie de Frayssinous*, II, 535–36.

71. *Ibid.*, p. 575. Subsequent quotations, pp. 576, 578.

72. *Quotidienne*, April 3, 1826.

73. Quoted in Guichen, *La France morale et religieuse*, pp. 111–12. Subsequent quotations, pp. 113–15.

74. Quoted in C. Lacombe, *La Jeunesse de Berryer* (1894), p. 304.

75. Guichen, *La France morale et religieuse*, p. 117.

76. Lacombe, *La Jeunesse de Berryer*, pp. 313, 314.

77. *Quotidienne*, April 24, 1826.

78. See Lacombe, *La Jeunesse de Berryer*, p. 310; Lamennais, *Correspondance*, I, 246.

79. The following works contain interesting appraisals of Lamennais's influence: Boutard, *Lamennais, sa vie et ses doctrines* (1905–13); Duine, *Lamennais. Sa vie, ses*

idées . . . (1922) ; C. Maréchale, *Lamennais, la dispute de l'Essai de l'indifférence* (1925).

80. *Annuaire historique* (1825), p. 224.

81. *Archives parlementaires,* May 26, 1826.

82. See Duine, *Lamennais,* p. 105, and Henrion, *Vie de Frayssinous,* II, 590, for light on this question of family connections.

83. Madrolle, *Défense de l'ordre social,* p. 403.

84. Lamennais, *Des Progrès de la Révolution,* in *Œuvres,* VI, 46. Subsequent quotations from the same volume.

85. Quoted in Duine, *Lamennais,* p. 131.

86. For details on these controversies, see Lamennais, *Sur une Attaque dirigée contre M. l'abbé de Lamennais et le Mémorial catholique,* in *Œuvres,* VI, 401–13, and *Lettres à l'archevêque de Paris* (second letter), *ibid.,* p. 348, for Flottes and Frénilly, respectively.

87. Lamennais, *Lettres à l'archevêque de Paris* (first letter), *ibid.,* p. 271.

88. *Ibid.* (second letter), p. 315.

89. *Ibid.* (first letter), p. 282.

90. Lamennais, *Lettre au rédacteur de la Quotidienne, ibid.,* VI, 262.

91. The newly elected Pope Pius VIII called *Des Progrès de la Révolution* "A book vomited from the volcano of Etna." Duine, *Lamennais,* p. 132.

92. Quoted in Lamennais, *Sur une Exposition des sentiments des Catholiques Belges,* in *Œuvres,* VI, 420.

93. *Ibid.,* p. 429.

NOTES TO CHAPTER VIII

1. Trognon's review of Reynouard, *Histoire de droit municipal* (1829), in *Etudes,* p. 187.

2. *Revue française* (May 1828), No. 3, p. 1.

3. Chateaubriand, *Analyse raisonée,* pp. 420–21.

Bibliography[1]

Achaintre, Picard, and L. N. Les Jésuites peints par Henri IV et jugés par Montesquieu, Voltaire, Raynal, Buffon, etc. 1825.

Agoult, Charles Constance. Lettres à un Jacobin, ou Réflexions politiques sur la constitution d'Angleterre et la charte royale considérée dans ses rapports avec l'ancienne constitution de la monarchie française. 1815.

Allison, John M. S. Thiers and the French Monarchy, 1788–1848. Boston, 1926.

Antoine de Saint-Gervais, A. Histoire des émigrés français. 2 vols. 1828.

Artz, Frederick B. France under the Bourbon Restoration. Cambridge, England, 1931.

Bagge, Dominique. Les Idées politiques en France sous la Restauration. 1952.

Bailleul, J. C. Examen critique de l'ouvrage posthume de Mme la baronne de Staël. 2 vols. 1818.

Baillot, D. Des Libertés de l'église gallicane. 1817.

———. Dialogue entre François I, Louis XI, Charles VII, et Louis XII sur le nouveau concordat. 1818.

Barante, A. G. P. de. Histoire des ducs de Bourgogne. 4th ed. 13 vols. in 12. 1826.

———. Mélanges historiques et littéraires. 3d ed. 3 vols. 1835.

———. Souvenirs. 5 vols. 1890–95.

———. La Vie politique de M. Royer-Collard. 2 vols. 1878.

Barbé, M. L'Etude historique des idées sur la souveraineté en France de 1815 à 1848. 1904.

Bardoux, Agénor. Le Comte de Montlosier et le gallicanisme. 1881.

Barruel, Augustin, abbé. Mémoires pour servir à l'histoire du jacobinisme. 5 vols. Hamburg, 1797–1803.

Barzun, Jacques. "Romantic Historiography as a Political Force in France," *Journal of the History of Ideas*, Vol. II, No. 3 (June 1941), pp. 318–29.

Bayle, Francis. Les Idées politiques de Joseph de Maistre. 1945.

Beau de Loménie, Emmanuel. La Carrière politique de Chateaubriand de 1814 à 1830. 2 vols. 1929.

Beaujour, Louis Auguste, baron de. Tableau des révolutions de la France depuis la conquête des Francs jusqu'à l'établissement de la Charte. 1825.

Beik, Paul. "The French Revolution Seen from the Right," *Transactions of the American Philosophical Society*, New Series, Vol. 46, Part I (February 1956) pp. 62–90.

Bellart, Nicolas de. Réquisitoire de M. le procureur général près de la cour royale contre le *Constitutionnel*. 1825.

Bellemare, J. F. Les Inquiétudes révolutionnaires. 1825.

———. Trois Procès en un. 1827.

———. Le Conseiller des Jésuites. 1827.

———. Le Collège de mon fils. 1827.

[1] Paris is the place of publication except when otherwise stated.

———. La Fin des Jésuites et de bien d'autres. 1828.
———. Le Siècle de fer des Jésuites. 1828.
———. Les Jésuites en présence des deux chambres. 1828.
Benoît, A. De la Liberté des cultes et du concordat. 1818.
Béranger, P. J. Procès fait aux chansons de P. J. Béranger. 1821.
———. Chansons. 1829.
Bergasse, Nicolas. Essai sur la propriété. 1821.
Bernard, L. Plaidoirie; Cause célèbre, plainte en diffamation des petits-fils de La Chalotais contre l'éditeur de *l'Etoile*. 1826.
Bernardi, Joseph. De l'Origine et des progrès de la législation française. 1816.
———. Lettre à M. le comte de Lanjuinais. 1818.
Berryer, A. P. Plaidoirie; Cause célèbre, plainte en diffamation des petits-fils de La Chalotais contre l'éditeur de *l'Etoile*. 1826.
Bertier de Sauvigny, Guillaume de. La Restauration. 1955.
———. Le Comte Ferdinand de Bertier (1789–1864) et l'énigme de la Congrégation. 1948.
Besnard, François Guillaume, abbé. Lettres sur la Révolution. 1828.
Billecocq, Jean Baptiste. Quelques Considérations sur les tyrannies diverses qui ont précedé la Restauration, sur le gouvernement royal et sur la dernière tyrannie impériale. 1815.
———. De l'Influence de la guerre d'Espagne sur l'affermissement de la dynastie légitime et de la monarchie constitutionnelle en France. 1823.
Biré, E. L'Année 1817. 1895.
Bodin, Félix. Résumé de l'histoire de France. 3d ed. 1823.
Boigne, Charlotte Louise, comtesse de. Mémoires. 1924.
Bonald, Louis de. Pensées sur divers sujets. 2 vols. 1817.
———. Observations sur l'ouvrage de Madame la baronne de Staël. 1818.
———. Réflexions sur le mémoire à consulter de M. le comte de Montlosier. 1826.
Boulogne, E. A. Instruction pastorale de Monseigneur l'évêque de Troyes sur l'impression de mauvais livres et notamment sur les nouvelles Œuvres Complètes de Voltaire et de Rousseau. 1821.
Boutard, Charles, abbé. Lamennais, sa vie et ses doctrines. 3 vols. 1905–13. Vol. I.
Boyer, Pierre Denis, abbé. Nouveaus éclaircissements sur quelques objections qu'on oppose au concordat, suivis de réflexions sur un écrit de M. Fiévée. 1818.
———. De la Liberté des cultes selon la Charte, avec quelques réflexions sur la doctrine de M. de Pradt. 1819.
Broglie, Achille Charles, duc de. Souvenirs de 1815 à 1870. 4 vols. 1886.
Brugerette, Joseph. Le Comte de Montlosier et son temps. 1931.
Burnichon, Joseph. La Compagnie de Jésus en France: histoire d'un siècle 1814–1914. 4 vols. 1914–22. Vol. I.
Carnot, Lazare. Memorial to the King. English translation. London, 1814.
———. Exposé de la conduite politique de M. le Lieutenant Général depuis le 1 juillet 1814. 1815.
———. Les Erreurs de la monarchie française. 1817.
Carrel, Armand. Œuvres politiques et littéraires. 5 vols. 1857–59.
Carrion-Nisas, A. De la Liberté et des factions, ou Coup d'œil sur l'état de la liberté publique aux diverses époques de notre histoire et sur son état présent. 1819.

———. La France au dix-neuvième siècle. 1821.
Carroll, Kieran J. Some Aspects of the Historical Thought of Augustin Thierry. Washington, D.C., 1951.
Chaillot, Pierre. Histoire des révolutions de France. 2 vols. 1817.
Charavay, Etienne. Le Général La Fayette (1757–1834). 1898.
Charléty, S. La Restauration. 1921. Vol. IV of Histoire de la France contemporaine, ed. by E. Lavisse.
Chateaubriand, François René, vicomte de. Œuvres complètes. 28 vols. 1826–31.
———. Memoirs . . . Translated by A. Teixeira de Mattos. 6 vols. London, 1842.
Chevalier, J. J. Histoire des institutions politiques de la France de 1789 à nos jours. 1952.
Chuquet, A., ed. Recollections of Baron de Frénilly. Translated by F. Lees. London, 1909.
Clausel de Coussergues, J. C. Quelques Considérations sur la marche du parti libéral dans les premiers mois de 1822. 1822.
———. Du Sacre des rois de France et des rapports de cette auguste cérémonie avec la constitution de l'état aux différens âges de la monarchie. 1825.
Clausel de Montals, Claude H., abbé. Questions importantes sur les nouvelles éditions des Œuvres Complètes de Voltaire et de J.-J. Rousseau. 1817.
———. De la Religion prouvée par la Révolution. 2d ed. 1817.
———. Réponse aux *Quatre Concordats* de M. de Pradt. 1819.
Collection des mémoires relatifs à la Révolution française. Edited by Berville and Barrière. 56 vols. 1821–27.
Collin d'Ambly, Pierre Nicolas. Les Jésuites condamnés par leurs maximes et par leurs actions. 1825.
Conny de la Fay, Félix de. La France sous le règne de la Convention. 1820.
———. De la Nécessité pour les rois des souvenirs de la Révolution. 1819.
———. Les Révolutionnaires de 1792 et les révolutionnaires de 1820. 1820.
———. Observations sur les confiscations révolutionnaires, et le projet de loi d'indemnité. 1825.
Constant, Benjamin. De la Doctrine politique qui peut réunir les partis en France. 2d ed. 1817.
———. "Des Effets du régime qu'on nomme révolutionnaire relativement au salut et à la liberté de la France" (1797), in Mélanges politiques et historiques relatifs aux événemens contemporains. 3 vols. 1829.
Cottu, Charles. De la Situation du clergé, de la magistrature, et du ministère. 1826.
———. Du Seul Moyen de sortir de la crise actuelle. 1829.
———. De la Nécessité d'une dictature. 1830.
———. Des Résultats nécessaires de la situation actuelle de la couronne et de la Chambre des Députés. 1829.
———. Des Devoirs du roi envers la royauté. 1830.
Courier, Paul Louis. Œuvres . . . précédées d'un essai sur la vie et les écrits de l'auteur par Armand Carrel. New edition. 1866.
———. Pamphlets politiques. 1839.
Cousin, Victor. Cours de l'histoire de la philosophie. 1829.
Le Cri des amis de la liberté sur un ouvrage intitulé *La France sous le règne de la Convention*. 1818.
Dampierre, Antoine Esmonin. Historique de la Révolution tiré des saintes écritures. Dijon, 1824.

Dauriat, Mme L. Extract from Commentaries of Mme. L. Dauriat on Mme. de Staël. London, 1818.
Debidour, A. Histoire des rapports de l'église et de l'état en France de 1789 à 1870. 1898.
Défense des résumés historiques. 1824. (Bound with Carrel, *Résumé de l'histoire d'Ecosse.*)
Delandine de Saint-Esprit, J. Le Panache de Louis XIV, ou Phalanges royales en 1815. 1817.
Delbare, F. T. Les Constitutions révolutionnaires en opposition avec la volonté générale de la nation. 1815.
———. Le Siècle de Louis XIV. 1823.
Des Granges, C. M. La Presse littéraire sous la Restauration, 1815–1830. 1907.
Dickinson, G. Lowes. Revolution and Reaction in Modern France. New edition. New York, 1927.
Dillon, H. Réponse . . . à la réplique de M. l'abbé Clausel. 1818.
Ducanel, C. P. La Constitution non écrite du royaume de France et les épreuves qu'elle n'a jamais cessé, un seul instant, d'être en vigueur depuis Clovis jusqu'à ce jour. 1814.
Duine, F. Lamennais: sa vie, ses idées, d'après les sources imprimées et les documents inédits. 1922.
Dulaure, Jacques Antoine. Histoire critique de la noblesse . . . 1790.
———. Causes secrètes des excès de la Révolution. 1815.
———. Equisses historiques des principaux événements de la Révolution. 5 vols. 1823–25.
Dupin, André. Mémoires. 2 vols. 1855.
———. Plaidoirie . . . du *Constitutionnel.* 1825.
Duroselle, Jean Baptiste. Les Débuts du catholicisme social en France (1822–1870). 1951.
Engel-Jánosi, Friedrich. Four Studies in French Romantic Historical Writing. Baltimore, 1955.
Examen des doctrines des Messieurs Fiévée et Chateaubriand dans leurs ouvrages intitulés *Histoire de la session de 1815* et *De la Monarchie selon la Charte.* 1816.
Férat, J. B. Une Révolution, est-elle encore possible? 1829.
Ferrand, A. Théorie des révolutions. 1817.
Fiévée, Joseph. Correspondance politique et administrative. 3 vols. 1815–19.
———. Histoire de la session de 1815. 1816.
———. Histoire de la session de 1816. 1817.
———. Histoire de la session de 1817. 1818.
Foy, M. S. Discours du Général Foy. 2 vols. 1826.
Frayssinous, D. L., abbé. Vrais Principes de l'église gallicane. 1818.
La Galère jésuitique. 1826.
Ganilh, Charles. De la Contre-révolution en France. 1823.
Georgel, J. F., abbé. Mémoires pour servir à l'histoire de la fin du dix-huitième siècle. 2d ed. 6 vols. 1820.
Geyl, Pieter. Napoleon: for and against. Translated by O. Renier. London, 1949.
Gilbert de Voisins, Pierre Paul Alexandre. Procédure contre l'institut et les constitutions des Jésuites suivie au Parlement de Paris. 1823.
Giroust, Jacques Charles. Une Erreur, ou Mille et mille erreurs, évitables ou inévitables, de mille et mille historiens, écrivains, discoureurs . . . 1816.

Gooch, G. P. History and Historians in the Nineteenth Century. 2d ed. London, 1935.
Goubeau de La Bilennerie, J. F. Histoire abrégée des Jésuites et des missionnaires Pères de la Foi. 2 vols. 1820.
Grandmaison, Geoffroy de. La Congrégation, 1801–1830. 2d ed. 1890.
Grégoire, H. B., abbé. Essai historique sur les libertés de l'église gallicane. 1820.
———. Histoire des confesseurs des empereurs, des rois, et d'autres princes. 1824.
Guichen, Eugène, vicomte de. La France morale et religieuse au début de la Restauration. 1911.
———. La France morale et religieuse à la fin de la Restauration. 1912.
Guillot, F. M. Le Jacobinisme réfuté, ou Observations critiques sur le mémoire de M. Carnot adressé au roi en 1814. 1815.
Guizot, François. Du Gouvernement représentatif et de l'état actuel de la France. 1816.
———. Discours prononcé pour l'ouverture du Cours d'histoire moderne. December 7, 1820.
———. Du Gouvernement de la France depuis la Restauration et du ministère actuel. 2d ed. 1820. Also Foreword to 3d ed. 1820.
———. Des Moyens de gouvernement et d'opposition dans l'état actuel de la France. 1821.
———. History of the Origin of Representative Government. Translated by Andrew R. Scoble. London, 1852.
———. Mémoires pour servir à l'histoire de mon temps. 3d ed. 8 vols. 1861.
———. History of Civilisation. Translated by William Hazlitt. 3 vols. London, 1873.
Halphen, Louis. L'Histoire en France depuis cent ans. 1914.
Hatin, E. Histoire politique et littéraire de la presse en France. 8 vols. 1859–61. Vol. VIII.
Hennequin, A. M. Plaidoirie; Cause célèbre, plainte en diffamation des petits-fils de La Chalotais contre l'éditeur de *l'Etoile*. 1826.
Henrion, Mathieu Richard, baron de. Vie de Monseigneur Frayssinous. 2 vols. 1844.
Henrion de Pansey, Pierre Paul. Des Pairs de France et de l'ancienne constitution française. 1816.
D'Herbelot, A. Lettres . . . à Charles de Montalembert et à Léon Cornudet (1828–1830). 1908.
Hudson, Nora. Ultra Royalism and the French Restoration. Cambridge, England, 1936.
J.A.P. De la Monarchie avec les philosophes, les révolutionnaires et les Jacobins. Lyon, 1817.
Jolly, T. F. Mémorial sur la Révolution française. 1824.
Jordan, Camille. La Session de 1817, aux habitans de Bain et du Rhône. 1817.
Jouffroy, Achille de. Les Fastes de l'anarchie, ou Précis chronologique des événemens mémorables de la Révolution française. 1820.
Jubé de la Perrelle, A. Lettre à M. le vicomte de Chateaubriand . . . concernant un pamphlet intitulé *De la Monarchie selon la Charte*. 1816.
———. Quelques Mots sur la proclamation de M. le comte de Chateaubriand. 1818.
Jullian, C. Historiens français du XIXe siècle. 1897.

Kentzinger, Antoine. Les Préceptes, ou la Religion sous les rapports politiques. 1820.
La Chalotais, Louis René de Caradeuc de. Mémoires. With an Introduction by Gilbert de Voisins. 1826.
———. Comptes rendus. 1826.
———. Essai sur l'éducation nationale. 2d ed. 1825.
———. Résumé des constitutions des Jésuites. 1826.
———. Résumé de la doctrine des Jésuites. 1826.
Lacombe, Charles de. La Jeunesse de Berryer. 1894.
Lacretelle, Charles. Précis historique de la Révolution française. New ed. 1821.
———. Histoire de l'assemblée constituante. 2 vols. 1821.
La Gorce, Pierre de. La Restauration: Louis XVIII, Charles X. 2 vols. 1926–28.
Lallemont, Guillaume, ed. Choix de rapports, opinions et discours prononcés à la tribune nationale. 24 vols. 1818–23.
La Luzerne, C. G., Cardinal de. Lettre du Cardinal de La Luzerne à l'éditeur de la *Quotidienne*. 1820.
Lamennais, Félicité de. Œuvres complètes. 10 vols. 1843–44.
Langeac, de Lespinasse de. Journal de l'anarchie, de la terreur et du despotisme. 1821.
Lanjuinais, J. D. Œuvres de J. D. Lanjuinais. 4 vols. 1832.
———. Appréciation du projet de loi relatif aux trois concordats. 1817.
———. Constitutions de la nation française. 2 vols. 1819.
Laroche, Benjamin. Considérations sur l'ouvrage de M. Guizot. 1820.
Laumier, Charles. Résumé de l'histoire des Jésuites. 1826.
Lemontey, P. E. Essai sur l'établissement monarchique de Louis XIV, et sur les altérations qu'il éprouva pendant la vie de ce prince. 1818.
Lepan, Edouard. Vie politique, littéraire, et morale de Voltaire, ou on réfute Condorcet et ses autres historiens. 2d ed. 1819. The first edition appeared in 1817.
L'Epinois, Henri de. Histoire de la Restauration, 1814–1830. 1873.
Le Sur, S. L. La France et les français. 2d ed. 1818.
Lirac, A. "La Guerre des Jésuites sous la Restauration," *Le Correspondant* (April–May, 1879), pp. 14–31, 226–48, 440–67.
"Des Livres et des pamphlets sur le concordat," in *Le Publiciste*. 1818.
Lombard de Langres, V. Histoire des sociétés secrètes. 1819.
———. Les Jacobins depuis 1789 jusqu'à ce jour, ou Etat de l'Europe en janvier 1822. 2d ed. 1822. The first edition appeared in 1820.
Lourdouieux, H. de. Opinion d'un citoyen sur la situation de la France et particulièrement sur les défections dans le ministère. 1818.
Madrolle, A. De la Révolution dans ses rapports avec ses victimes et particulièrement avec les émigrés. 1824.
———. Défense de l'ordre social, attaqué dans ses fondemens . . . par M. de Montlosier, ou l'on défère au roi, aux chambres et aux cours les œuvres de cet écrivain comme le résumé des erreurs avec lesquels la philosophie a fait la Révolution. 1827.
Maistre, Joseph de. Œuvres complètes de J. de Maistre. New ed. 14 vols. Lyon, 1884–86.
Maréchal, C. La Jeunesse de Lamennais. 1913.
———. Lamennais: la dispute de l'Essai de l'indifférence. 1925.
———. Lamennais et Lamartine. 1907.
Marchangy. Plaidoyer de M. de Marchangy . . . prononcé le 29 août 1822,

devant la cour d'assises de la Seine, dans la conspiration de La Rochelle. 1822.
Maritain de Neuwaches, C. Les Jésuites dévoilés à leurs amis et à leurs ennemis. Lyon, 1829.
Martinet, Mme. Aperçu historique de la Révolution française. 1827.
Mauduit, Roger. Les Conceptions politiques et sociales de Bonald. 1913.
Mazade, Charles de. L'Opposition royaliste. 1894.
Merlet, Gustave. Tableau de la littérature française, 1800–1815. 3 vols. 1883.
Meunier, Georges. Les Grands Historiens du dix-neuvième siècle. 1894.
Michaud, E. Le Jésuitisme politique et le comte de Montlosier en 1826. Berne, 1889.
Mignet, François. History of the French Revolution. English translation. London, 1846.
Monod, G. La Vie et la pensée de Jules Michelet, 1798–1852. 2 vols. 1923. Vol. I.
Montfleury, J. P. P. Le Mensonge détruit par la vérité, ou Réfutation des erreurs politiques et religieuses contenues dans l'ouvrage intitulé *Le Jésuitisme de M. de Pradt.* 1826.
Montgaillard, abbé de. Histoire de France. 2d ed. 9 vols. 1817.
Montlosier, François de. De la Monarchie française. 4 vols. 1815.
———. Mémoire à consulter sur un système religieux et politique tendant à renverser la religion, la société et le trône. 1826.
———. Dénonciation aux cours royales. 1826.
Moulinié, Henri. De Bonald. 1915.
N., chevalier de. Des Ultras en 1818 et de la note secrète. 1818.
Nettement, Alfred. Histoire de la littérature française sous la Restauration. 3d ed. 2 vols. 1874.
Norvins, Jacques de. Tableau de la Révolution française. 1819.
O'Connor, Mary. The Historical Thought of François Guizot. Washington, 1955.
Ollé de Mantet. Dialogue historique entre un royaliste et un libéral. 1830.
Plamenatz, John. The Revolutionary Movement in France, 1815–71. London, 1952.
"Plan des libéraux pour recommencer la révolution," in *La France Chrétienne.* 1821.
Pouthas, C. H. Guizot pendant la Restauration. 1923.
Pradt, Dominique Georges, abbé de. Les Quatre Concordats. 3 vols. 1818.
———. Du Jésuitisme ancien et moderne. 1826.
Preuves frappantes de l'imminence d'une seconde révolution. 1827.
Prudhomme. Histoire impartiale des révolutions de France. 1826.
Quélen, Louis Hyacinthe de. Oraison funèbre . . . [du] duc de Berry. 1820.
Remède unique aux maux de l'église et de l'état, par un curé de campagne. 3d ed. 1817.
Rémusat, Charles de. Critiques et études, ou Passé et présent. New edition. 1857.
"De la Révolution qui nous menace," *Journal du Nord* (January 18, 1830).
Riambourg, Jean Baptiste. Les Principes de la Révolution française. Chalons-sur-Saône, 1820.
Richard, C. H. Aperçu de la Révolution française et des véritables intérêts de la royauté dans l'état actuel des choses. 1820.
Rienzi, Domeny de. Adresse au gouvernement et au peuple français. 1820.
Rioust, M. N. Carnot. 1817.

———. Procès du Sr. M. N. Rioust pour son ouvrage ayant pour titre Carnot. 1817.

Rivarol, C. F. de. Essai sur les causes de la Révolution française. 1827.

Roche, Achille. Histoire de la Révolution française. 1825.

Roche, J. L. H. F. Essai analytique sur l'histoire universelle. 2 vols.

Sagnac, P. "Le Concordat de 1817," *Revue d'histoire moderne et contemporaine* (December 1905 and March 1906), pp. 189–210, 261–88, 433–53.

Saint-Chamans, A. de. Du Croque-mitaine du comte de Montlosier, de M. de Pradt, et de bien d'autres. 1826.

Sainte-Aulaire, Louis Clair de Beaupoil de. Histoire de la Fronde. 3 vols. 1827.

Saint-Roman, Alexis Jacques, comte de. Opinion de M. le comte de Saint-Roman sur le projet de loi tendant à indemniser les anciens propriétaires des biens-fonds confisqués . . . , Session de 1825, séance du 11 avril. 1825.

Saint-Victor, J. de, ed. Documents historiques, critiques, apologétiques concernant la Compagnie de Jésus. 3 vols. 1827–30.

Salaberry, C. M. "Aux Hommes de bien," in *Le Conservateur de la Restauration.* 1828.

———. Souvenirs politiques sur la Restauration. 2 vols. 1900.

Santo-Domingo, Joseph Hippolyte. Les Jésuites en action sous le ministère Villèle. 1828.

Silvy, L. Les Jésuites tels qu'ils ont été . . . 1815.

———. Difficulté capitale proposée à M. l'abbé Frayssinous. 1818.

Siret, C. J. C. Précis historique du sacre de S.M. Charles X. Reims, 1826.

Stadler, Peter. "Politik und Geschichtschreibung in der französischen Restauration, 1814–1830," *Historische Zeitschrift*, Vol. 180, No. 2 (October 1955), 265–96.

Staël, Mme de. Considerations on the Principal Events of the French Revolution. English translation. 3 vols. London, 1818.

Stendhal (Henri Beyle). The Red and the Black. English translation. 2 vols. in 1. New York, 1926.

Stenger, Gilbert. The Return of the Bourbons. English translation. New York, 1909.

Tabaraud, Mathieu Mathurin. Du Pape et des Jésuites. 1814.

Tableau des trois époques, ou les Philosophes avant, pendant et après la Révolution. 1829.

Taillandier, R. G. L'Anti-révolutionnaire, ou Lettres à mon fils sur les causes, la marche et les effets de la Révolution française. 2d ed. 2 vols. 1830.

Teuteberg, René. Prosper de Barante: Ein romantischer Historiker des französischen Liberalismus. Basel, 1945.

Thierry, Augustin. Lettres sur l'histoire de France. New ed. 1859. This work was first published in 1827.

———. Dix Ans d'études historiques. New ed. 1859. This volume first appeared in 1834.

———. Histoire de la conquête de l'Angleterre par les Normands. 1825.

Thiers, Adolphe. Histoire de la Révolution française. 1823–27.

Thiessé, Léon. Résumé de l'histoire de la Révolution française. 1828.

Thureau-Dangin, Paul. Royalistes et républicains. 1874.

Tild, Jean. L'Abbé Grégoire. 1946.

Tissot, P. T. Précis, ou Histoire abrégée des guerres de la Révolution française. 3 vols. 1821.

Tocqueville, Alexis de. Democracy in America. Translated by Henry Reeve. 2 vols. New York, 1945.
Trognon, Auguste. Etudes sur l'histoire de France. 1836.
Vatout, J. De l'Assemblée constituante, ou Réponse à M. C. Lacretelle. 1822.
Vaulabelle, Achille de. Histoire des deux restaurations. New ed. 10 vols. 1874.
Villèle, Jean Baptiste, comte de. Mémoires et correspondance. 5 vols. 1891–92.
Vitet, Louis. La Ligue. 1824.
Vitrolles, Eugène François, baron de. Mémoires et relations politiques. Published by E. Forgues. 3 vols. 1883.
Weill, Georges. La France sous la monarchie constitutionnelle (1814–1848). 1912.

NEWSPAPERS AND PERIODICALS

Annuaire historique, 1821–30
Archives parlementaires. 2d ser. Vols. 12–62.
Archives philosophiques, politiques et littéraires, July 1817–December 1818
Bibliothèque historique, March 1818–April 1820
Bibliothèque royaliste, 1819–26
Le Conservateur, October 1818–March 1820
Le Constitutionnel, 1819–30
Le Courrier français, 1819–30
Le Drapeau blanc, 1819–27
L'Etoile, 1820–27
Le Globe, 1824–30
Journal des débats, 1815–30
La Minerve française, February 1818–March 1820
Le Moniteur, 1815–30
Le Nain jaune, December 1814–July 1815
Le National, January 1830–August 1830
Le Nouvel homme gris, 1819–20
Le Producteur, 1825–26
La Quotidienne, 1815–30
Revue encyclopédique, 1819–30
Revue française, January 1828–September 1830
Revue des deux mondes, 1829–30

Index